A SHADOW OF GLORY

A SHADOW OF GLORY

Reading the New Testament after the Holocaust

Tod Linafelt, Editor

Routledge
Taylor & Francis Group
NEW YORK AND LONDON

Published in 2002 by
Routledge
29 West 35th Street
New York, NY 10001
www.routledge-ny.com

Published in Great Britain by
Routledge
11 New Fetter Lane
London EC4P 4EE
www.routledge.co.uk

Routledge is an imprint of the Taylor & Francis Group.

Printed in the United States of America on acid free paper.

Library of Congress Cataloging-in-Publication Data
A shadow of glory: reading the New Testament after the Holocaust / Tod Linafelt, editor.
p. cm.
Includes index.
ISBN 0-415-93793-0 (hardback)—ISBN 0-415-93794-9 (pbk.)
1. Bible. N.T.—Criticism, interpretation, etc.
2. Holocaust
(Christian theology)
I. Linafelt, Tod, 1965–
BS2370 .S53 2002
225.6'09'045—dc21

2002004904

Contents

Acknowledgments

Material in Susannah Heschel's article, "Reading Jesus as a Nazi," was previously published in her earlier article, "Redemptive Anti-Semitism," in R. Thompson and T. Phillips, eds., *Literary Studies in Luke-Acts: Essays in Honor of Joseph B. Tyson* (Macon, GA: Mercer University Press, 1998). A slightly different, earlier version of James D. G. Dunn's article, "The Jew Paul and His Meaning for Israel," was previously published in Udo Schnelle and Thomas Söding, eds., *Paulinische Christologie: Festschrift Hans Hübner* (Göttingen: Vandenhoeck & Ruprecht, 2000). Gary A. Phillips's article, "The Killing Fields of Matthew's Gospel," was first published in Fiona Black, Roland Boer, and Erin Runions, eds., *The Labour of Reading: Desire, Alienation and Biblical Interpretation*, Semeia Studies (Atlanta: Scholars Press, 1999). I gratefully acknowledge permission to reprint all three pieces.

I am also grateful to Kathryn McMahon and to Mythri Jegathesan, both of Georgetown University, for their help in preparing the manuscript for publication, and to Nick Street, of Routledge, for patiently seeing it through.

T.L.

Introduction

TOD LINAFELT

In attempting to articulate the ways in which the sacrifice of Jesus Christ has superceded the sacrificial system of Judaism, the author of the New Testament letter to the Hebrews draws heavily on the image of the shadow. The Israelite priestly service is deemed "a shadow of heavenly things" (8:5), and the Torah merely "a shadow of the good to come" (10:1). In short, Judaism before Christ is presented as *a shadow of glory*, a religion that was useful in a fallen and limited way, but must now be abandoned in light of the fullness of Christ. For a thinker steeped in Platonic thought and struggling to encourage what was likely a small, threatened community, the characterization is an effective rhetorical maneuver. But for readers today the "shadow of glory" takes on a more unsettling meaning. For after nearly two millennia it is clear that such Christian supersessionism has had dire consequences for Jews and Judaism. From forced conversions, to countless pogroms, to the systematic murder of six million Jews in Nazi Germany, the "glory" of Christianity's triumph in the West has indeed cast a long and baleful shadow. The present volume looks out from this shadow back at the texts of the New Testament and explores how those texts might be read differently in light of the Holocaust.

One cannot, of course, simply lay the blame for a long and baleful history of Christian antisemitism at the feet of the New Testament writers. Indeed, for most of those writers there did not even exist a separate religion known as "Christianity," and none could have foreseen the unholy mixture of religious ideology, nineteenth-century racial theory, and modern technology of mass death that resulted in the Holocaust. Rather, the issue is how our present interpretive horizon, shaped as it inevitably is by events of the twentieth century, impinges upon this ancient literature. Put simply, the contributors to this volume all respond in one way or another to the question: How has the historical web of events known as the Holocaust affected—or how *should* it affect—the way we read the founding texts of Christianity?

A few words about the very term "Holocaust" is in order. The term is a shorthand, in some ways inappropriate, way of referring both to the *official*, state-sponsored attempt to annihilate European Jewry by the National Socialist (Nazi) party in Germany during the 1930s and early 1940s and to the *unofficial*, yet sometimes equally deadly, pogroms and looting that took place in Nazi-occupied territories, especially in central and eastern Europe. The word Holocaust comes from the Greek translation (*holocaustos*) of the Hebrew word *`olah*, which designates in the Hebrew Scriptures the whole burnt offering that is sacrificed to God. Current usage of the term came to prominence in the 1960s and was solidified in the American imagination by the widely seen television miniseries from 1978, "The Holocaust," and more recently by the United States Holocaust Memorial Museum in Washington, D.C. Yet many have objected to the term being applied, given its religious and sacrificial overtones, to the murder of six million Jews, and one often finds the term *Shoah* (Hebrew for "destruction") substituted instead.

We tend to associate the Holocaust with killing centers such as Auschwitz-Birkenau and Treblinka, where together more than two million people were murdered, but it would more properly include as well the forced marches, roaming death squads, disease, and starvation that came with the Nazi persecution of Jews. It is certainly true, of course, that many non-Jews died in similar circumstances, and often side by side with Jews, yet it is also true that Jews and Judaism held a unique place in Nazi ideology and were singled out for persecution in a way that other political, ethnic, and religious groups were not. It is this ideological freight placed on Judaism, combined with the sheer scale of the killings (fully two-thirds of world Jewry and one-third of European Jewry perished between 1933 and 1945), that makes the Holocaust the massive and tragic phenomenon that it is.

Although countless volumes have been written on the Holocaust, and its philosophical, ethical, and theological implications have been explored from numerous perspectives, there is a conspicuous poverty of works that reflect explicitly and in a sustained manner on the impact of the Holocaust on the practice of biblical interpretation. This impact is, as the range of essays in the present volume show, vast and complex and is impossible to put into a single, summary statement. On the one hand, our attention is focused more keenly on issues that have been raised independently of any consideration of the Holocaust. Thus, for example, the topics of anti-Judaism in the Gospels or the ambiguities of Paul's thinking on God's continuing faithfulness to Israel have received a fair amount of attention in recent decades, and several of the essays here will revisit these issues, albeit with the expressed intention of offering a distinctive engagement with the post-Holocaust milieu. On the other hand, there are certain issues and questions that arise from the quite specific events that constitute the Holocaust. For example: How did New Testament scholars who were also Nazi party members deal with the Jewish identity of Jesus? How is the objectivity striven for in historical criticism called into question by the real ethical demands of contemporary Jewish–Christian relations? What is it about the erection of a cross at Auschwitz that is so controversial, and how might that give us new insight into the passion narratives of the Gospels? And what might all this mean for theological interpretation?

These and other issues are raised in the essays that follow—essays by internationally renowned scholars, as well as by younger scholars who bring fresh perspectives and cutting-edge interpretive work. The writers hail from both biblical studies and from Jewish studies, and the combination of Jewish and Christian, male and female, European and American, makes for a vigorous and diverse collection of essays, united nonetheless by a passionate commitment to facing squarely the ethical implications of reading and writing after the Holocaust.

PART I

The Holocaust in the History of Interpretation

CHAPTER 1

The Christian Canon and the Problem of Antisemitism

PAMELA EISENBAUM

Many Christians and Jews today are genuinely interested in promoting positive relations between the two faith communities.[1] Often an explicit awareness of living in a post-Shoah world is articulated by the various organizations devoted to Jewish–Christian relations. But even when such awareness is not explicitly articulated, most of these individuals and organizations have been at least implicitly motivated by the Shoah and the long history of Christian brutality toward Jews.[2] This desire for better relations between Christians and Jews often inspires statements stressing our common heritage. The place where this common heritage is most plainly evident is in the sharing of some scriptures, what Christians commonly call the Old Testament and Jews call the Tanakh or Hebrew Bible.[3] The sharing of scriptures thus constitutes the starting point for Christians and Jews as they enter into dialogue with one another; this seems especially true for Christians.[4]

Although the sharing of scriptures evokes the sentiment that we have a common heritage, it also disguises the profound differences in the meaning of the Bible for Jews and Christians. When American Jews are speaking in their own circles (that is, not in interfaith gatherings), they commonly use the term "Bible" to refer to their scripture. But "Bible" means something different for Christians. Not only are the contents different (a Christian Bible contains a New Testament as well as the Old Testament), but, by the fourth century C.E., the two Testaments together were thought of holistically as *Christian* scripture. The earliest extant Christian Bibles contain both the Old and New Testament, with all of the texts written in Greek.[5] The Greek Old Testament was based on the Septuagint, a translation made by Jews during the third and second centuries B.C.E. The process of canonization therefore caused a vast rereading of the scriptures of ancient Israel, a Christianizing of those scriptures that differed tremendously from the way the rabbis came to understand those same texts.[6]

One common assumption embedded in the notion that Jews and Christians share a common scriptural heritage in the Old Testament/Tanakh is that the New Testament (and its call to belief in Jesus) is the only thing that divides Judaism and Christianity. For Jews, much of the New Testament sounds violently anti-Jewish. Many Christians themselves have recognized this problem and been troubled by it. The origins of Christian supersessionism, it is often assumed by Christians and Jews, can be found in the New Testament. I intend to refute this assumption by proposing that the *texts* of the New Testament themselves are less of a problem in Jewish–Christian relations than the *process of canonization* among Christians in antiquity.[7]

Modern Jews and Christians often do not realize that for most of the past 2000 years, our "common heritage" in the scriptures of Israel has produced more antipathy than comradery.[8] That Christians canonized many of the same scriptures as Jews did not create common ground; rather, it created a battleground that drove a deeper wedge between the two groups. As Christians came to see the Holy Bible as made of two parts, the Old Testament and the New Testament, they came to redefine Jews, Judaism, and Jewish scripture as having been superseded by Christianity. In this essay I will highlight some events that led to the canonization of the Christian Bible from the first to the fourth centuries while emphasizing the rhetoric that made up the debates about canonization. Historically, there were some Christians who had different ideas about what writings should constitute the Christian canon. Thus the biblical canon modern Christians take for granted was hardly a historical inevitability. I will then demonstrate how the debates of antiquity were eerily replayed by Christian theologians during the Third Reich. I hope not only to show the dangers inherent in too facile an understanding of our "sharing of scriptures," but also to offer some insights about deepening our understanding of this common textual heritage.

The First Century

In the beginning, the only sacred texts known to believers in Jesus were those texts deemed sacred by Jews. The New Testament (hereafter, NT) is full of references to "scripture" by which NT authors always mean the writings generally considered sacred by Jews of the first century.[9] With one or two possible exceptions, NT authors never quote other early Christian writings as authorities.[10] Paul certainly would not have envisioned his letters having the status of scripture. With the possible exception of the Apocalypse of John, which presents itself literally as a revelation of the heavenly realm, none of the writers who produced the documents that now comprise the NT believed their writings had the same scriptural authority of, say, the Torah and the Hebrew Prophets. Thus, during the first century there was no debate about the canon: Christian scripture was identical to Jewish scripture. To be sure, there were debates among Jews of different sects about the interpretation of the Bible, but not about the contents of the Bible.[11]

Although Christians have traditionally credited Paul with the notion that the covenant with Christ has supplanted the covenant with Moses—thus setting up the Old Testament/New Testament paradigm—a wave of scholarship has been building in Pauline studies (often referred to as the "new perspective on Paul")[12] that argues that Paul never had any such supersessionist ideas. There is no doubt that many negative statements about Torah can be found in Paul's letters. But many scholars have convincingly argued that these statements are not intended as a wholesale rejection of Jewish law. There are far too many positive statements Paul makes about Jewish law for such a view to be tenable. The more convincing explanation of Paul's negative statements about Jewish law is that he opposes Jews or Judaizing Christians who wish to impose Jewish law on Gentiles as a prerequisite for being in Christ; he is not rejecting the Mosaic covenant per se.[13]

Rather, building on the vision found in the Prophets, Paul wants to include all the "nations" (the Greek word is *ethne*, which can be translated either "gentiles" or "nations") in the same covenant Israel already enjoys. In other words, gentiles—at least gentile believers in Jesus—can now be included in the heritage of the Jews as made known in the scriptures, but they do not need to become Jews (thus do not need to be circumcised) to partake of that heritage. In Romans 4, Paul makes sophisticated use of the Abraham saga to argue that Abraham is not just the patriarchal ancestor of the Jews, but of the gentiles, too; in other words, of *all* the nations. The linchpin of Paul's argument is Genesis 17:5 in which God promises that Abraham will be the "ancestor of a multitude of nations (*ethne*)."[14] As Paul says, "according to grace, the promise is guaranteed to all [Abraham's] descendants, not to those who belong to Torah only, but rather to those who belong to the faith of Abraham, who is the father of us all! As it is written, 'I have made you the ancestor of many nations (*ethne*)'" (Romans 4:16b–17a; translation mine).

Paul's vision of Judaism had been expanded to a greater point of inclusivity than many other Jews (including other followers Jesus) were willing to accept. But Paul's sense of continuity between first-century Judaism and Israel's history as related in scripture remains firmly in place. There can be no supersessionism for Paul, because Judaism has not been replaced by anything. What will later become the Old Testament for Christians is still very much the sum total of Holy Writ for Paul.

The Second and Third Centuries

The unquestioning authority of Jewish scripture that prevailed in the first century began to change in the second century. The *Epistle of Barnabas*, a document usually dated somewhere within the first half of the second century, is an excellent example of how thinking for some Christians had begun to change, moving far beyond anything seen among NT documents.[15] The primary focus of the writer of *Barnabas* (whom I will hereafter call Barnabas) is to argue that the scriptures of Israel have been completely misunderstood by the Jews, both because the Jews have consistently been disobedient and because they have taken the scriptures literally and thus have not been able to see how they point to Christ. Interestingly, Barnabas takes some texts literally, usually those that recount the disobedience of the people.

Barnabas provides a good example of how a few generations after Paul some Christians began to develop a different scriptural hermeneutic. Barnabas writes: "What then does [God] say to Abraham, when he alone was faithful, and it was counted him for righteousness? 'Behold I have made thee, Abraham, the father of the Gentiles (*ethne*), who believe in God in uncircumcision.'"[16] Here Barnabas both mimics Paul's use of Genesis 17:5 in Romans 4:16–17, and yet he turns it upside down. Barnabas replaces Paul's inclusive vision with an exclusivist one. No longer is Abraham father of *all* the *ethne* as Paul says in Romans 4:16, or even a *multitude* of *ethne*, as the text of Genesis 17:5 itself says, but only the *ethne* who specifically reject circumcision, namely non-Jews. In Barnabas's understanding of salvation history, gentiles have *replaced* Jews as the children of Abraham (see also *Barnabas* 14.1–4). Barnabas thereby creates discontinuity between the people spoken of in scripture and his contemporary Jews.

As Hans von Campenhausen put it, *Barnabas* represents "the most thoroughgoing attempt to wrest the Bible absolutely from the Jews, and to stamp it from the very first word as exclusively a Christian book."[17] But von Campenhausen also points out that Barnabas does not deal adequately with questions about circumcision, the Sabbath, and food laws as they apply to a gentile context. Although Barnabas used symbolic exegesis to dismiss peculiarly Jewish commandments, his interpretations jeopardized the continuity of the two Testaments (von Campenhausen, 70–71).

It is no surprise, then, to discover that some Christians of the second century began to doubt the validity of the scriptures. They began to question how these scriptures, which contained so much about Jewish history and practices, bore relevance for Christians. By the second century, writings by Christians were beginning to circulate more widely. There is strong evidence that Paul's letters, for example, originally written to individual churches, were copied and gathered together into collections. In addition, by the beginning of the second century, there are at least four gospels in circulation.[18] Although none of these early

Christian writings hold scriptural status in the second century, they are gaining in importance and availability. Furthermore, as more gentiles came to dominate Christian communities, they understandably lacked the sentimental attachment to the history and tradition of Israel that Paul and many of the gospel writers had. Thus, Christians began to see the negative statements about the Torah made by Paul as applicable to Jews and Judaism.

The first and most devastating argument for a full-scale rejection of the scriptures of Israel came from a radical Paulinist named Marcion (c. 84–160). He was excommunicated by Rome because of his radical ideas and subsequently founded his own church (which survived until the fifth century). Marcion believed that the God who plays such an important role in the scriptures of Israel is not the same God who is represented by Jesus Christ.[19] They are literally different Gods. He identified the Jewish God as a creator-god, who meted out justice to human beings as they deserved. The God of Jesus Christ was a Savior-God from another transcendent realm who was far superior to the creator-god.

Marcion's hermeneutics and theology meant that he could no longer regard the scriptures of Israel as divinely authoritative. Thus he identified a small selection of more recent Christian writings as having scriptural status. He included only an edited collection of Paul's letters and an abridged version of the Gospel of Luke. Aside from his dogmatic allegiance to Paul, the reason for such a slim canon was that he was forced by his theological convictions to expunge everything that referred to the scriptures of Israel. Many if not most of the writings that now make up the NT include citations of, paraphrases of, and references and allusions to these texts. Put simply, Marcion's position was that these few Christian writings should replace the texts of ancient Israel as scripture for Christians.

Although Marcion is not necessarily thought of as a "gnostic" Christian, gnostic Christians of the second and third centuries also typically believed that the God of Israelite scripture was a lower god. There is no one consistent hermeneutical orientation to scripture in the writings deemed "gnostic" by scholars—some gnostic writers ridiculed it and some revered it as holding secret knowledge if interpreted correctly. Many if not most gnostic Christians seemed to have studied it earnestly and used it to justify their arguments. In most cases, like Marcion, gnostic exegesis stressed the discontinuity between the revelation of scripture and the revelation that had occurred in Jesus Christ (and their own revelatory writings).

These attitudes prompted a fierce debate about what constituted scripture for Christians that continued throughout the second and third centuries. Eventually, the writings of Marcion and the gnostics were deemed heretical by the "orthodox" church. But the arguments of these "heretics" must have been a severe threat and perhaps compelling to a number of Christians, precisely because the church fathers began to construct a much more self-conscious and sophisticated hermeneutic regarding the role of scripture within the context of Christian belief. Justin Martyr, whose dates are roughly contemporary with Marcion's, converted to Christianity because he was transformed by the teachings of the Hebrew Prophets, taught to him by an old Christian. Von Campenhausen credits Justin with being the first Christian to develop "a doctrine of holy scripture" (von Campenhausen, 88). Although most Christian authors before Justin use scripture as evidence that Jesus is the Christ, in Justin's *Dialogue with Trypho*, he reverses the argument. Because everything foretold about Christ in scripture came true, the scriptures must be the essential witness to the divine plan. In other words, Justin makes an argument for the validity of Israelite scripture for Christians, rather than simply assuming it. But Justin, like those before him, must explain those peculiarly Jewish parts of the Bible—circumcision, the food laws, the Sabbath, i.e., the ceremonial law—in this new Christian context. Whereas Barnabas engaged in symbolic and allegorical exegesis, Justin opts for a more literalistic, historical approach. The law was a kind of ad hoc necessity because of the disobedience of the Jews. "Thus, 'circumcision, which derives from Abraham,' was ordained simply in order that, even in the dispersion, the Jews might remain identifiable, and not escape their merited punishments."[20] Justin appeals to the prophets to demonstrate what he sees as the obduracy of the Jews. Elsewhere in the *Dialogue with Trypho*, Justin refers to Israelite scripture as "your scriptures, or rather not yours, but ours." In other words, the Law, the Prophets, the Psalms, and the rest of what made up scripture at that point properly belonged to Christians. At the close of the second century there still was no NT. Thus, there was not yet a textual concept of the Old Testament, just the "scriptures" (that is, the scriptures of Israel), for which some Christians had no use. Against the influence of Marcion and gnostic Christians, the church fathers followed Justin in constructing arguments for the continuing validity of scripture in order to create a sense of unity between those sacred writings, to which Jews also laid claim, and Christian faith. Meanwhile, Christian writings, particularly those that had the status of apostolic authority—in other words, writings having a close chronological connection to the life, death, and resurrection of Jesus—were becoming more revered. Perhaps the first person to express textual unity between the scriptures of Israel and these Christian writings comes from Tertullian (c. 155–220), who says,

> [The Church] knows one Lord God, Creator of the universe, and Christ Jesus, born of the Virgin Mary, Son of God the Creator, and the resurrection of the flesh; she unites the Law and the Prophets with the writings of the evangelists and the apostles; from that source she drinks her faith and

> that faith she seals with water, clothes with the Holy Spirit, feeds with the Eucharist, encourages to martyrdom; and against that teaching she receives no one.[21]

Although Tertullian writes before there is an official Christian canon, he clearly stresses the unity of "the Law and the Prophets" and "the evangelists and the apostles," thus setting the stage for the concept of the unified Christian canon, one made up of the Old Testament and the NT. Moreover, Tertullian clearly defines a boundary between those who hold the correct view of scripture and those who do not.

Many of the arguments of the church fathers of the second and third centuries were directed mainly at other Christians, but these arguments were made at the expense of the Jews and Jewish claims to the same scriptures. The more Christians argued for continuity between the scriptures of Israel and the life, death, and resurrection of Jesus, the more they worked to sever the connection between those same scriptures and their contemporary Jews.

The Fourth Century

It is surely no coincidence that in the same century that Christianity moves from being a marginalized, often persecuted religion to being the official state religion under Constantine, it finally produces its official scriptural canon, made up of Old Testament (hereafter, OT) and NT.[22] State sponsorship of Christianity led to the mass production of Christian Bibles, which is the primary reason our earliest biblical codices derive from the fourth century. Although the word "canon" is not used to refer to Christian scripture until Athanasius of Alexandria in 367, it was Eusebius of Ceasarea in the early fourth century who, by virtue of his research interests as a historian and having access to the works of Origen (c. 185–253), made available to Constantine Origen's revision of the Septuagint, which Origen had referred to as the "Old Testament." More importantly, Eusebius constructed a comprehensive understanding of history that made seamless the material contained in the Old and New Testaments.

In his *Preparation for the Gospel*, Eusebius explains why Christianity is founded upon the "oracles of the Hebrews" (as opposed to the sacred writings of other cultures). First on his agenda is the distinction between "Hebrews" and "Jews."

> And you may know the difference between Hebrews and Jews thus: the latter assumed their name from Judah, from whose tribe the kingdom of Judah was long ages afterward established, but the former from Eber, who was the forefather of Abraham. And that the Hebrews were earlier than the Jews, we are taught by the sacred writings.[23]

He goes on to explain the Jews' "manner of religion," which is dependent on the laws of Moses. The reader learns that the Mosaic legislation and the establishment of the Jewish nation was caused by the people's "moral weakness" at the time, making them unable to "emulate the virtue of their fathers, inasmuch as they were enslaved by passions and sick in soul . . ." (*Preparation*, 7.9d).

Eusebius builds on Justin's arguments, in which there is a pristine early period, followed by disobedience and the giving of the law at Sinai out of necessity. Christians are of course descended from Hebrews. The patriarchs, Moses, and the prophets become the ancestors of the Christians; the biblical heroes are seen as pre-Christ Christians. The Jews, on the other hand, are seen as illegitimate offspring, a people rightfully deprived of their heritage because of their depravity. By making this neat distinction between Hebrews and Jews, Eusebius is able to maintain continuity between the OT writings and Christianity, while at the same time denying the continuity between the people of God spoken of in the OT and Jews.[24]

Eusebius's writings are not polemically directed against Jews; he writes for Christian Rome. One of the strongest motivations for retaining the scriptures of Israel as the Christian OT was to demonstrate to Rome that Christianity was not a new-fangled cult. For Christians to gain stature in the eyes of Rome they had to demonstrate they had deep roots in antiquity. Rome's tolerance for Judaism and peculiar Jewish practice was largely predicated on Judaism's claims to a long-standing tradition extending far back in time. The need to prove to Rome that Christianity represented a long tradition exacerbated the need to push Jews out of the historical picture and claim the scriptures of Israel as exclusively Christian.

Robert Wilken has made the point that Christians probably suffered from a kind of inferiority complex as they tried to define themselves over against Judaism. "That Christians only had copies of the Jewish books, that few Christians knew Hebrew, and that Christians read and studied the Bible only in translations put them on the defensive. Possession of the original books was no small matter, for the rightful possession implied that one understood their contents."[25] Precisely because Christians had to make a case for the OT in the second through the fourth centuries, had to argue for its validity as *Christian* Holy Writ, they were led to dispossess the Jews of their scripture. For if "scripture" was equivalent to the sacred writings of Jews, then how could it truly belong to Christians? For Jews of the rabbinic period, they understood their sacred writings to be the story of God's covenantal relationship with them in particular. Jews understood themselves as constituting the exact same people as spoken of in the Bible. They saw no historical break between ancient Israel and themselves, much as Paul had. There is nothing comparable in rabbinic writings to the sense of newness reflected in the OT/NT schema constructed by Christians.[26] For Christians of the second through the fourth centuries, the essence of the OT was that it constituted a harbinger of Christ; everything in scripture pointed toward Christ. The OT by itself was, at best, incomplete.[27]

Thus, the OT was retained as scripture but it was, well, old. It was scripture in so far as it related to the NT. But because Jews did not read it this way, and because Jews had traditionally been the caretakers of scripture, Christians had to undermine the rival Jewish understanding of the Bible to establish their interpretation as legitimate. Interestingly, Marcion's rejection of Israelite scripture was largely due to his rather "Jewish" understanding of it.[28] He saw the OT as too particularistic. What was prophesied was a kingly messiah who would restore the Jews to the land. Marcion agreed with the Jews that a suffering messiah was never envisioned by the Hebrew Prophets. For Marcion, all of this was proof that Jesus and the message he brought was unprecedented, having nothing to do with the Jews or their Bible. Thus, those Christian writers who wanted to defend the Christian OT had to debunk completely the Jewish understanding of the Bible, and thoroughly Christianize the texts of the OT. Of course, this hermeneutical move saved the OT as scripture in a Christian context. The irony is that the rhetoric of the church fathers that preserved the scriptures of Israel and provides a common textual tradition for Jews and Christians today is the same rhetoric that constructed a view of Judaism and Christianity as mutually exclusive.

Nazi Theologians Revive the Debates of Antiquity

Strikingly, Christian theologians of the Third Reich reflect the same ironic tension regarding debates about the canon as had occurred in antiquity. Many *Deutsche Christen* theologians who were loyal to Nazi ideology rejected the OT, precisely because they thought of it as a Jewish book.[29] But even before the rise of Nazism, the famous Christian historian and theologian Adolf von Harnack argued that the OT should be published separately from "Christian scripture" because it is contradictory to the New Testament—a suggestion resembling the thought of Marcion, about whom Harnack had written the definitive study.[30]

Of course, others argued against those theologians who wanted to reject the OT. These Christians—who include both Protestants and Catholics, those who were Nazi party members and those who were not—employed the same kind of rhetoric used by orthodox Christians during the second through the fourth centuries. In their attempt to maintain the traditional Christian canon comprised of OT and NT, they completely disassociated the OT from contemporary Jews, Judaism, and Jewish culture. Cardinal Faulhaber, the relatively moderate archbishop of Munich, preached passionately against any rejection of the OT. In defense of the OT he says:

> By accepting these books Christianity does not become a Jewish religion. These books were not composed by Jews; they are inspired by the Holy Ghost, and therefore they are the word of God, they are God's books. The

> writers of them were God's pencils, the Psalm-singers were harps in the hand of God, the prophets were announcers of God's revelation. It is for this reason that the Scriptures of the Old Testament are worthy of credence and veneration for all time. Antagonism to the Jews of today must not be extended to the books of pre-Christian Judaism.[31]

The cardinal makes three distinctions or disassociations: that between ancient Israel and postbiblical Judaism, that between the OT scripture and other Jewish writings like the Talmud, which are not divinely inspired, and that between what is of permanent value in the OT and what is of transitory value. Of the first distinction he says:

> We must first distinguish between the people of Israel before and after the death of Christ. Before the death of Christ during the period between the calling of Abraham and the fullness of time, the people of Israel were enlightened men who by the law, the Mosaic Torah, regulated their religious and civil life, by the Psalms provided them with a prayer book for family devotion and a hymn book for the public liturgy, by the Sapiential books taught them how to conduct their lives, and as prophets awakened the conscience of the nation with the living word.... After the death of Christ, Israel was dismissed from the service of Revelation. She had not known the time of her visitation. She had repudiated and rejected the Lord's Anointed, had driven Him out of the city and nailed Him to the Cross. Then the veil of the Temple was rent, and with it the covenant between the Lord and His people. The daughters of Sion received the bill of divorce.... (Faulhaber, 257–258).

Like his predecessors in antiquity, Cardinal Faulhaber's defense of the OT is made at the expense of the Jews, not because he felt any "common heritage" with the Jewish people.

One particularly interesting Christian thinker who allied himself with the Nazis but also argued against the *Deutsche Christen* rejection of the OT was Gerhard Kittel.[32] Kittel was a New Testament scholar and one of the foremost authorities on ancient Judaism. Kittel took pains at his trial in 1946 in Nuremberg to defend his views, because they were based on his historical expertise, not on vulgar antisemitism. He, too, made a distinction between the good Jews of ancient times and contemporary Jews who were corrupt, only he did not make the cut-off the death of Christ, but the Babylonian exile. Prior to the exile, Israel was a state with its own laws and boundaries and land. But after the exile, some Jews chose not to return home. Thus, the diaspora led to a wholly new form of Judaism; "Jewry became a religion and a race without a homeland."[33] Furthermore, because they had no actual political power, they became parasitic on other nations. The "Jewish Question" in Kittel's view could therefore be intellectually and historically substantiated within OT scripture itself. Although Kittel's interpretation of biblical history reveals his own perspective—obviously informed by the concept of nationalism that so dominated postenlightenment thought—making the point of disconnection between Israel and Judaism the Babylonian exile, rather than the death of Christ, offered one more argument in favor of seeing the OT as an exclusively Christian book. His interpretive context may have been different than that of Tertullian or Eusebius, but like them, Kittel defended the OT as a Christian book by seeing it as the history of the Jews' failure and God's eventual rejection of the Jewish people. Christians were therefore the true Israel, whereas the Jews were God's outcasts, or, worse yet, God's enemies.

Concluding Thoughts

It took nearly 300 years to establish the Christian canon. Not only did Christians have different views on the matter, but the Jewish connection to the Hebrew scriptures, through language, culture, and observances, made claims to continuity seemingly easier. That is why Christians of the past worked so hard to construct a rhetoric of exclusion toward Judaism; that was the only way to be persuasive in retaining the OT. Since part of the meaningfulness of the study of the past is to see that historical events are not inevitabilities, but develop through a series of choices people make, I cannot help but wonder what would have happened if Christians had settled on a canon that did not overlap with the Hebrew Bible? Would there have been the same hostility?

At the same time, I recognize that there were good reasons for the Christian canon to turn out as it did. For at least the first 200 years of Christian history, the only sacred authority to which Christians could appeal was Israelite scripture, and many Christians, whether of Jewish or gentile origin, revered those texts as much as any rabbinic Jew. Justin was converted by studying the Prophets, not by reading the gospels. Furthermore, many of the texts that would eventually make up the NT are so full of quotations, allusions, and paraphrases of the Septuagint, that some of these writings would barely be comprehensible if the OT had not been included in the Christian Bible.

The resemblance of ancient debates about the Christian canon to debates during the Third Reich provides not only one more connection between ancient Christian anti-Judaism and modern antisemitism (and thus, at least implicitly, the Shoah itself), but should force Jews and Christians to ask whether their "common" heritage is really something we hold in common. Indeed in most recent scholarship, there is widespread acknowledgment that both Judaism and Christianity represent radical transformations of the religion of Israel, and that the meaningfulness of Israel's sacred writings was dependent on reinterpreting them so as to make them vital in a world profoundly transformed during the Hellenistic and Roman periods.[34] It may sound outrageous initially, but the premise upon which Kittel based his antisemitic view of Jewish history was not totally unfounded. There is no doubt that modern Judaism differs immensely from the religion of Israel. The question is whether the difference reflects degeneration, as Kittel, like Eusebius and so many other Christians, had argued. Christianity, too, differs radically from Israelite religion. Kittel's primary criterion for seeing Judaism as degenerate was that it no longer had the status of nationhood. Ironically, Christianity was from the start supranational—"no longer Jew or Greek," as Paul had said—much as diaspora Judaism was and still is.

For most of history, having a set of sacred texts in common has led to a rhetoric of hostility, not a sentiment of kinship. The reason is obvious: the interpretation of those scriptures within the respective faith communities of Judaism and Christianity mattered more than the texts themselves, and that interpretation was one of the keys to self-definition between the two religions. Jews and Christians must both recognize that they each constructed their understanding of scripture within the contexts of their separate faith communities after the biblical period. The rabbis of the Mishnaic and Talmudic period *made* the writings of Israel into the Tanakh. The church fathers *made* those same writings, together with the NT, into the Christian Bible. Both were born out of a creative need to retain the past and yet make it vital to the present. Historically, the most important difference between the two is that Christianity grew much larger in number and stature once it allied with Rome and, from then on, its rhetoric was backed by political power and force. Ultimately, Jews suffered horrendously. Christians today, therefore, should not simply assume a common textual heritage with Jews and Judaism as a starting point for Jewish–Christian dialogue. As a Jew, I encourage Christians to acknowledge the historical relationship that exists between the making of the Christian Bible and the anti-Jewish attitudes that resulted from the rhetoric of canonization. That would be the first step toward recognizing the otherness of the Jewish understanding of scripture and the otherness of Judaism. If that were the starting point, I think we could work toward a genuine sense of what we share in scripture, but that sense of commonality would come at the end of a dialogical process, not at the beginning.

NOTES

1. An earlier version of this article was presented at the Fiftieth Annual Conference of the American Theological Library Association, held at the Iliff School of Theology, June 1996.
2. Perhaps the best place to go for information on organizations devoted to Jewish–Christian relations is the Jewish–Christian Relations Net (*www.jcrelations.net*).

3. "Tanakh" is an acronym composed of the first letter of the Hebrew word for each of the three parts of the Hebrew Bible: Torah, Nevi'im (Prophets), Kethuvim (Writings).
4. See, for example, the founding statement by the International Council of Christians and Jews (*www.jcrelations.net/stmnts/iccj_theol_statement.htm*).
5. Our earliest extant codices of the Christian Bible are all dated to the fourth and fifth centuries. They include Codex Sinaiticus, Alexandrinus, Vaticanus, Ephraemi, Bezae.
6. For a concise explanation of the differences between the Jewish and Christian canons, see the entry on "Canon" in the *HarperCollins Bible Dictionary*, ed. P. J. Achtemeier et al., rev. ed. (New York: HarperCollins, 1996).
7. For the purposes of this essay, my focus will be almost exclusively on the Christian canonization process; I will say little about the process among Jews of the same period. Although I occasionally use the word "canon" when speaking of the scriptures of Israel in the first and second centuries C.E., to emphasize that they were widely regarded as having divine authority, the term oversimplifies the matter. Whether there was a well-defined Jewish biblical canon by the first century is highly debatable. In my own view, Israelite scripture was constructed into the official Jewish canon by the rabbis at about the same time that Christians were establishing their canon, during the second to the fourth centuries C.E. (although for Jews if may have been more firmly fixed by the end of the second century). Evidence from the Dead Sea Scrolls, for example, indicates a freer and more fluid understanding of sacred texts during the first century C.E. For an excellent discussion of the development of the Hebrew canon using evidence from the Dead Sea Scrolls, see E. Ulrich, *The Dead Sea Scrolls and the Origins of the Bible* (Grand Rapids, MI: Eerdmans, 1999).
8. I will use the phrase "scriptures of Israel" in this essay as a neutral (and historically more appropriate) way of describing the texts that become the Tanakh for Jews and the Old Testament for Christians.
9. The scriptures of Israel are referred to in a variety of ways in the New Testament. Even the same author can refer to it in different ways. See, for example, Romans, where in 3:2 Paul calls them "the oracles of God;" in 3:21 "the law and the prophets;" and in 4:3 "scripture." The point, however, is that there is no ambiguity about the scriptural authority of the texts cited.
10. See 2 Peter 3:15–16, which mentions the writings of Paul. Although some writings of the New Testament use the writings of other New Testament authors, e.g., Matthew and Luke use the Gospel of Mark as a source, there is no evidence that such sources have any kind of scriptural status.
11. See J. Blenkinsopp, "Interpretation and the Tendency to Sectarianism: An Aspect of Second Temple History," in *Jewish and Christian Self-Definition*, Vol. 2 (Philadelphia: Fortress, 1981), 1–26.
12. The new perspective on Paul is represented in the works of K. Stendahl, L. Gaston, J. Gager, D. Boyarin, N. T. Wright, and J. D. G. Dunn, to name just a few. They themselves hardly comprise a perfect unity of perspective, but they all read Paul as standing well within the context of first-century Judaism.
13. For a good discussion of the problem of negative and positive statements about Jewish law, see J. Gager, *Reinventing Paul* (New York: Oxford University Press, 2000), 1–15.
14. All biblical quotations come from the NRSV unless otherwise indicated and will be cited in text.
15. Some scholars have argued that an attitude of supersessionism is already present in Hebrews or Luke-Acts, if not in Paul or other NT writings. Although I do think Hebrews represents a significant hermeneutical shift from Paul—to be sure, Hebrews speaks of the new covenant in Christ as having replaced the old, which is even called "obsolete" by the author—Hebrews

treats the scriptural texts reverently and sees the old covenant as having established certain paradigms that are continued in the new covenant; they have just been perfected.

16. *Epistle of Barnabas* 13:7; hereafter cited in text as *Barnabas*. Translations for *Barnabas* are taken from *The Apostolic Fathers* (LCL; London: Heinemann, 1919). For a more detailed discussion of the role of Abraham in *Barnabas*, see J. Siker, *Disinheriting the Jews* (Louisville, KY: Westminster/John Knox, 1991), 148–151.
17. H. von Campenhausen, *The Formation of the Christian Bible* (Philadelphia: Fortress, 1972), 70; hereafter cited in text as von Campenhausen.
18. It is likely there were more than four. Some scholars argue that the Gospel of Thomas can be dated to the first century. See also Luke 1:1–4, in which the gospel writer reports that "many have undertaken to set down an orderly account" of the story of Jesus' life, death, and resurrection.
19. The classic study of Marcion was done by A. von Harnack in 1921. A later English translation was made entitled *Marcion: The Gospel of the Alien God* (Durham, NC: Labyrinth, 1990). More recent is the study by R. J. Hoffman, *Marcion: On the Reinstitution of Christianity: An Essay on the Development of Radical Paulinist Theology in the Second Century* (AAR Academy Series 46; Chico, CA: Scholars, 1984).
20. See Justin's *Dialogue with Trypho* 16.2; 19.2; 19.5; 23.5; 92.3.
21. *Prescriptions Against Heretics*, 36. Translation taken from S. L. Greenslade, *Early Latin Theology* (Library of Christian Classics; Philadelphia: Westminster, 1956).
22. See the discussion by J. Carroll in *Constantine's Sword: The Church and the Jews, A History* (Boston: Houghton Mifflin, 2001), 178–207. Carroll argues that Constantine was driven by the need to unify the empire (which was divided at the time) and virtually all his political, religious, and military undertakings, including his attempts to unify Christians, were designed to establish a singular, common understanding of what it meant to be part of Rome.
23. *Preparation for the Gospel*, 7.6c; hereafter cited in text as *Preparation*. Translations for Eusebius are taken from *Preparation for the Gospel*, Part I (Grand Rapids: Baker, 1981).
24. For a fuller discussion, see P. Eisenbaum, *The Jewish Heroes of Christian History: Hebrews 11 in Literary Context* (Atlanta: Scholars Press, 1997), 218–225.
25. R. Wilken, *John Chrysostom and the Jews: Rhetoric and Reality in the Late 4th Century* (Berkeley: University of California, 1983), 81.
26. S. Cohen, *From the Maccabees to the Mishnah* (Philadelphia: Westminster, 1987), 21, 230–231.
27. See E. E. Ellis, "Biblical Interpretation in the New Testament Church," *Mikra: The Translation, Reading and Interpretation of the Hebrew Bible in Ancient Judaism and Early Christianity*, ed. M. J. Mulder (Minneapolis: Fortress, 1990), 691–725.
28. See S. G. Wilson, *Related Strangers: Jews and Christians 70–170 C.E.* (Minneapolis: Fortress, 1995), 215–216.
29. See E. C. Helmreich, *The German Churches Under Hitler* (Detroit: Wayne State University Press, 1979), 150.
30. See H. J. Kraus, *Geschichte der historisch-kritischen Erforschung des Alten Testaments von der Reformation biz zur Gegenwart* (Neukirchen Kries Moers: Buchhandlung des Erziehungsvereins, 1956), 351; and R. Ericksen, *Theologians Under Hitler* (New Haven: Yale University Press, 1985), 50, 209. See also n. 19.
31. English quotations for Cardinal Faulhaber are taken from *Nazi Culture: Intellectual, Cultural and Social Life in the Third Reich*, ed. George L. Mosse (New York: Schoken, 1981), 258–259; hereafter cited in text as Faulhaber.
32. Kittel was a Nazi party member but he was often critical of the *Deutsche Christen* theologians, because they argued for historically untenable views such as that Jesus was not Jewish, which

Kittel knew to be ridiculous. The best discussion I have found of Kittel is in Ericksen, *Theologians Under Hitler*, 28–78.

33. Ericksen, *Theologians Under Hitler*, 61. Ericksen refers to an article by Kittel entitled "Die Entstehung des Judentums und die Entstehung der Judenfrage," *Forschungen zur Judenfrage* 1 (1936): 47–48.
34. See, for example, A. Segal, *Rebecca's Children: Judaism and Christianity in the Roman World* (Cambridge, MA: Harvard University Press, 1986).

CHAPTER 2

Higher Critics on Late Texts

Reading Biblical Scholarship after the Holocaust

DEBORAH KRAUSE AND TIMOTHY K. BEAL

The Holocaust casts an unfathomably dismal shadow across the history of modern thought. When we face it honestly and self-critically, all our old proclamations of progress and the upward March of History lose their bearing. So too when it comes to the history of Christian thought and biblical interpretation. Indeed, the crisis of the Holocaust demands that we reread the Christian Bible and the history of Christianity in ways that acknowledge the future that haunts it. This means not only rereading New Testament texts and interpretations made of it by preachers and theologians. It also means rereading the ostensibly non-Christian and nontheological academic heritage of modern, so-called "Higher" biblical criticism.

In this light, or rather under this shadow, we want to revisit a particular historical paradigm that took hold within Higher Criticism in the late nineteenth and early twentieth centuries, a result especially of the work of Julius Wellhausen in Old Testament studies and Ferdinand Christian Baur in New Testament studies. Influential among many biblical scholars to this day, we contend that this historical paradigm serves a certain anti-Jewish and anti-Catholic orientation within the academic culture of biblical criticism, revealing its own deep historical affiliation with European Protestant theological tradition.

In general this paradigm presents Israelite history and early Christian history as parallel stories of degeneration and corruption, moving from vital religious beginnings to staid priestly hierarchies. Within this framework, late biblical texts, that is, texts identified with these later, degenerate periods, are treated as priestly, legalistic, institutional corruptions of earlier, vital traditions. In the Old Testament, these late texts are often identified with Judaism, as distinct from earlier Israelite religion, and in the New Testament these late texts are identified with early Catholicism, as distinct from the earlier Jesus movement. Within this historical framework for biblical interpretation, then, Judaism and Catholicism come to stand for priestly corruptions of earlier religious epochs, which are idealized when compared with them.

The Law Sidled In

Although earlier biblical scholars such as Karl Heinrich Graf and Edouard Reuss had made similar arguments, it is primarily to Julius Wellhausen's 1878 *Prolegomena zur Geschichte Israels* (*Prolegomena to the History of Israel*) that we owe the establishment in German and English biblical criticism of the hypothesis that the Priestly (P) literary strand represents the latest material in the Torah.[1] Indeed, no one would deny the astounding impact of Wellhausen's *Prolegomena* on the academic culture of late nineteenth- and early twentieth-century biblical criticism. Within a few years of its publication we find a "sudden halting of new theories and the formation of an impressive critical consensus."[2] No longer was the Priestly material considered to be the *Grundschrift* of Israelite history and canonical development. On the contrary, it quickly came to be regarded as the latest material in the Pentateuch, its content reflecting a great chasm between postexilic Judaism and the vital Israelite traditions.

Many studies have noted the anti-Jewish (and at times anti-Catholic) bias evident in Wellhausen's rhetoric. But the ideological force of his work concerns far more than surface rhetoric. It is built into the very historical framework he uses for reconstructing Israelite and Jewish history.

Central to Wellhausen's historical reconstruction is the sharp distinction he makes between *Israel* before the Babylonian exile and *Judaism* after the Babylonian exile. Indeed, exile appears in his history as an unbridgeable chasm between Israel and Judaism. It "tore the nation from its native soil for half a century—a breach of historical continuity, greater than which it is scarcely possible to conceive."[3]And the mark of this breach on the literature of the Torah is the legal material of the Priestly strand. Wellhausen's concluding motto, which he takes from Vatke, puts it most succinctly: "Das Gesetz ist zwischenein getreten," that is, "the law sidled in." Between Israel and Judaism is the law. The legal material of the Priestly strand, which Wellhausen identifies with postexilic Judaism as opposed to preexilic Israelite religion, "rears the hierocracy on the tabula rasa of the wilderness." It is "the negation of nature, by means of the bald statutes of arbitrary absolutism."[4]

> Is it to be supposed that it was (say) Moses, who encouraged his people as they were struggling for bare life in the wilderness to concern themselves about a superabundantly rich endowment of their clergy? . . . For all these

> dues . . . flowed into a common coffer, and benefitted those who had the control of this, the priestly aristocracy of Jerusalem, whom it helped to rise to a truly princely position.[5]

Wellhausen illustrates his historical account of the degenerative path from preexilic Israel to postexilic Judaism through the metaphor of a tree. The Jahwist (J) strand, which, for Wellhausen, reflects the earliest period in Israelite religion, is a "green tree" in its natural, wild form. In the subsequent Deuteronomic (D) strand, that green tree is "polled, [but] not uprooted." But in the Priestly strand, the green tree is logged and hewn into "the regularly shapen timber, ever more artificially shaped with square and compass. . . . It is dry wood that is cut and made to a pattern."[6]

As this illustration makes particularly clear, Wellhausen's history is kin in many respects to other nineteenth-century romantic ideas about the history of religion, representing the social hierarchies and legal codes of organized religion as lamentable institutional corruptions of a wilder, more pristine and more universal natural religion. What makes his historical reconstruction of Israelite history particularly problematic is not this romantic orientation in and of itself, but his association of early preexilic Israelite religion with the former and postexilic Judaism with the latter. In this way Judaism is made to stand for all that is degenerative and corrupt, as far removed from its natural origins as a board in a prison wall is from the wilds of the forest. It is divorced from its own religious heritage.

Wellhausen's scholarly contribution to anti-Judaism goes far beyond any personal biases he had. It is structural, built into the very framework of his history. As such it provides academic grounding for Christian supersessionism. For it strips Judaism of its identity with Israel, giving it no legitimate claim to its own theological heritage.

Robbing Peter to Pay Paul

To the extent that Wellhausen established the paradigm for the "Higher Critical" interpretation of Israelite history, Ferdinand Christian Baur and the Tübingen School accomplished a similar paradigmatic shift in the study of the history of early Christianity. In an important article and in later works, Baur argued that the New Testament literature not only contains history, but that as a whole it presents a history of early Christianity.[7] Baur impelled the critic to trace the relationships between the New Testament books, and to perceive them as a development of teachings.

As did Wellhausen, Baur required a framework in order to trace a history out of the relationships between the New Testament books. Within a Hegelian model of dialectic history, Baur portrayed early Christianity as a struggle of ideas between the "thesis" of Jewish or Petrine Christianity (evident in Petrine material such as Matthew and Revelation) and the "antithesis" of Gentile or Pauline Christianity (evident in Paul's letters: Romans, Galatians, and 1–2 Corinthians). Within this paradigm, Paul's gospel was fundamentally at odds with the gospel of the original, "Judaizing" apostles. These gospels Baur characterized, respectively, as "freedom from the law" and "circumcision." Although Baur noted that the church required the structure of the Judaizing gospel for the Pauline gospel to endure through history, the gospel he preferred is obvious. As Peter Hodgson notes:

> Baur's special interest and preference lies with the Pauline tendency; without it, the purely hierarchical and dogmatic would result in a 'wounding of the faith.' Paulinism embodies and expresses the *fundamental* thought from which Christianity originally proceeded and which is the moving principle of its entire historical development.[8]

Baur categorized the New Testament literature according to three historical phases of teachings (*Lehrbegriffe*): the earliest phase included the first four letters of Paul; the second phase included Hebrews, the shorter Pauline letters, 1–2 Peter, James, the Synoptics, and Acts; and the latest phase included the Pastoral Epistles and the Johannine literature. Through these phases Baur saw a steady dissipation in historical value, from Paul's fiery presentation of the gospel of freedom from the Law to ever more conciliated presentations of this gospel in the face of the Judaizing opposition and later Gnostic heresies. As such, early Christian history develops from a religious expression emphasizing freedom in the spirit to one ever more bound by encroaching elements of the cult, of law and institutionalization. In this sense, sacred history is construed as a drama detailing the loss of divine presence through the cult, thereby setting the stage for the righteous reforms of Jesus on the one hand and Luther on the other.

Baur's understanding of the relationship between the unmediated Pauline gospel and later New Testament literature echoes his view of the relationship between the Reformed Protestant and Roman Catholic churches. Peter Hodgson quotes Baur: "Protestantism breaks with Catholicism because it becomes convinced that the unity of God and man, which is the absolute content of Christianity . . . cannot be envisioned in such a form as that represented by the Papacy."[9] In Roman Catholicism, Baur believed that the idea of the church had been absolutized, and its historical reality had not been kept in check by the suprahistorical idea. Thus its dynamism was lost. The Reformed church, on the other hand, had not absolutized itself as idea, but had continually maintained a dynamic tension between the idea and its historical manifestation.

Baur's framework for reconstructing the history of early Christianity functions like Wellhausen's for reconstructing Israelite history. Wellhausen's paradigm works to denigrate literature identified with the established, centralized Jerusalem cult of postexilic Judaism (and later Jewish religion). Baur's paradigm works to denigrate literature identified with the established, centralized cult of the church (and later Roman Catholicism). Baur's work also shows how an interpretative strategy that denigrates texts reflective of an organized cult has functioned to marginalize the place of both Jewish and Roman Catholic tradition in biblical criticism. Nowhere is this more clear than in Baur's characterization of Peter as the representative of "Jewish" Christianity. Here the rock on which the Roman Catholic Church is built is the emissary of the "Judaizing" tendencies in Christianity. In this model, everything before and after the Pauline teachings is ascribed marginal (and at times heretical) status.

Baur's formulation of the history of early Christianity as one of a struggle between Petrine and Pauline fronts has been attacked on many sides. The sharp divisions seen between Pauline and Petrine Christianity have been questioned.[10] Beyond this, his dependence on a Hegelian understanding of the dialectic development of "early catholicism" has often been noted.[11] Nonetheless, Baur is still ascribed the role of charting New Testament historical critical research.[12] As such, his paradigm of the relationship between the literature of the New Testament as a "development" that progresses from early unmediated revelation (the ideal free gospel) to later mediated and hierarchically structured institution (the early Catholic Church) has exerted an alarming force throughout New Testament interpretation, one that readily serves both anti-Judaism and anti-Catholicism. A brief review of how this paradigm has worked in criticism of the Pastoral Epistles (which Baur designated as some of the New Testament's latest literature) reveals the extent to which the ideology of Baur's historical interpretation still holds sway in modern biblical study.[13]

The force of Baur's historical model may be seen, for example, in Martin Dibelius and Rudolph Bultmann's notions of the dissolution of Pauline revelation in the Pastoral Epistles. Dibelius characterized them as reflective of a "Bourgeois Christianity."[14] Bultmann likewise assessed the Pastoral Epistles as a "somewhat faded Paulinism," characterizing them as "ploddingly one sided" in their movement from Paul's conception of personal piety to a culturally accommodated "religion."[15]

Ernst Käsemann linked the mediation of Pauline revelation in later New Testament literature to the delay of the parousia. As such, Käsemann's articles on the Pastoral Epistles present the later literature as a dissolution of Pauline eschatology.[16] Käsemann's *Jesus Means Freedom* makes the ideological function of this reading glaringly apparent. Here his characterizations of the New Testament literature serve as apologia for a nonstructured and noninstitutionalized church that follows Jesus as Lord. In a fascinating move, Käsemann uses his chapter on the Pastoral Epistles to demonstrate how they assert the Church as absolute over Jesus. He then compares the absolutization of the church in the Pastorals with Roman Catholicism: "With Rome, here is the symbol of the church which chooses to make itself absolute, and which in its tradition, its official capacity, and its legal claims avoids the judgment of the crucified Lord."[17]

Lest we think that such denigrating readings of late New Testament literature are the sole property of German scholarship, James Barr, a British Scholar, has offered a pointed characterization of the later texts of the Hebrew Bible and New Testament. In his reflections on the nature of Christian scripture he examines what the early or late nature of a tradition might say about its authority. In this he reveals his disdain for the theological content of the Pastoral Epistles (and other late texts).

> Thus the earlier text is not, because it is earlier, automatically superior to the later, but the later, just because it is final, is certainly not superior to the earlier. On the contrary, if we take the main central material as our basis, in either Old or New Testament, it is difficult to doubt that the approach to completeness is signalized by a certain deterioration, by a failure to understand what the basic insights of the contents of the traditions were, by a tendency to compromise on the one hand and to harden into rigid systems on the other. This can sometimes be seen in the latest touches added to books, sometimes in the more marginal books added last to the canon. Who will suppose, for instance, that 2 Peter really understood Christianity as well as 1 Peter, or that letters to Timothy are in theological content comparable with Romans or Galatians?[18]

Operating within the same historical paradigm, J. D. G. Dunn, also of Great Britain, concludes his work on the New Testament literature with a chapter entitled "Early Catholicism." Here he not only claims that the Pastoral Epistles are late and reflect the rebuttal of Gnostic heresy; he wonders if they might reflect their own heresy as well: namely "too little recognition that church life . . . can be grievously over structured, and the spirit bottled up in office and ritual." He concludes with this Baurian echo: "perhaps . . . the tragedy of early catholicism was its failure to realize that the biggest heresy of all is the insistence that there is only one ecclesiastical obedience, only one orthodoxy."[19]

Baur's paradigmatic framework continues to dominate much of New Testament criticism, but there are scholars who are working to find alternative models for reconstructing the history of early Christianity. Elisabeth Schüssler Fiorenza is a noteworthy example.[20] Although she does read 1–2 Timothy and Titus as "patriarchalizations" of the *ekklesia* and departures from the earlier *agape* fellowship of the Jesus movement, she sees these changes as the result of efforts to accommodate the church to Greco-Roman cultural models of organization. Moreover, she suggests that these texts are not descriptive but prescriptive, thereby challenging the very idea that they represent a later phase in the general history of the church.[21] This is a revolution in thought about these "later" texts. Rather than representing a general loss of Idea and Spirit, these texts represent one position within a much larger ongoing argument about the church.[22] They represent one voice within a field of contending voices. As such these texts should not be read as a stop along the way in the historical degeneration of the Pauline (or pre-Pauline) gospel.[23] History (particularly women's history) is studied not as a linear development of teachings, but rather as an ongoing, contextually specific struggle for liberation.

Conclusion

Others have acknowledged the anti-Jewish and anti-Catholic biases in our Higher Critical forebears.[24] But few have offered structural–ideological critiques of the interpretive frameworks upon which they depend, frameworks that remain dominant in many academic circles even today. There is more to ideology than bias, and more to its social power than that which resides in the interpreter's intentions. Until we acknowledge this, our well-intentioned readings remain naive about the ideological mission they might well be serving.

Academic biblical criticism after the holocaust is charged with a new sense of ethical accountability. Large narratives of original blessing and degenerative loss, of redeemed blessing and exclusive promise, such as those found within the historical constructions of Wellhausen and Baur, serve to charter chauvinistic communal identities that can easily characterize others as a threat to blessing, and thereby justify their annihilation. Clothed within the saving purposes of God, the "Higher Critical" making of biblical history has been complicit in creating religious identities that have justified a horror of human suffering for Jews, indigenous people, women, and children. Where we locate sacred origins and how we render them in relation to our current situation is never an objective or value-free endeavor. How we carve the lines and construe the historical evidence, particularly in relation to our own communities, will always require a combination of utmost ethical vigilance and modest historical vision.

NOTES

1. The first English edition, *Prologomena to the History of Israel*, trans. J. Sutherland Black and Allan Menzies (Edinburgh: A. & C. Black, 1885), was prefaced by W. Robertson Smith and included a reprint of Wellhausen's article, "Israel," from *Encyclopaedia Britannica.*
2. Brevard S. Childs, *Introduction to the Old Testament as Scripture* (Philadelphia: Fortress, 1979), 113.

3. Wellhausen, *Prolegomena zur Geschichte Israelis*, 29; translated in Lou H. Silberman, "Wellhausen and Judaism," *Semeia* 25 (1982): 77.
4. Wellhausen, 104.
5. Wellhausen, 164–165.
6. Wellhausen, 81, 361.
7. Ferdinand Christian Baur, "Die Christuspartei in der korinthischen Gemeinde der Gegensatz des petrinischen und paulinischen in der ältesten Kirche, der Apostel Petrus in Rom," *Tübinger Zeitschrift für Theologie* 4 (1831): 61–208; reprinted in *Ausgewählte Werke in Einzelausgaben, I: Historisch-kritiische Untersuchungen zum Neuen Testament*, ed. Klaus Scholder (Stuttgart-Bad Cannstatt: Freidrich Frommann Verlag, 1963).
8. Peter Hodgson, *The Formation of Historical Theology: A Study of Ferdinand Christian Baur* (New York: Harper & Row, 1966), 211.
9. Hodgson, 131–132.
10. Ernst Haenchen, *The Acts of the Apostles, a Commentary* (Philadelphia: Westminister Press, 1971), 17.
11. Robert L. Brawley, *Luke-Acts and the Jews: Conflict, Apology, Conciliation* (Atlanta: Scholars Press, 1987), 3. In addition, see the comments of William Baird, *History of New Testament Research*, Vol. 1 (Minneapolis: Fortress Press, 1992), 269, who notes "Had Baur been an uncritical devotee to Hegel, he would have affirmed the synthesis of the Jewish thesis and the Pauline antithesis in the accommodation of the second century. In actuality, Baur's own theological sympathies are solidly on the side of Paul."
12. Gerhard Kümmel, *The New Testament: The History of the Investigation of its Problems*, trans. S. McLean Gilmour and H. C. Kee (Nashville: Abingdon Press, 1972), 142–143; Baird 258–269.
13. Ferdinand Christian Baur, *Die sogenannten Pastoralbriefe des Apostles Paulus aufs neue krtisch untersucht* (Stuttgart and Tübingen: J. G. Cotta, 1835).
14. Martin Dibelius and Hans Conzelmann, *The Pastoral Epistles*, trans. Philip Buttolph and Adela Yarbro (Philadelphia: Fortress Press, 1972), 10: "The church (of the Pastoral Epistles) has obviously adjusted to the thought of the world's duration and has learned to become at home in it."
15. Rudolph Bultmann, *Theology of the New Testament*, Vol. 2, trans. Kendrick Grobel (New York: Scribners, 1955), 186.
16. Ernst Käsemann, "Paul and early Catholicism," *New Testament Questions of Today*, trans. Wilfred F. Bunge (New York: Harper & Row, 1969), 239.
17. *Jesus Means Freedom: A Polemical Survey of the New Testament*, trans. Frank Clarke (Philadelphia: Fortress Press, 1968).
18. James Barr, *Holy Scripture: Canon, Authority, Criticism* (Philadelphia: Westminster Press, 1983), 93.
19. James D. G. Dunn, *Unity and Diversity in the New Testament: An Inquiry into the Character of Earliest Christianity* (Philadelphia: Westminster Press, 1977), 365. Of late, Dunn has tempered his stance toward the Pastorals in relation to Paul. In his recent commentary on 1–2 Timothy and Titus, he notes that the Pastorals, although later than Paul's letters, ought not to be categorized as "sub-Pauline." In a footnote to this comment, Dunn offers a fascinating parallel that relates to the chronological division of Isaiah: "Isaiah 40–55 is usually classified as Deutero-Isaiah, but who would even begin to think of these chapters as 'sub-Isaiah'" ["The Pastoral Epistles," *The New Interpreters Bible*, Vol. 11 (Nashville: Abingdon, 2000), 781, n. 24]. In response to Dunn's claim we would note that, indeed, Isaiah 40–55 provided some of the most important prophetic tradition for early Christian midrash, especially for the development of Christology. On the other hand, "third Isaiah" (Chapters 56–66), deemed late and priestly by scholars since Dunn, is often denigrated or ignored as "sub-Isaiah."

20. Elisabeth Schüssler Fiorenza, *In Memory of Her: A Feminist Theological Reconstruction of Christian Origins* (New York: Crossroad, 1983), 107, writes: "The praxis and vision of Jesus and his movement is best understood as an inner-Jewish renewal movement that presented an *alternative* option to the dominant patriarchal structures rather than an oppositional formation rejecting the values and praxis of Judaism."
21. Schüssler Fiorenza, 310.
22. Schüssler Fiorenza, 310.
23. Other studies of the Pastorals reflect Schüssler Fiorenza's practice of viewing the Pastorals not as a development in early Christian history, but rather as an expression of a particular manifestation of the church. For examples, see Dennis R. MacDonald, *The Legend and the Apostle: The Battle for Paul in Story and Canon* (Philadelphia: Westminster, 1983); Luise M. Schottroff, "Oppression of Women and Hatred of Women's Liberation," in *Lydia's Impatient Sisters: A Feminist Social History of Early Christianity* (Louisville: Westminister/John Knox, 1995), 69–78; and Vincent L. Wimbush, ed., *Rhetorics of Resisitance: A Colloquy on Early Christianity as Rhetorical Formation, Semeia* 79 (1997).
24. For example, Robert P. Ericksen, "Assessing the Heritage: German Protestant Theologians, Nazis, and the 'Jewish Question,'" in *Betrayal: German Churches and the Holocaust*, eds. Robert P. Ericksen and Susannah Heschel (Minneapolis: Fortress Press, 1999), 22–39; and William R. Farmer, "A Social History of Markan Priority," in *The Gospel of Jesus: The Pastoral Relevance of the Synoptic Problem* (Louisville: Westminster/John Knox Press, 1994), 146–160.

CHAPTER 3

Reading Jesus as a Nazi

SUSANNAH HESCHEL

I

In an obsequious act of submission to Nazi ideology, many German theologians in the Third Reich transformed the central teachings of the New Testament into Nazi principles. Judaism was said to pose a violent and dangerous threat to Germans, and Jesus became an Aryan whose teachings were essentially the same as those of Hitler. That such a massive corruption of Christian teachings was possible, even under Hitler, should bring pause to theologians. That some of the theologians involved in creating the Aryan Jesus continued to teach theology in postwar Germany, often repeating the very same ideas, albeit couched in less inflammatory language, sets an important agenda for contemporary Christians, as well as all scholars of religion concerned about political misuses of religion.

The declaration during the Nazi era that Jesus was an Aryan was political shorthand. Claiming that Jesus was a Jew did not necessarily mean a rejection of National Socialism, but stating that Jesus was an Aryan made it clear that one was a Nazi and an antisemite, and also willing to modify Christian Scripture and liturgy to bring them in accord with Nazi principles. The Aryan Jesus was the confession of those who sought a teutonic brand of Christianity, rejecting the Old Testament and anything else that smacked of Jewish influence in the church, as the slogan of the pro-Nazi German Christian movement proclaimed: "Unsere Aufgabe ist Deutschland, Unsere Kraft ist Jesus" ["Our task is Germany, our strength is Jesus"]. The question of Jesus' Jewishness came to the fore in heavy debate during 1936–1937, and by the war years it became difficult, in Protestant circles, to deny that Jesus was an Aryan.

Several of the ideas central to the Aryan Christian movement were already under discussion long before 1933: whether the Old Testament should remain in the biblical canon, the racial background of Jesus, and the relationship between Christian and Jewish ethics and spirituality. Once Hitler came to power, however, the main question was how the church could play a significant role in the new state of affairs. Nazi ambivalence toward Christianity as a rival ideology, and toward the churches as potentially competing sources of authority, led some Nazi theorists, such as Alfred Rosenberg, to call for the elimination of Christianity from Germany. On one point, however, both sides were in agreement: Christianity was thoroughly infiltrated by Jewish elements. For Nazis such as Alfred Rosenberg, that meant Christianity was anathema to Germans. For church leaders, eager to defend their positions of power, it simply meant a reformation that would purge Christianity of all Jewish taint. That reformation constituted the central focus of Aryan Christian efforts throughout the Third Reich. No other issue, political or theological, occupied their attention to the same degree. Nor did the Aryan Christians hesitate when they realized the political implications of the theological position they were taking. On the contrary, they embraced whole-heartedly Nazi efforts to eliminate Jews from Germany and presented their own purging of Jewish elements from Christianity as a theological justification for their government's Final Solution.

II

Let us take, for example, Walter Grundmann,[1] professor of New Testament at Jena from 1936 to 1945 and academic director of the Institute in Eisenach, who wrote in 1941 in the preface to his book, *The Religious Face of Judaism*:

> This book will be an attempt to answer, in a generally understandable way, the question of the origins of Judaism and the nature of its general appearance. . . . One fact will remain fixed at all times: a healthy Volk must and will reject Judaism in every form. This fact is justified before history and through history. If someone is upset about Germany's attitude toward Judaism, Germany has the historical justification and historical authorization for the fight against Judaism on its side! To prove this statement is the special concern of this work; and on this statement also later research will be able to alter nothing! So this work serves the great fateful fight of the German nation for its political and economic, spiritual and cultural and also its religious freedom.[2]

The "Institute for the Study and Eradication of Jewish Influence on German Religious Life," known during the Third Reich as the "Entjudungsinstitut" [De-Judaization Institute], was established at the initiative of the Evangelical Church of Thuringia, whose leaders were early and staunch supporters of Nazism. The Thuringian region itself was nazified early; by 1930 the NSDAP controlled the regional government, establishing Wilhelm Frick as state minister. The Party's success was due, in large measure, to the work of Julius Leutheuser and Siegfried Leffler, two Bavarian pastors who organized support for the Nazi Party among the farmers of Western Thuringia in the late 1920s. Both were veterans of World War I, active in the Freikorps, and became early members of the NSDAP, joining on June 1, 1929. Leutheuser and Leffler had been asked to leave the Bavarian church in 1927 as a result of their völkisch activities and became the early forces behind the most radical wing of the Aryan Christian movement, which they based in Thuringia.[3] Their agitations among Thuringia's rural population contributed significantly to the markedly high support in that region for the NSDAP in the elections of 1928–1932.

The Landeskirchenrat, the church governing council, in Thuringia was controlled by early Nazi party members, including Leffler,[4] who became one of the regional leaders of the Aryan Christians. The bishop of Thuringia from May 1934 until his death in August 1942, Martin Sasse,[5] was an early Nazi party member and an ardent antisemite. In response to Kristallnacht Bishop Sasse published a pamphlet, on November 15, 1938, entitled, *Martin Luther on the Jews: Away with Them*, containing excerpts from Luther's notorious diatribe. In his forward Sasse wrote that Luther was the greatest antisemite of his day, the warner of his people against the Jews. Sasse condemned Ernst vom Rath's murder at the hands of a Jew and stated that the church would fight against the "corrosive spirit of Judaism . . . and every praise of the Jewish people." By 1939 the church issued laws exempting pastors from examinations in Hebrew, forbidding church membership to non-Aryan Christians, and outlawing any contact by pastors with Jews.[6]

Given the temper of the regional church, its initiative in establishing the Institute is not surprising. Hugo Pich, church superintendent, first submitted a proposal in October 1938 to Friedrich Werner, president of the Church in Berlin, outlining the goals and structure of an "Amt für Entjudung der Kirche," which would expose and eliminate "the degenerate Jewishness in Christianity and the church."[7] The Amt would carry the authority of both state and church, and, according to Pich, it would be part of Hitler's "Weltkampf gegen das Weltjudentum."[8] Pich's proposal was circulated by church officials in Berlin to the regional bishops on November 15, 1938, one week after Kristallnacht. Several months later Siegfried Leffler submitted a similar proposal, with a more detailed description of the structure of an institute to be established in Thuringia. The central functions of the institute, according to Leffler, would be scholarly, producing a journal and a monograph series, as well as offering courses for pastors and religious teachers. The director and co-workers would be university theology professors and dozenten. The Institute was formally opened in April 1939, in ceremonies on the Wartburg in Eisenach. Leffler served as general director and Grundmann as academic director. Published membership records include the names of over forty university professors, and several hundred church officials, pastors, and religious teachers. Included as academic members were Adolf Bartels, Georg Beer, Georg Bertram, Walter Birnbaum, Gustav Entz, Johannes Hempel, Johannes Leipoldt, Wolf Meyer-Erlach, Theodor Odenwald, Rudi Paret, Herbert Preisker, Martin Redeker, Hartmut Schmoekel, and Georg Wobbermin, among others.

The Institute's two main functions were sponsoring conferences and publications. Large conferences were annual events, and smaller lectures were scheduled frequently in different parts of Germany, usually in connection with a university theology faculty. The conferences began and ended with hymns, Bible readings, prayers, and the Hitler salute, and attendance included academics, lay people, and clergy, for whom the church paid travel costs. Among the papers delivered at the conferences were whether Jesus' mother tongue was really a Semitic language (Prof. Hugo Odeberg of Lund, Sweden, 1942); the danger of Judaization in religious education (Prof. Hermann Werdermann, Dortmund, 1942); the difference between prophetic understandings of God and that of Jesus (Pastor Hans Pohlmann, Schneidemühl, 1942); Philo and Jewish propaganda in the ancient world (Prof. Georg Bertram, Giessen, 1939); the influence of modern Jewish thinkers, especially Spinoza and Mendelssohn, on German culture (Grundmann, 1942); and the application of racial historical methods on the study of the Old Testament (Prof. Karl Friedrich Euler, Giessen, 1941). The papers delivered were published in three volumes, edited by Grundmann, in 1940, 1942, and 1943.[9]

Additional publications of the Institute included an annual report of activities, with articles describing the Institute's mission and successes; monographs by Grundmann and others on Judaism and early Christianity; and revised liturgical materials, including a hymnal, *Grosser Gott Wir Loben Dich*, and a New Testament, *Die Botschaft Gottes*,[10] both of which were purged of all Jewish references. The New Testament, for example, contained no references to the genealogy of Jesus from David, expunged Jewish terms, such as Jehovah, Israel, Zion, and Jerusalem, and eliminated the Last Supper, John the Baptist, and Paul. In the forward Grundmann compared his work to that of Luther, writing, "This work, arising at the time of the decisive struggle of the Germans, will be a service for the soul of the German volk." This version of the New Testament was distributed to German soldiers on the front.[11]

The Institute's financing came from the church. Each of the German state churches was asked to make annual contributions of several thousand Reichmarks. Substantial contributions also came from a bank account under the private control of church president Friedrich Werner in Berlin. The Institute itself was housed in a large villa in Eisenach that belonged to the church, and which today serves as the Predigerseminar for Thuringia. With the onset of the war, the Institute grew and flourished. Hitler had called for a suspension, in early 1940, of state harassment of the churches, in order to encourage total support for the war effort. The alliance with the Soviet Union undermined Rosenberg's position by forcing an end to anticommunist rhetoric, thereby weakening the power of one of the most ardent Nazi opponents of Christianity[12] and granting increased attention to anti-Jewish propaganda.

The theology formulated by the Institute had a dual function: to provide unqualified support to Nazi government policies and to create a niche for Christianity in the new Nazi order. Above all, church leaders wanted to be important to the government, to protect their own interests and to take part in a revolution they found fascinating. The main contribution the church could make was through propaganda. Certainly, a sermon from a pastor, preaching each week from the chancel, carried a far greater impact than the weekly newspaper, *Der Stürmer*, with its semipornographic offenses to bourgeois values. The Aryan Christians sought to carry out their mission with eagerness.

Moreover, Grundmann and his colleagues at the Institute were not simply local pastors; they were professors of theology at German universities, training the coming generation of pastors. Some held positions of high importance in the academic world of German theology; Johannes Hempel, for example, who chaired the Institute's working group on the Old Testament, held the professorship of Old Testament at the University of Berlin and served as editor of the *Zeitschrift für die alttestamentliche Wissenschaft*. Most of the most active members, however, were professors of New Testament, which gave their writings on Judaism added weight. Within the German university, the study of Judaism was located primarily in the theological faculties, among the professors of New Testament. The study of Christian origins necessitated knowledge of rabbinic and Hellenistic Judaism, although that knowledge was generally used to draw a contrast between a degenerate ancient Judaism and early Christianity. Grundmann himself studied at the University of Tübingen under the New Testament scholar Gerhard Kittel, whose expertise on the history of Judaism was esteemed both by his academic colleagues and by Nazi party officials who consulted him on the so-called "Jewish Question."[13] Indeed, it was during his studies in Tübingen, while serving as an assistant to Kittel in preparing the *Theological Dictionary of the New Testament*,[14] that Grundmann joined the Nazi party, becoming one of its earliest members.

The Christian theology developed by Grundmann was a Nazified Christianity. He justified Nazi antisemitism by arguing that Jesus himself was utterly opposed to everything Jewish, that Jesus came from a racially non-Jewish background in the Galilee, that Jewish influences present within the New Testament were the result of early Jewish Christian dogmatic falsifications, and that the de-Judaization of Christianity would continue the work of the Lutheran Reformation. Grundmann's formulations did not stem from any original research on his part; rather, he was able to draw on existing arguments published by other scholars. Ernst Lohmeyer, in 1936, contended there was a two-site origin of Christianity, in Galilee and Jerusalem, representing Gentile and Jewish viewpoints, respectively.[15] Lohmeyer argued for a two-site eschatology, a son of man eschatology that developed in the Gentile Galilee and a messiah eschatology that developed in Jewish Judea. Adolf Schlatter, with whom Grundmann studied in Tübingen, had earlier contended, in his *Geschichte Israels*, that whatever Jewish religious presence did exist in the Galilee in the first century had resulted from forced conversion of non-Jews to Judaism.[16]

The devastation of the Jewish population of the Galilee by the Babylonian conquest in 587 B.C.E. was a well-known fact. Modern scholars, however, were confronted by a myth of an Aryan Galilee that became popular among German nationalists seeking to purge Jesus of any Jewish associations. The argument that Jesus was an Aryan first arose during the nineteenth century in Germany as nationalists questioned whether Christianity was a suitable religion for Germans, since Jesus was a Jew. The philosopher Johann Fichte was among the first to question the ethnic origins of Jesus, and Paul de Lagarde argued that Jesus, in proclaiming himself the son of man, was actually saying, "I am not a Jew." Houston Stewart Chamberlain's best-seller of 1900, *Foundations of the Nineteenth Century*, popularized the idea that Jesus was most likely Aryan, while Artur Dinter, in his popular 1934 pamplet, *War Jesus Jude?*, declared Jesus an Aryan, the destroyer of Judaism and the Old Testament, and the greatest Nazi and antisemite of all times. Emanuel Hirsch's denial of Jesus' Jewishness, in *The Essence of Christianity*, published in 1939, gave the claim added academic prestige.

In his 1941 life of Jesus, *Jesus der Galiläer*, Grundmann presented evidence for Jesus' distinctiveness from Judaism and his repudiation of it. Most of his arguments were drawn from the work of other scholars and nothing was strikingly original. Still, given the context of the Nazi era, even his repetition of old anti-Jewish canards take on an ominous ring. For example, Grundmann cited rabbinic claims that Jesus was the illegitimate child of Mary and a Roman soldier to assert that Jesus' father was not Jewish. Because Mary is a non-Jewish name, he argued, Jesus' parentage could not have been Jewish. Citing Lohmeyer, Grundmann argued Jesus' use of the Galilean title "son of man," rather than the Jewish title "messiah" was further proof of his Gentile identity. To prove that Jesus' own piety stood in opposition to Judaism Grundmann cited his intimate relationship with God as father, Abba; his sense of authority rooted in himself, rather than in Torah; and his teaching while wandering, rather than in a rabbinical school. Although Jesus cited the prophets and psalms of the Old Testament, Grundmann argued that this was insignificant because "so much more that is in the Old Testament was not cited by Jesus."[17] Most important was the distinction between Jesus' intimacy with God and the master–slave relationship that Grundmann argued was promoted in the Old Testament and postbiblical Jewish literature.[18] Jesus' central teaching of the fatherhood of God and the sonship of the believer was drawn not from Judaism, but from Epictetus and Seneca.[19] Finally, Grundmann uses the crucifixion in a circular argument: because Jesus rejected Judaism so completely, he was crucified by the Jews; and the fact that the Jews crucified Jesus is proof that Jesus repudiated Judaism.[20] Grundmann's conclusion: "We can . . . with the greatest probability, [assert] that Jesus was no Jew. . . . However, the other question, to which people he did belong, cannot be answered."[21]

The most important element of the Aryan argument, however, was the claim that Jesus's spirituality was radically different from Judaism. Relatively little attention is given to defining the positive content of the Aryan Geist, while most of the attention goes to defining the nature of the repugnant Jewish Geist. For Grundmann and other members of his institute, the most common distinction was between Jesus' intimacy with God, as a father–son relationship, and the master–slave relationship characteristic of the Old Testament and postbiblical Jewish literature.[22] This "Abba argument," which was popularized by Joachim Jeremias after the war, was first developed by Grundmann in a 1938 book, based on Kittel's article on "Abba" in the *Theological Dictionary*. Jesus, Grundmann said, addressed God as Abba, father, which no Jew did, since the Jews' relationship with God was distant and remote. Jews called God "Father," whereas Jesus called God "Abba," or "my father."[23] Jesus' central teaching of the fatherhood of God and the sonship of the believer stands in opposition to Judaism, and is drawn from the teachings of Epictetus and Seneca.[24] The implications of the Abba argument were important: the God of the Jews was remote and the Jews were devoid of inner devotion and were stuck in legalism, exemplified, Grundmann writes, by the ten commandments.[25] The God of Judaism is determined by "Vergeltungsgedanken," or retaliation, whereas "the Sermon on the Mount of Jesus is the source of the unmediated relationship with God, exemplified in the appearance of Jesus of Nazareth himself."[26] The distinction is not an accident; Jesus undertook a fight against Jahwe as a tribal God and against Judaism.[27] In contrast, Jesus did not proclaim the Jewish God, but rather a spiritual experience of God. As a result, Christians, like Aryans, have a closeness to God, a spiritual experience of divine presence, and judge ethical situations individually, not on the basis of general laws; the Semitic is intellectual, the Aryan is moral.

In avowing the political goals underlying his theology Grundmann was quite direct. In a lecture delivered at an institute-sponsored conference held in 1941, Grundmann explains the importance of his view of Jesus for the present political strivings of Germany: "Our Volk, which stands above all else in a struggle against the satanic powers of world Jewry for the order and life of this world, dismisses Jesus, because it cannot struggle against the Jews and open its heart to the king of the Jews."[28] Not to worry, Grundmann reassures his readers; Jesus was no Jewish messiah. The struggle against the satanic Jews can be carried forth without having to abandon Jesus. Neither a messiah nor a Jew, Jesus presents no obstacle to bringing an end to Judaism. To alleviate any possible moral concerns about Germany's treatment of the Jews, Grundmann wrote, "To this very day Jewry persecutes Jesus, and all who follow him, with unreconcilable hatred. By contrast, Aryan people in particular can find in Jesus Christ an answer to every and the deepest question."[29]

Finally, in an article on Moses Mendelssohn, published in 1943, Grundmann blames modern Jewish theologians for intolerance toward Christianity in the Third Reich. Because Mendelssohn and others had written that Christianity was Judaism for non-Jews, and that Jesus was a Jewish teacher, some Nazis had attacked Christianity as a Jewish religion. Even Nazis could be duped by Jewish propaganda. As always, Grundmann's solution was the elimination of Jews from Germany and of Jewishness from Christianity.[30]

In the summer of 1944 Church Superintendent Hugo Pich, whose 1938 report had served as the basis for establishing the Institute, sent a proposal to church officials for a more thorough de-Judaization of the Scriptures, entitled "The Jew Saul and his Proclamation of Christ in the Light of the Fire of the Jewish Global Conflagration." Pich called for a thorough overhaul of the Pauline epistles, arguing that they were infected with Jewish notions that had contaminated Christianity. By this time, both church and Institute officials were unsympathetic, given the war conditions.[31] Moreover, as Bishop Walther Schultz of Mecklenburg, an early supporter of the Institute, argued, Pich's proposal regarding the Pauline epistles would imply that for so many centuries the church had been held hostage by a Jew: "I consider Pich's report absolutely bizarre and for that reason an insult to our Volk, whom one here indirectly blames, that in their miserable narrowness and lack of instinct they were seduced for 1500 years by some stinking Jew."[32]

In Grundmann's massive quantity of publications after 1945 he does not refer to his Nazi-era writings, nor does he refer to Jesus as an Aryan. But Jesus remains a Galilean utterly opposed to everything Jewish, which is why the Jews crucified him, and Judaism remains a spiritually degenerate religion that promoted violence and intolerance in the Hellenistic world, including forcible conversion and circumcision, at point of death, of the Galilean community. Take, for example, his 1956 description of the Jewish rebellions against the Romans: "The demons of a fanatical nationalism pushed Israel into the abyss; in the Jewish war these words were fulfilled in terrible ways."[33]

With the end of the war and the entrance of the American Armed Forces into Thuringia in the spring of 1945, efforts were made to maintain the Institute. Grundmann had been drafted into the army in 1943, with Bertram succeeding him as academic director of the Institute. In a report to the church in May 1945, Bertram requested permission to retain his leadership of the Institute and urged that it continue its research efforts.[34] The new members of the Landeskirchenrat, however, were no longer the Aryan Christians of the Nazi era, but had been replaced by members of the Confessing Church, and they denied Bertram's request. Grundmann returned to Thuringia in the fall of 1945, after serving as a prisoner of war for several months, and he learned that he had been dismissed from his position as Professor of New Testament at the University of Jena, because he had joined the Nazi party so early—in December 1930. He applied, in December 1945, to the Landeskirchenrat to continue the work of the Institute, and was rejected. Grundmann was asked by the Thuringian church to leave the region and return to his home church of Saxony, where he had been born. The church of Saxony was unwilling to accept him, so he reapplied for admission in Thuringia in 1947 and was finally assigned pastoral duties. By 1954 Grundmann's academic career was once again blossoming; he was appointed Rektor of the Katechetenseminar in Eisenach, lectured at the theological seminary in Leipzig, and became the academic advisor to the Evangelische Verlagsanstalt, the Protestant publishing house of the German Democratic Republic. In 1974 he was appointed Kirchenrat in Thuringia, an honorary position.

The postwar careers of other members of the Institute also flourished. Most of his colleagues from the Institute retained their university appointments, as well as their positions within their respective churches. Martin Redeker, a noted Schleiermacher scholar, remained at the University of Kiel, and Johannes Hempel retained both his professorship at Berlin and his editorship of the distinguished *Zeitschrift für die alttestamentliche Wissenschaft.* Similarly, Wilhelm Koepp remained at Greifswald, Gustav Entz at Vienna, Walter Birnbaum at Göttingen, and Hugo Odeberg, professor at the University of Lund, Sweden, retained his prominent reputation as a scholar of Judaica. Grundmann was replaced at the University of Jena by Herbert Preisker, who had been a member of the Institute, and Rudolf Meyer, another one-time Institute member, also joined the Jena faculty. Johannes Leipoldt retained his position at Leipzig and collaborated with Grundmann on a large, three-volume collection of primary texts from the Greco-Roman world, together with extensive commentaries, promoting Grundmann's reputation even further.[35]

Grundmann's output of publications in the postwar years prior to his death in 1976 was enormous. His gospel commentaries in particular were widely read by pastors and theology students in both East and West Germany, replacing as the standard works the commentaries of Adolf Schlatter, his former teacher. Although he ceased discussing the question of Jesus' racial identity, his postwar writings continue his central argument that Jesus' teachings stand in fundamental opposition to those of Judaism. What is striking is that his postwar readers found nothing objectionable to his theological arguments. Within the context of a long tradition of anti-Judaism within New Testament scholarship, there was nothing unusual in Grundmann's characterizations of Judaism. The "hatred" and "demonic nationalism" that he ascribes to Palestinian Jews at the time of Jesus continue in his postwar writings, as does his insistence on Jewish responsibility for the crucifixion. That the denigration of Judaism presented in his writings participated in the Holocaust is never acknowledged by him.

In 1941 Pastor Karl Dungs of Essen wrote a long letter to the Ministry of Propaganda in which he declared, "The Jewish question is the central issue of the church struggle."[36] In the debates that took place among the different factions of the Aryan Christians, and between the Aryan Christians and the Confessing Church, the element that bound them together was antisemitism. Different positions were defined in relation to the assessment of the "Jewish threat." Dungs himself concluded his letter by asserting that the problem that the church must now address is what to do with the Old Testament, now that the Jews have disappeared from Germany. The depraved indifference to the fate of the Jews on the part of so many pastors and theologians is a scandal that will confront us for generations to come.

III

At stake, however, is not simply the activities of a group of theologians during the Third Reich, but their participation in a larger pattern of thinking that began long before and continued long after. Indeed, postwar German scholarship on the New Testament shows a striking combination: some theologians who show remarkable attentiveness to removing anti-Judaism from the Christian tradition, and others whose work betrays a striking indifference. Traces of Grundmann can still be found in some popular writings in Germany. A German feminist theologian, Christa Mulack, blamed Nazism on Judaism, which she identified as a "male" religion, in contrast to the "female" morality of Jesus:

> We can say that the relations of Jesus with the law corresponded to typically female ideas, while those of the Pharisees and Scribes were at home in a typically male mental world. . . . It is always the same thing: Within patriarchy no man takes responsibility for his deeds, because he acts on the command of someone higher. The men themselves wash their hands in innocence. These men would have done exactly as Pilate, if Jesus had let them, but also exactly like Rudolf Hess or Adolf Eichmann, who pleaded 'not guilty,' because in the last analysis they had only followed the com-

> mand of a Führer. And if this Führer commanded murder, then his followers would certainly have to murder. With all the differences that are certainly present here, the inner methods of argumentation are still the same. It always shows the same obedience to authority that is so typical for the male gender.[37]

Her argument was popularized in a best-seller that appeared in Germany in 1989, in which journalist Franz Alt identified Nazism with Pharisaism, suggesting that Judaism was to blame for the Holocaust.[38] In his book, which was described as "the first antisemitic best-seller since 1945,"[39] Alt described the Nazi murder of Jewish women and children in August 1941:

> The murder of children at Biela-Zerkov happened because there was a command for it. The near stoning of the adulterous woman [described in the gospels] happened, because there was a law for it. But where was the conscience in both of these stories about men? Christa Mulack: 'It is always the same thing: Within patriarchy no man takes repsonsibility for his deeds, because he acts on the command of someone higher. The men themselves wash their hands in innocence.'[40]

The conclusion that Mulack draws is that Hess and Eichmann are typical examples of patriarchal morality that disclaims responsibility by appealing to a "higher authority," a morality that, Mulack argues, characterizes Judaism. In an assertion that aroused no comment by reviewers of her book, Mulack maintains that Jewish adherence to divine commandments is equivalent to Nazi obedience to the criminal orders of their superiors. Nazism is the result of the triumph of Jewish patriarchal morality over Jesus' feminist morality. German Christians are thus in no way responsible for the Holocaust; Jews are made by Mulack into victims of their own religion. And who is washing her hands in innocence?

IV

Scholars in several fields have articulated their conviction that the Holocaust calls into question the basic frame of reference of their fields. Edith Wyschogrod writes that "the meaning of self, time, and language are all affected by mass death. . . . We are in the grip of immense experiential changes which both create and reflect new philosophical perspectives."[41] No other field has been challenged as severely by the Holocaust as that of Christian theology. Held responsible as a major source for antisemitism in Europe, its moral legitimacy is called into question. Not only its specific teachings about Jews and Judaism, beginning in the New Testament, but one or another of its modes of thinking—apocalyptic, gnostic, redemptive—are interrogated as the modes by which Nazism structured its ideology. Yet some historians studying the churches during the Nazi period hold the church exempt from responsibility for the Holocaust, as persecuted victims of National Socialism along with the Jews, as Kurt Meier argues, or as independent wellsprings of theological purity, as Trutz Rendtorff argues.[42] Such conclusions are possible only when disconfirming data are ignored, or the wrong questions are posed. Numerous studies of the churches in the Third Reich avoid the Holocaust, defining Nazism solely in terms of its nationalism and war mongering. Few provide information about membership of church officials in the Nazi party and related organizations. Antisemitism is too often defined solely as a biological hatred of Jews, as if it were unrelated to the moral and spiritual denigration of Judaism found in Christian writings. Others define Hitler's hatred of Jews as symbolic of his deeper hatred of Christianity.[43]

The theological problem is whether the Aryan Jesus movement is a product of Christianity, or of Christianity gone awry. What the experience of the churches in Nazi Germany makes clear is that no mechanism exists within Christian theology that was capable of excluding Nazi excesses as un-Christian. The story of the Institute calls into question whether German Protestant theology has an intrinsic moral commitment and self-judgment, as it is clear that Grundmann's efforts would have been praised had the Nazis won; the sympathetic judgment of several contemporary church historians makes that clear. I would argue that Christian inhibitions against violent atrocities were eroded once four conditions were met: the institutional church gave its approval; the actions and beliefs were routinized by citing older, well-known theological anti-Judaism; the Jews were presented as a moral danger to Christians; and a theological appeal to so-called higher authority, values, or spirituality was formulated. That the German Christian movement emerged out of liberal Protestantism is crucial; it presented itself as a modern, scientific theological movement, not as a religious faith rooted in the supernatural; it was a religion that affirmed society, its political structures, and its intellectual discourse.

In his critique of Emil Durkheim's claim that "man is a moral being only because he lives in society," Zygmunt Bauman has argued for the social production of immoral behavior. Morality, Bauman writes, "may manifest itself in insubordination towards socially upheld principles, and in an action openly defying social solidarity and consensus."[44] Morality is not the product of society, but is presocial, Bauman argues, and it is something that society manipulates and exploits. If responsibility, as Levinas argues, is the essential structure of subjectivity, morality is the primary structure of intersubjective relation, and its creation is presocial, Bauman argues. Morality is not a product of society, but is something that society manipulates and exploits. So, too, with theology. Although it claims to be the creator and upholder of morality, morality is both prior and independent of theology. The Institute functioned as the religious justification for the social production of Nazi antisemitism. What the German Christian movement created was a theology able to manipulate and exploit morality.[45]

NOTES

1. Grundmann, born in in Chemnitz in 1906, joined the NSDAP on December 1, 1930, shortly after arriving in Tübingen to serve as assistant to Gerhard Kittel on the *Theologisches Wörterbuch zum Neuen Testament*; his membership number was 382544.
2. Walter Grundmann and Karl Friedrich Euler, *Das religiöse Gesicht des Judentums: Entstehung und Art* (Leipzig: Verlag Georg Wigand, 1942).
3. Anja Rinnen, *Kirchenmann und Nationalsozialist: Siegfried Lefflers ideelle Verschmelzung von Kirche und Drittem Reich* (Weinheim: Deutscher Studien Verlag, 1995), 65–67.
4. Siegfried Leffler, born in 1900, joined the NSDAP on June 1, 1929; his membership number was 138841. Julius Leutheuser, also born in 1900, joined the NSDAP the same day; his membership number was 138836. BDC, Leffler, and Leutheuser materials.
5. Martin Sasse, born in 1890, joined the NSDAP on March 1, 1930; his membership number was 204010 BDC, Sasse materials.
6. Copies of the regulations are found in the Archive of the Evangelische Church in Thüringen (LKA) in Eisenach.
7. Friedrich Werner, born in 1897, joined the NSDAP on January 1, 1931; his membership number was 411184.
8. Pich's proposal is found in the Zentral Archiv der evangelischen Kirche, Berlin.
9. *Christentum und Judentum: Studien zur Erforschung ihres gegenseitigen Verhältnisses* Sitzungsberichte der ersten Arbeitstagung des Institutes zur Erforschung des jüdischen Einflusses auf das deutsche kirchliche Leben vom 1. bis 3. März 1940 in Wittenberg, hrsg. Walter Grundmann. (Leipzig: G. Wigand, 1940). *Germanentum, Christentum und Judentum: Studien zur Erforschung ihres gegenseitigen Verhältnisses*, Vol. 2. Sitzungesberichte der zweiten Arbeitstagung des Instituts zur Erforschung des jüdischen Einflusses auf das deutsche kirchliche Leben vom 3. bis 5. März 1941 in Eisenach. Hrsg. Walter Grundmann. (Leipzig: Verlag Georg Wigand, 1942). *Germanentum, Christenum und Judentum.* Studien zur Erforschung ihres gegenseitigen Verhaeltnisses. Dritter Band. Sitzungesberichte der dritten Arbeitstagung des Instituts zur Erforschung des jüdischen Einflusses auf das deutsche kirchliche Leben vom 9. bis 11. Juni 1942 in Nuernberg. Hrsg. Walter Grundmann. (Leipzig: Georg Wigand, 1943).
10. *Die Botschaft Gottes*, hrsg. vom Institut zur Erforschung des jüdischen Einflusses auf das deutsche kirchliche Leben. (Leipzig: Otto Wigand, 1940). The forward was signed by Grundmann, Wilhelm Büchner, Erich Fromm, Heinz Hunger, and Heinrich Weinmann.
11. According to information from the Archivist of the LKA in Eisenach, Pfarrer Heinz Koch; Grundmann's own Personal Akten are closed until 2006.
12. See J. S. Conway, *The Nazi Persecution of the Churches* (New York: Basic Books, 1968), 284.
13. Robert P. Ericksen, *Theologians Under Hitler: Gerhard Kittel, Paul Althaus and Emanuel Hirsch* (New Haven and London: Yale University Press, 1985).
14. Grundmann contributed over twenty articles to the *Theologisches Wörterbuch zum Neuen Testament*, which was edited by Gerhard Kittel; volumes began to appear in 1933. Kittel himself joined the NSDAP in May 1933.
15. Ernst Lohmeyer, *Galiläa und Jerusalem* (Göttingen: Vandenhoeck & Ruprecht, 1936).
16. Adolf Schlatter, *Geschichte Israels von Alexander dem Grossen bis Hadrian* (3rd Auflage; Stuttgart: Calwer Verlag, 1925), 13, based on Josephus, *Antiquities*, 13, 318f. "Die Unterwerfung der Galiläer unter die Juden erfolgte durch Zwangsbeschneidung und Zwangsannahme der

jüdischen Religion. Wer sich weigerte, wurde von seinem Boden vertrieben." Cited by Grundmann, *Jesus der Galiläer*, 169. For a description of his closeness to Schlatter during his student days, see Grundmann's unpublished autobiography, *Erkenntnis und Wahrheit*, LKA Eisenach, 19–21.

17. *Jesus der Galiläer*, 143.
18. Walter Grundmann, *Die Gotteskindschaft in der Geschichte Jesu und ihre religionsgeschichtlichen Voraussetzungen* (Weimar: Verlag Deutsche Christen, 1938), 31.
19. Ibid., 15.
20. *Jesus der Galiläer*, 162.
21. Ibid., 199.
22. Walter Grundmann, *Die Gotteskindschaft in der Geschichte Jesu*, 31. See also Walter Grundmann, *Aufnahme und Deutung der Botschaft Jesu im Urchristentum* (Weimar: Verlag Deutsche Christen, 1941), 27; Schenk, 65.
23. Walter Grundmann, *Wer Ist Jesus von Nazareth?* (Weimar: Verlag Deutsche Christen, 1940), 22.
24. Grundmann, *Die Gotteskindschaft*, 15.
25. Grundmann, *Wer Ist Jesus von Nazareth?*, 22.
26. Walter Grundmann, *Die Bergrede Jesu* (Schriften zur Nationalkirche Nr. 10; Weimar: Verlag Deutsche Christen, 1939), 16.
27. Walter Grundmann, *Der Gott Jesu Christi* (Weimar: Verlag Deutsche Christen, n.d.). Delivered at a conference in 1936.
28. Walter Grundmann, "Das Messiasproblem," in *Germanentum, Christentum und Judentum: Studien zur Erforschung ihres gegenseitigen Verhältnisses*, Vol. 2, ed. Walter Grundmann, (Sitzungesberichte der zweiten Arbeitstagung des Instituts zur Erforschung des jüdischen Einflusses auf das deutsche kirchliche Leben vom 3. bis 5. März 1941 in Eisenach), 381.
29. *Deutsche mit Gott: Ein deutsches Glaubensbuch* (Weimar: Verlag Deutsche Christen, 1941).
30. Walter Grundmann, "Mendelssohn und Hamann," in *Germanentum, Christenum und Judentum* (Leipzig: Georg Wigand, 1943), 1–48.
31. Sievers to Pich, 15 August 1944, re. "Der Weg zur entjudeten deutschen Reichskirche in der Glaubensgefolgschaft Jesu: . . . nachdem der totale Krieg in schärfster Form eingesetzt hat, wir nur einen Gedanken haben dürfen, wie wir unserem Vaterland in diesem Schicksalskampf dienen und helfen können. Ich muss es sowohl persönlich, als auch als Vorsitzender der Arbeitsgemeinschaft evangelischer Kirchenleiter und als stellvertretender Leiter des Instituts zur Eforschung . . . ablehnen, mich jetzt mit der Neugestaltung der Kirche zu befassen und ich möchte auch Ihnen dringend empfehlen, diese Sache jetzt ruhen zu lassen."
32. Bishop Walther Schultz to President Rönck, 2 August 1944 re. Pich's Denkschrift, *Der Jude Schaul*. LKA Thüringen, Personalia: Leffler, Grundmann: Institut, 1938–1944.
33. Walter Grundmann, *Die Geschichte Jesu Christi* (Berlin: Evangelische Verlagsanstalt, 1956), 160.
34. Georg Bertram, *Denkschrift betr.* Aufgaben eines theologischen Forschungs-Instituts zu Eisenach 6 May 1945, 1. LKA Thüringen, Bestand A921: Akten des Landeskirchenrats der Evangelisch-Lutherischen Kirche in Thüringen über Entjudung der Kirche, 1939–1947.
35. Walter Grundmann and Johannes Leipoldt, *Umwelt des Urchristentums*, 3 vol. (Berlin: Evangelische Verlagsanstalt, 1965–1967).
36. YIVO Archive, New York, Berlin Collection Reel G135.
37. Christa Mulack, *Jesus: der Gesalbte der Frauen* (Stuttgart: Kreuz Verlag, 1987), 155–156.
38. Franz Alt, *Jesus—der erste neue Mann* (München: Piper Verlag, 1989).
39. Micha Brumlik, *Der Anti-Alt* (Frankfurt am Main: Eichborn Verlag, 1991).
40. Alt, *Jesus*, 84.

41. Edith Wyschogrod, *Spirit in Ashes: Hegel, Heidegger, and Man-Made Mass Death* (New Haven: Yale University Press, 1985), ix.
42. Trutz Rendtorff, "Das Wissenschaftsverständnis der protestantischen Universitätstheologie im Dritten Reich," in *Theologische Fakultäten im Nationalsozialismus*, eds. Leonore Siegele-Wenschkewitz and Carsten Nicolaisen (Göttingen: Vandenhoeck and Ruprecht, 1993), 19–44.
43. Karl Barth, "The Protestant Churches in Europe," *Foreign Affairs* 21 (January1943): 263.
44. Zygmunt Bauman, *Modernity and the Holocaust* (Ithaca: Cornell University Press, 1989), 177.
45. The author would like to thank the archivist of the Landeskirchenarchiv Thüringen, Pfarrer Heinz Koch, for his very gracious assistance and advice.

CHAPTER 4

Shoah Consciousness and the Silence of American Christian Biblical Scholarship

MARK K. GEORGE

I have found in my conversations with American Jews that the Shoah is something about which many of them, if not all of them, are continually aware. Many American Jews born after World War II spent hours watching movies on the Shoah as part of their religious school training, and thus the Shoah has become a central part of their self-understanding as Jews.

As an American Christian biblical scholar, I find myself keenly aware that my own self-understanding, at least professionally, is not shaped to the same degree by the Shoah, and I find this to be rather curious. On a professional level, Jewish religious scholars have grappled with the significance of the Shoah for a number of years, and it has been a central focus of their work. Indeed, Richard L. Rubenstein argued that "the question of God and the death camps . . . is *the question* for Jewish theology in our times."[1] But why hasn't this question been "the question" of *Christian* theologians and biblical scholars in our time? Granted, unlike the Jews, Christians were not the target of systematic Nazi violence. But certainly Christian theology, scholarship, and attitudes toward Judaism and Jews contributed to Nazi ideology and the Shoah. Thus Rubenstein's question seems to me to be a very important question for Christianity and Christian theologians to address, and leads to my question about why the question of God (or perhaps more appropriately, the Christian understanding of God) and the death camps has not become "the question" for Christian theologians and biblical scholars.

To be fair, several Christian theologians have grappled with the significance of the Shoah, such as P. van Allen, F. Littell, and R. R. Ruether. But these scholars are the exceptions, and their numbers are relatively few. Furthermore, there have been more Christian theologians, rather than biblical scholars, who have taken up this question. Where are the Christian biblical scholars? Why haven't they taken up this question? Certainly this volume as well as an earlier volume, *Strange Fire*, on reading the Hebrew Bible after the Shoah, have begun to correct this lacuna in biblical studies, but the response has been slow in coming.[2] At a minimum, it seems to me that those scholars who understand themselves to be Christian biblical theologians and who write biblical theologies should have taken up this question, although in general they have not done so.

My question could be addressed from a variety of angles, and my hope is that these angles will be explored by others. The answer is complex, and exploring all (or even a significant number of) the reasons for this lacuna in biblical studies is beyond the scope of this essay. So here I want to formulate one response, namely how Christian biblical studies go about the task of interpreting biblical texts in terms of the methodologies employed, particularly at the beginning of the twenty-first century, and how these methodologies address or fail to address the question of the Shoah. The disturbing conclusion of this analysis will be that although the methodologies currently used in the field of Christian biblical studies make it possible to address the question of (the Christian) God and the death camps, the question still remains largely unanswered. This raises another question, namely, is there an ethical or moral obligation on the part of Christian biblical scholars (and biblical theologians) to address this question, to seek to answer, as Christians, what Jewish theologians have found to be a very difficult question? Perhaps there is no such obligation for Christian biblical scholars. But if we fail to provide a response to this question, then it seems to me that our silence perpetuates the long history of anti-Judaism and Christian supersessionism that has characterized Jewish–Christian relations since the beginning of Christianity.

The Search for History

"Modern" Christian biblical studies in the Western world began during the Reformation and Enlightenment periods.[3] Historical criticism emerged as the dominant form of Christian biblical criticism among Protestant biblical critics as a result of the emphasis Luther, Calvin, and other reformers placed on the priority of the biblical text and on interpreting the Bible in terms of other biblical texts, rather than according to Church teachings on the Bible.[4] This emphasis on the biblical text gradually developed into the historical critical method, a means of reading the Bible that would reveal the meaning of the text for Christians and Christianity.[5] Historical criticism has provided important insights into the Bible, and was the primary means of critically interpreting the biblical text through the mid-twentieth century.

Historical criticism sought to achieve several goals, one of which was to take seriously the study of the language and grammar of the biblical text. Each biblical author has used language in a particular way, and historical critics sought to understand the biblical languages better in order to understand the way in which those authors used their language. The concern with language and grammar also led to the rise of textual criticism and the attempt to understand how differences between copies ("witnesses") of the biblical texts arose and then to evaluate which copies were more original than others.

Related to this goal is the assumption by historical critics that history can be studied objectively, and therefore it has sought to develop a means to reconstruct and evaluate that history. Historical criticism assumes texts have meanings that were shaped by the historical contexts in which those texts were produced, and thus one of the primary tasks of historical criticism is to use linguistic and grammatical evidence, archaeological finds, literary and cultural remains from surrounding cultures, and other artifacts to reconstruct those historical contexts and to determine those original meanings. This "original" meaning is a text's true meaning and contains the meaning and truth a historical critic's contemporaries need to understand and apply that biblical text to their own contexts.

In developing these guidelines and methods for their work, Christian historical critics sought to break with the way in which the Bible had been read and interpreted throughout much of the Church's history. Prior to the rise of historical criticism, the Bible had been acknowledged as having multiple meanings, and interpreters employed the exegetical principle of the four senses of the Bible when reading the text. These four senses, which developed by the end of the fourth century C.E. and were then used throughout the Middle Ages in the West, were the literal, the allegorical, the tropological (or moral), and the anagogical.[6] Of these four senses, allegory, with its pattern of type–antitype, was the most important.[7] The exegetical principle of the four senses allowed interpreters of the Bible to read the text and move from the literal meaning of the text to its significance for interpreters and their contemporary communities. As such, biblical criticism was done within particular Christian faith communities and with current issues in mind, an approach to the text that historical critics came to find untenable because of its subjectivity.

To correct for the "subjectivity" of interpretations based on the four senses of the Bible, historical criticism sought the original, historical meaning of biblical texts in order to identify the timeless, God-given truths of the Bible, so that those truths could, in turn, be applied to various situations and contexts. The truths themselves, however, would remain constant, even if their application varied from context to context. This search therefore required that biblical critics set aside their own presuppositions and notions about history or the biblical text and investigate the text on its own.[8] The attempt to maintain critical distance from one's own context in order to interpret the biblical text led to many advances in biblical criticism, such as H. S. Reimarus's study of Jesus, which raised the problem of the historical Jesus (Reimarus argued that Jesus' preaching differed from what the early Church proclaimed about Jesus and his message). The question of the written development of the New Testament was initiated by J. J. Griesbach, who emphasized the distinctions between the gospels, argued that the Gospel of John was markedly different from the other three gospels, and then sought to explain the literary interrelationships among Matthew, Mark, and Luke. J. G. Eichhorn demonstrated the differences between the Pastoral Epistles and the other Pauline epistles. These and other arguments about issues in the New Testament set the stage for the critical study of the Bible, and are the basic questions that continue to be debated and discussed by Christian biblical scholars.

Problems and Shortcomings

The gains in understanding the Bible made by historical criticism, however, have come at a cost. First, although historical criticism no longer assumed allegorical interpretation was the best means of determining the truth of the biblical text, it retained from earlier Christian exegetes the belief that Christianity had superceded Judaism, and Christian historical critics read the biblical texts accordingly.[9] Thus as historical criticism arose and developed a new set of methods for determining and reconstructing the historical background of the biblical texts, the Christian perspective from which this work typically was done typically produced interpretations of the Bible and of history (that of ancient Israel, early Judaism, and early Christianity) that demonstrated Christianity's superiority over Judaism. The Christian desire to reveal the truth of the Bible was ultimately the desire to demonstrate that Jesus and his message were the fulfillment of God's plans for humanity.[10]

Historical criticism also suffered from its desire to be as objective as possible in its reading of the biblical text. Because historical critics were exhorted to lay aside their biases, presuppositions, and other influences from their own social, historical, and political contexts in order to determine what the text meant in its original context, these same critics often failed to explain how their interpretations impacted and related to their own historical contexts. They also failed to realize they could not completely lay aside biases and presuppositions from their own contexts (such as the view that Christianity superceded and completed Judaism). The failure to attain objectivity and the focus on the historical past often left Christian biblical scholars silent on contemporary events, unable to provide commentary on current events informed by their work on the Bible. Whether conscious or not, this public silence on current events perpetuated Christian biases and attitudes about Judaism and Jews.

Jewish biblical scholars have argued that historical criticism's attempt at objectivity is fundamentally flawed, because historical criticism is deeply imbued with Christian theological and dogmatic influences.[11] Indeed, the fundamental attitude toward the biblical text reveals historical criticism's Christian bias. Christian historical critical readings of the Bible have tended to emphasize issues of faith, spirituality, and morality, while matters of ritual and laws have received less attention (a result not only of anti-Judaism, but of Protestant anti-Catholicism). Jewish biblical and textual exegesis, by contrast, has tended to remain in the midrashic and talmudic tradition of studying texts for the validation of halakic norms and interpreting the Bible for its relevance to each generation.[12] From this perspective, Christian biblical scholars have not addressed the question of (the Christian) God and the death camps because they have been too busy seeking the eternal truths of the Bible, which they see as locked in the ancient, original text. Perhaps this search precludes admitting the possibility that this Christian God would have allowed or participated in the Shoah.[13]

Post-Shoah Historical Criticism

The failure of historical critical objectivity and the impossibility of a Christian biblical scholar completely laying aside her or his biases and presuppositions have been made clear in recent years by biblical scholars themselves. R. Bultmann's article "Is Presuppositionless Criticism Possible?" in 1957 marked a watershed in the level of awareness among Christian biblical scholars about the impossibility of being objective interpreters.[14] In 1963, K. Stendahl, drawing on the work of J. Munck, published what was to become a groundbreaking article on Paul in which Stendahl acknowledged the Lutheran bias of Pauline scholars in reading Paul, a bias that denigrated Judaism and the Torah in favor of Christianity.[15] Stendahl argued such readings were misreadings of Paul and Paul's views of Judaism and the Law, and Stendahl's arguments set Pauline scholarship on a new course. W. D. Davies' *Paul and Rabbinic Judaism* (1948) and his student E. P. Sanders's *Paul and Palestinian Judaism* (1977) were immensely important works that focused on the Jewish background of the New Testament and brought about a greater appreciation for the diversity of the Jewish backgrounds of the New Testament and the anachronistic understanding of Judaism that had been propounded by Christian biblical scholars since Luther and the beginning of historical criticism.[16]

It is important to note that all of these works appeared after the Shoah and that they reflect a reappraisal of the assumptions made by Christian biblical scholars concerning the use of the historical critical method, the Jewish background of the New Testament, and of the relationship between Judaism and Christianity. The discovery of the Dead Sea Scrolls, which also helped illuminate the historical context out of which Christianity arose, further encouraged Christian biblical scholars to reevaluate their assumptions about early Judaism and early Christianity as they worked on the New Testament. Thus there has been at least implicit acknowledgment by some Christian biblical scholars in the post-Shoah period of the horror of the Shoah and of Christianity's role in making the Shoah possible, even if these scholars have not explicitly taken up the question of (the Christian) God and the death camps. Christian biblical scholars also have made efforts to improve relations with Jewish biblical scholars by forming collaborative working groups, such as the formation in 1989 of the Early Jewish/Christian Relations section in the Society of Biblical Literature (one of the primary scholarly associations for American and international biblical scholars).

Alternative Methodologies

In the post-Shoah period of Christian biblical studies, historical criticism has not been the only methodological tool for interpreting biblical texts. Beginning in the 1960s, American doctoral programs in biblical and religious studies began to admit more women and minority candidates into their programs, and these students and scholars brought about a number of changes in traditional Christian biblical interpretation. These scholars used historical criticism to ask different questions of the biblical text, such as where were the women in the biblical texts and why didn't they receive the same critical attention as did male characters in the text. They also brought to bear on the Bible important new social and cultural understandings and perspectives based on the different social and cultural contexts out of which these scholars came. At the same time, Christian biblical scholars began to grow dissatisfied with historical criticism and its tendency to ignore the literary qualities of the biblical texts in favor of trying to determine and reconstruct the historical contexts of the text.[17] These various changes in the field of American Christian biblical studies led to the emergence of new methods for interpreting the Bible. Of the various methods that have gained acceptance in the field in the twentieth century, I will consider three here: literary criticism, feminist criticism, and postmodern criticisms. These methodologies present new opportunities and ways for Christian biblical scholars to address the question of (the Christian) God and the death camps, because they correct some of the deficiencies of historical criticism. At the same time, however, they present their own shortcomings and problems for addressing this question.

The rise of literary critical approaches to the biblical text began in the 1960s. The roots of literary criticism lie in the New Criticism, which flourished in the United States from the mid-1930s to the late 1960s. Literary critical readings of the Bible have bracketed out questions of history, both the history out of which the text arose and the interpreter's own historical context, to focus on various literary aspects of the biblical text, such as setting, word play, character development, plot, and narrative voice.[18] The use of literary criticism by Christian biblical scholars has brought about a new awareness of the literary characteristics of the biblical text, of its holistic nature, of the internal conversations and connections that exist within and between biblical texts, and of the fact that there are truths and meanings conveyed in the text apart from those based on history. The work of A. N. Wilder on the rhetoric of the gospels, for example, raised awareness of the way in which the biblical text operates and communicates as a literary and social product.[19] R. C. Tannehill's work on Luke-Acts likewise raised awareness of the narrative unity between two different New Testament texts of different genres.[20]

"Feminist interpretation" is an inexact way to describe a variety of approaches to the biblical text that arise out of women's interpretations of the Bible as well as their experiences with various contemporary social and political realities and academic institutions.[21] Feminist interpretations of the Bible in America began in the late nineteenth century with the publication of E. C. Stanton's *The Woman's Bible*.[22] The second wave of feminist interpretation began in the 1960s and 1970s as female Christian biblical scholars began to challenge the silence about women in biblical studies and the stereotypical ways in which women in the Bible were viewed, as well as the ways in which women were oppressed in contemporary society (oppressive situations due in part to interpretations of women of the Bible). Feminist biblical scholars have combined their political strategies of justice for women with historical critical and other methodologies for interpreting the biblical text, and their interpretations have spanned a range of objectives, from recuperating women's stories in the Bible (which is the primary approach in *The Woman's Bible*), to a hermeneutics of suspicion about biblical stories (a perspective most closely associated with the work of E. Schüssler Fiorenza, who begins with the assumption that the biblical texts and their interpretations are androcentric and serve patriarchal functions), to postmodern feminist critiques of the text and interpretation (such as T. Pippin's work on John).[23] Schüssler Fiorenza's work on the hermeneutics of suspicion has been quite important in feminist biblical interpretation (despite receiving significant critique), because it has opened up both the understanding of the biblical text and the how the biblical text was produced, and how the biases and presuppositions of biblical interpreters and their interpretations affect the practice of Christian biblical interpretation (especially as these biases involve gender). Such work has brought to the fore issues not only of the meaning of texts in antiquity but also their meaning in contemporary situations and how those meanings create, support, and perpetuate contemporary cultural norms and biases.

Postmodern readings of the biblical text have appeared since the mid-1980s, as the impact of postmodernism began to be felt beyond the field of philosophy and critical theory. Postmodern readings cover a range of methodological approaches, and thus "postmodern biblical interpretation" is difficult to define. Like feminist interpretations, however, such readings are characterized by an awareness that interpretations of texts are historically and culturally conditioned and therefore infused with the biases and assumptions of the interpreter and the method employed by the interpreter; a questioning of objectivity and the notion of a singular truth; their interdisciplinary nature; and by a greater awareness of the multiplicity of meanings that are possible in literary texts. This last characteristic, postmodernity's awareness and celebration of multiple meanings of the text, provides a connection between this approach and premodern readings of the Bible, although the reasons for postmodernism's celebration of multiple meanings is quite different from that of the premodern period.[24]

Christian biblical scholars who have employed postmodern approaches to biblical texts have been able, like Schüssler Fiorenza (who is not herself a postmodern interpreter), to interpret critically not only the text but the very process of interpretation and the active role of the interpreter in creating meaning from the text. E. A. Castelli's work on Paul and S. D. Moore's work on the gospels demonstrate the possibilities for greater self-critical awareness on the part of the interpreter as she or he creates meaning out of the biblical text.[25]

Missed Opportunities

Although these alternative approaches to interpreting the biblical text have challenged historical criticism and brought about helpful correctives to some of its shortcomings, none of these methods leads automatically to addressing the question of (the Christian) God and the death camps. Indeed, each has its own shortcomings and challenges when it comes to responding to this question. The bracketing of history in literary critical readings has enabled greater appreciation of the literary nature of the biblical texts. Such readings, however, fail to acknowledge the historically conditioned nature of reading or of the impact such readings have on the interpreter's social–historical context. In a post-Shoah world, the bracketing of history ignores the fact that six million Jews died in the Shoah, thereby ignoring their suffering and the circumstances that brought about their deaths and effectively perpetuating the systems of hate, discrimination, and oppression that sent these people to their deaths. Thus, although literary critical readings revive some of the practices of premodern readings of the biblical text (due to their attention to the text's literary characteristics), they do not accomplish as much as those earlier readings if they fail to consider the context in which literary critical readings of the Bible occur.

One of the primary shortcomings of Christian feminist biblical interpretation has been its too narrow focus on sexism and women's experience, and this narrowness of focus has led to critiques by both minority and Jewish women.[26] B. Brooten, J. Plaskow, and K. von Kellenbach, among others, have pointed out the anti-Judaism in much Christian feminist biblical scholarship, which has tended to portray Judaism in one of three ways: in a dualistic pattern in which Judaism is the negative element and Christianity is the positive element; as the scapegoat, in which Judaism and Jews are to blame for the evils of the world; and as the precursor to Christianity.[27] This anti-Judaism in Christian feminist interpretation is one reason why the question of (the Christian) God and the death camps has not been taken up by Christian feminist biblical scholars. Nevertheless, Christian feminist biblical scholars can address this question and their own anti-Judaism if, as Plaskow argues, they will work to become aware of the anti-Judaism in Christian feminist theory; problematize anti-Judaism in the Christian tradition as part of the feminist analysis of the Bible; address anti-Judaism in Christian sources and begin to appreciate Judaism as an autonomous, changing, and diverse religion; read the New Testament as an important source for Jewish women's history; and engage in dialogue with Jewish feminist biblical scholars and interpreters.[28]

Finally, postmodern approaches to the biblical text run the risk being unable to evaluate various interpretations of the text and being unable to use the results of their biblical interpretations to speak to contemporary situations. Much depends in this regard on how those who employ postmodern approaches to biblical texts understand these approaches as having arisen in response to the tradition of philosophy and theology in the West (which is certainly how the French scholars upon whose work and thought most postmodern approaches rely—J. Lacan, M. Foucault, R. Barthes, J. Derrida, J. Kristeva, and L. Irigaray, among others—understood their work). American appropriations of postmodern thought have tended to jettison the historical, social, cultural, and intellectual contexts out of which postmodernism arose in Europe, a tendency that has made postmodernism in America susceptible to charges that it rejects critical thought and celebrates nihilism and anarchy. If postmodern approaches engage only in a carnivalesque play of meanings in the text and fail to engage in critical discussion of why a rejection of objectivity and other totalizing claims for meaning are oppressive, they too will fail to address the question of (the Christian) God and the death camps.

Conclusion

There are many reasons why Christian biblical scholars have not addressed the question of (the Christian) God and the death camps. I have provided one reason here, namely the methodologies that have been used by Christian biblical scholars since the Reformation to interpret the biblical text. Historical criticism, the most prominent of these methodologies, has been deeply influenced by

Christian theological assumptions, and this influence has perpetuated anti-Judaism biases, although post-Shoah use of this method has begun to correct for these influences. Other methodological approaches have arisen in the post-Shoah period, and these methodologies have provided helpful correctives to the shortcomings of historical criticism, such as acknowledging other aspects of the biblical text (literary features, the presence of women, and so on). But these methods, too, have yet to lead a significant number of Christian biblical scholars to address the question of (the Christian) God and the death camps. The potential for addressing this question is present in all these methodologies, but it will require Christian biblical scholars to be willing to address this question and use these methods to provide responses to it.

There are hopeful signs that more Christian biblical scholars will take up this question. One is the fact that Jewish scholars are beginning to be trained in the New Testament and to interpret the New Testament from a Jewish perspective (using a variety of methods for their interpretations). These interpretations of the New Testament are changing the way in which Christian biblical scholars read the text and are raising their awareness of the shortcomings and assumptions of their methods. Likewise, the rise of postcolonial criticism as an approach to the biblical text is making Christian New Testament scholars (and biblical scholars in general) aware of how interpretive methods "colonize" texts and people, legitimating the interpretations of one group or culture (e.g., Christians) over those of other groups or cultures.[29] Finally, the essays in this volume are raising awareness of the need to address this question and pointing the way to how such a response can be formulated and can influence interpretations of the biblical text.

In the end, however, it will be up to individual Christian biblical scholars to take up this question and wrestle with it. To do so will require increased awareness of several facts: of the history of anti-Judaism that has been integral to Christian biblical interpretation and theology for centuries, of the ways in which this history has influenced Christian understandings and interpretations of the Bible, of how this history has influenced the methodological tools employed by Christian biblical scholars, and of the need to question Christian theology and Christian views of God. Increased awareness of these facts, however, will not be enough if Christian biblical scholars are to take up the question of (the Christian) God and the death camps. To paraphrase Plaskow, all Christian biblical scholars must work to problematize the anti-Judaism in the Christian tradition. We must acknowledge and address the anti-Judaism that is present in the source texts of Christianity, including those New Testament texts (e.g., Hebrews) that promulgate anti-Judaism. We must work to correct the claim that Judaism is the negative antithesis to Christianity, that it is Christianity's precursor, and that Christianity has superceded Judaism. The theological assumption that Jesus is the messiah, the fulfillment of Hebrew Bible prophecy, and thus that Christianity is *the* way of salvation for all the world, needs to be questioned by Christian biblical scholars, for it is precisely this theological assumption about Jesus and (the Christian) God that made (and makes) the death camps possible. We also must be willing to question directly our theological images and assumptions about God and ask how our Christian notions of God made the Shoah possible (if they did not outright demand the Shoah). Our Jewish sisters and brothers have led the way with these theological questions, and it is time we joined them in asking and seeking answers to these difficult questions.

NOTES

1. R. L. Rubenstein, *After Auschwitz: Radical Theology and Contemporary Judaism* (New York: Bobbs-Merrill, 1966), x (italics original). Rubenstein's argument is but one response by Jewish theologians and philosophers to the Shoah in the post-Holocaust era. For a brief survey of responses, see M. Berenbaum's "Theological and Philosophical Responses," in *The Holocaust Encyclopedia*, ed. W. Laqueur (New Haven: Yale University Press, 2001), 625–631.
2. *Strange Fire: Reading the Bible after the Holocaust*, ed. T. Linafelt (New York: New York University Press; Sheffield: Sheffield Academic Press, 2000). Linafelt also provides a review of biblical responses to the Shoah in his "'Mad-Midrash' and the Negative Dialectics of Post-Holocaust Biblical Interpretation," in *Bibel und Midrasch: Zur Bedeutung der rabbinischen Exegese für die Bibelwissenschaft*, eds. G. Bodendorfer and M. Millard (Tübingen: Mohr Siebeck, 1998), 263–274.
3. There are differences in Christian biblical interpretation in the traditions of the Eastern and Western Church. Because the Shoah occurred at the hands of the Nazis, I will consider only the Western Church in this essay. As for the point at which "modern" Christian biblical studies begin, many scholars point to the Enlightenment period, although some [see J. Barton, "Historical-critical approaches," in *The Cambridge Guide to Biblical Interpretation*, ed. J. Barton (Cambridge companions to religion; Cambridge: Cambridge University Press, 1998), 16] argue that the origins of historical criticism are to be found in the Reformation period.
4. For a review of the Reformation period and its impact on biblical criticism, see H. Frei, *The Eclipse of Biblical Narrative: A Study in Eighteenth and Nineteenth Century Hermeneutics* (New Haven: Yale University Press, 1974), 18–37; W. G. Kümmel, *The New Testament: The History of the Investigation of its Problems*, trans. S. M. Gilmour and H. C. Kee (Nashville, TN: Abingdon, 1972), 20–39.
5. The development of historical criticism as the method for interpreting biblical texts and examining issues in the Bible was left almost exclusively to Protestant biblical critics until the mid-twentieth century. The Roman Catholic Church, at the Council of Trent (1546 C.E.), reaffirmed the priority of Church interpretation against Luther's assertions of the priority of the Bible, thereby effectively suppressing the use of historical criticism by Roman Catholics until the mid-twentieth century, when the Roman Catholic Church took a series of steps (which culminated at the Second Vatican Council) to change its position on the use of historical criticism.
6. This is the distinction given to the multiple levels of meaning in the biblical text by John Cassian (c. 360–435 C.E.).
7. M. Reeves, "The Bible and Literary Authorship in the Middle Ages," in *Reading the Text: Biblical Criticism and Literary Theory*, ed. S. Prickett (Oxford: Basil Blackwell, 1991), 14.

8. Historical critics have long debated the relationship between the critical study of the biblical text and the critic's own faith position [i.e., are critics interpreting biblical texts over their faith position, or from the perspective of (and in service to) their faith position?]. The inaugural lecture of J. P. Gabler in 1787 provides a classic formulation of the distinction between biblical exegesis and biblical theology [as opposed to dogmatic theology; for a translation and discussion of this work, see J. Sandys-Wunsch and L. Eldredge, "J. P. Gabler and the Distinction Between Biblical and Dogmatic Theology: Translation, Commentary, and Discussion of His Originality," *Scottish Journal of Theology* 33 (1980): 133–158]. For a review of this discussion, see Kümmel, *New Testament*, especially Parts III and VI.
9. In the premodern period before historical criticism arose, the exegetical principle of the four senses of the Bible, and especially allegory (with its pattern of type–antitype), was susceptible to being used by Christian exegetes to reinforce this idea of Christian supersessionism, because New Testament texts were routinely cited as the fulfillment of Hebrew Bible texts, the antitype to the Hebrew Bible's type.
10. This desire is easily seen in the *Heilsgeschichte* (salvation-history) school of interpretation (one of several competing proposals about the relationship between the Old and New Testaments in the Christian Bible and of its central themes), in which the entire Bible is thought to reveal God's acting through history to bring about the salvation of humanity. It also is evident in the terminology Christians use for their canon: Old Testament and New Testament, nomenclature that presupposes Christianity supercedes Judaism.
11. See J. D. Levenson, *The Hebrew Bible, the Old Testament and Historical Criticism* (Louisville, KY: Westminster/John Knox Press, 1993); E. L. Greenstein, *Essays on Biblical Method and Translation* (Brown Judaica Series 92; Atlanta: Scholars Press, 1989).
12. A helpful evaluation of Christian biblical criticism as compared with Jewish biblical criticism is S. C. Reif's essay "Aspects of the Jewish Contribution to Biblical Interpretation," in *The Cambridge Companion to Biblical Interpretation*, ed. J. Barton (Cambridge: Cambridge University Press, 1998), 143–159.
13. Although I am concerned in this essay with Christian biblical scholars and their silence about the Shoah, I must note here that a similar situation exists among Jewish biblical scholars as exists for Christian biblical scholars. Jewish theologians have taken up the question of God and the death camps, but what about Jewish biblical scholars? Few such scholars have addressed the question of God and the death camps in their work.
14. R. Bultmann, "Is Exegesis Without Presuppositions Possible?," in *Existence and Faith: Shorter Writings of Rudolf Bultmann*, selected and trans. S. M. Ogden (New York: Meridian, 1960), 289–297. Originally published as "Ist voraussetzungslose Exegese möglich?," *Theologische Zeitschrift* XIII (1957): 409–417.
15. K. Stendahl, "The Apostle Paul and the Introspective Conscience of the West," *Harvard Theological Review* 56 (1963): 199–215; reprinted in K. Stendahl, *Paul among Jews and Gentiles and Other Essays* (Philadelphia: Fortress, 1976), 78–96.
16. W. D. Davies, *Paul and Rabbinic Judaism: Some Rabbinic Elements in Pauline Theology* (London: S.P.C.K., 1948); E. P. Sanders, *Paul and Palestinian Judaism: A Comparison of Patterns of Religion* (Philadelphia: Fortress, 1977).
17. To my knowledge, none of the new methodologies and approaches that have been developed in the post-Shoah period by Christian biblical scholars received their impetus directly from awareness of or reaction to the Shoah.
18. There are many essays in print that describe the rise and goals of literary readings of the Bible, such as R. Detweiler and V. K. Robbins, "From New Criticism to Poststructuralism: Twentieth-Century Hermeneutics," in *Reading the Text: Biblical Criticism and Literary Theory*, ed. S. Prick-

ett (Oxford: Blackwell, 1991), 225–280.

19. A. N. Wilder, *The Language of the Gospel: Early Christian Rhetoric* (New York: Harper & Row, 1964).
20. R. C. Tannehill, *The Narrative Unity of Luke-Acts: A Literary Interpretation*, 2 vols. (Philadelphia: Fortress, 1986; Minneapolis: Augsburg/Fortress, 1990).
21. This characterization of feminist interpretation draws on that made in The Bible and Culture Collective's essay "Feminist and Womanist Criticism," in *The Postmodern Bible* (New Haven: Yale University Press, 1995), 225–271, especially 234–235.
22. E. C. Stanton, *The Woman's Bible*, 2 vols. (New York: European Publishing Co., 1895–1898).
23. E. Schüssler Fiorenza, *In Memory of Her: A Feminist Theological Reconstruction of Christian Origins* (New York: Crossroads, 1983); E. Schüssler Fiorenza, *Bread Not Stone: The Challenge of Feminist Biblical Interpretation* (Boston: Beacon, 1984); T. Pippin, *Death and Desire: The Rhetoric of Gender in the Apocalypse of John* (Louisville, KY: Westminster, 1992). This typology of feminist interpretation is a modification of that given by The Bible and Culture Collective, "Feminist and Womanist Criticism," 244–267.
24. There have been a number of characterizations of postmodern biblical interpretation that suggest the connection between postmodernism and premodern readings of the text lies in their rejection of "critical" readings of the biblical text (so R. Carroll, "Poststructuralist Approaches, New Historicism and Postmodernism," in J. Barton, *The Cambridge Companion to Biblical Interpretation*, 51). In my view, this is a misreading and misunderstanding of postmodernism and how it differs from premodern readings of the Bible. Premodern readings of the Bible, which acknowledged the existence of multiple meanings in the Bible, understood those meanings to have their ultimate unity in God. Postmodern readings, with their rejection of notions of absolute or eternal truths, make no such totalizing or unifying claim.
25. E. A. Castelli, *Imitating Paul: A Discourse of Power* (Louisville, KY: Westminster/John Knox Press, 1991). S. D. Moore, *Literary Criticism and the Gospels: The Theoretical Challenge* (New Haven: Yale University Press, 1989); *Mark and Luke in Poststructuralist Perspective: Jesus Begins to Write* (New Haven: Yale University Press, 1992).
26. R. Weems, who was influenced by the work of b. hooks, has argued that the experiences of racism, oppression, and discrimination experienced by minority women in America is not acknowledged by feminist biblical interpretation, and thus she calls for a Womanist interpretation of the biblical text that *does* account for these experiences [R. Weems, *Just a Sister Away: A Womanist Vision of Women's Relationships in the Bible* (San Diego: Lura Media, 1988)]. A helpful discussion of the differences between feminist and womanist interpretations of the Bible can be found in The Bible and Culture Collective, "Feminist and Womanist Criticism."
27. B. Brooten, "Early Christian Women and their Cultural Context: Issues of Method in Historical Reconstruction," in *Feminist Perspectives on Biblical Scholarship*, ed. A. Y. Collins (Chico, CA: Scholars Press, 1985), 66–91; J. Plaskow, "Anti-Judaism in Feminist Christian Interpretation," in *Searching the Scriptures, Volume 1: A Feminist Introduction*, ed. E. Schüssler Fiorenza (New York: Crossroads, 1995), 117–129; K. von Kellenbach, *Anti-Judaism in Feminist Religious Writings* (Atlanta: Scholars Press, 1994). My portrayal of Judaism in Christian feminist biblical scholarship is based on von Kellenbach's work.
28. Plaskow, "Anti-Judaism," 124–127.
29. Postcolonial interpretations of the biblical text have appeared in F. F. Segovia, *Decolonizing Biblical Studies: A View from the Margins* (Maryknoll, NY: Orbis, 2000); F. F. Segovia, ed., *Interpreting beyond Borders* (Bible and postcolonialism 3; Sheffield: Sheffield Academic Press, 2000); R. S. Sugirtharajah, ed., *The Postcolonial Bible* (Bible and postcolonialism 1; Sheffield: Sheffield Academic Press, 1998).

PART II

Reading as Jews

CHAPTER 5

Blood on Our Heads

A Jewish Response to Saint Matthew

STEVEN L. JACOBS

Introduction: The Problem Yet Remains

In her important study of German military chaplains in the Third Reich, Doris L. Bergen relates the following incident:

> Another Catholic priest at the front contrasted his (silent) opposition to the Holocaust with the enthusiasm of his co-religionists. He recalled his shock at hearing Hitler in a radio speech proclaim that "Jewry must be destroyed, and not only in Germany. The hour of reckoning has come." The priest himself witnessed a forced transport of Jews from a marketplace piled high with bodies; he saw train cars jammed with people he knew were to be killed. But what surprised him the most was the discovery that "various people welcomed the destruction of the Jews." *Even a fellow priest told him at the time, "There is a curse on this people ever since the crucifixion of Jesus when they cried: 'Let his blood be on our heads and the heads of our children.'"* [1]

More than fifty years after the horrific events of the Holocaust/Shoah, how are good-faith Christians to deal with contemporary implications and understandings of Matthew 27:25 in a world that continues to practice genocide, not only against Jews, but against anyone who falls "outside the universal of moral obligation" (to use Helen Fein's felicitous phrase).[2] How will religiously committed Jews, interested in dialogue with their Christian neighbors in a world in which support for the very survival not only of the State of Israel but the Jewish People itself appears to be diminishing, move forward, still burdened by the events of this past and knowledge not only of Christian complicity but of New Testament foundational complicity as well? Beyond both, how can good people of conscience—whatever their religious traditions and/or orientations—continue to affirm *any* manner of scriptural literalism of the past and its relevance to the present, given its continuing use *against* individual persons and communities? Further, in a modern world that continues to experience a growing and incresingly violent and textually based fundamentalism, not only by Christians but by Jews and Muslims as well, where are the religious voices of reason, moderation, and tolerance to be found rather than drowned out in these same communities? Questions such as these—and there are others—gnaw at the very essence of what it means to be human in the aftermath of such genocides, and raises the pain-filled question of whether religion, both institutional and theological, has proven itself so morally and ethically deficient and bankrupt as to be both meaningless and irrelevant in this twenty-first century.

The Scene Itself

After the apparent suicide of Judas, the betrayer of the Christ, who returns his "blood money" of thirty pieces of silver to the chief priests in the Temple, these same chief priests, together with the elders, bind the Christ and hand him over to Pontius Pilate, governor of Judea, after having conferred together "to bring about his death" (v. 1). Pilate, in turn, interrogates him with two questions, neither of which elicits a direct answer: "Are you king of the Jews?" (He responds, "You say so," v. 11) and "Do you not hear how many accusations they make against you?" Again, no direct answer whatsoever.

According to the text, it is Passover time, and the governor is prepared to release a prisoner, a supposed goodwill gesture. Turning to the assembled Jews, he asks, "Whom do you want me to release for you, Jesus Barabbas or Jesus who is called the Messiah?" (v. 17).[3] After Pilate's own spouse sends word not to have anything to do with this second Jesus, the dialogue intensifies. He again asks the crowd which of the two to release, and they respond, "Barabbas" (v. 21). He then asks, "What should I do with Jesus who is called the Messiah?" (v. 22). Evidently, turning ugly, the crowd, now becoming somewhat unruly, shouts its answer twice, "Let him be crucified!" (vs. 22 and 23).

Pilate then literally "washes his hands" of the whole affair and says, "I am innocent of this man's blood; see to it yourselves" (v. 24).[4] Then the people as a whole answer, "His blood be on us and on our children!" (v. 25)

As it presents itself, this horrific response does not appear in either the Markan or the Lukan parallel, and, most assuredly, not in the Johanine text of the Gospels. What does, however, appear in the first two is the stridency of the

Jewish crown and their desire for Jesus' crucifixion. Luke, however, ends his own account with comments that appears neither in Matthew nor Mark, "but Jesus he delivered up to their will" (23:25), again assessing primary responsibility for the crucifixion and death of the Christ on the part of the Jews.

The Ambivalence of the Christian Commentaries

Historically, scriptural literalism on the part of Christians (and Jews) was normative up until the end of the 1700s, when a newer, more objective scientific line of reasoning, a product of the European Enlightenment, crept into the study of the Bible. Questions of authorship, textual accuracy, Divine inerrancy, and the like now made their appearances in both the study of the Hebrew Bible and the New Testament. Commentaries on the texts, however, still largely the domain of the religious and denominational communities, did not reflect this newer thinking. Thus, we find in the older Christian commentaries an expansion of the condemnation of the Jews as reflected in Matthew 27:25.

Two examples of what may be termed "classical" or "historical" Christian commentaries are those of John Gill and Matthew Henry. The former writes:

> **Then answered all the people . . .** They were as unanimous in their imprecations upon themselves, as in desiring the crucifixion of Christ.
>
> **and said, his blood be on us, and on our children; . . .** so this phrase is used in (Joshua 2:19) (2 Samuel 1:16), and in other places, and in the Talmud (BT Pesachim 11a; Yoma 21a; Avoda Zara 12b), and it is a notion of the Jews, that the guilt of innocent blood, and the blood of that innocent means children, lie not only upon the persons immediately concerned, but upon their children to the end of the world; and so the judges used to address the witnesses upon a trial after this manner. (Maimonides, *Hilchot Sanhedrin* 12:3)[5]

Thus, according to Gill, are the Jews also condemned by their own textual words in both Bible and Talmud.

Still in much use today in many Protestant communities, and, therefore, much more important, are the words of Matthew Henry. Commenting on Matthew 27:25, we find the following:

> **His blood be on us and on our children**—If this man be innocent, and we put him to death as a guilty person, may the punishment due to such a crime be visited on us, and upon our children after us! What a dreadful imprecation! *and how literally fulfilled!* The notes on Chap. 24 will show how they fell victims to their own imprecation, being visited with a series of calamities unexampled in the history of the world. They were visited

with the same kind of punishment; for the Romans crucified them in such numbers when Jerusalem was taken, that there was found a deficiency of crosses for the condemned, and of places for the crosses. *Their children or descendants have had the same curse entailed upon them, and continue to this day a proof of the innocence of the Christ, the truth of his religion, and of the justice of God.*[6]

Thus, again, Jewish tragedies subsequent to the death of the Christ, including the destruction of Jerusalem, are the (direct) result of Jewish perfidy in the death of this same Christ. By extension, then, Henry would have to conclude that the Holocaust/Shoah, too, was, equally, the result of such criminal behavior.[7]

Turning more to the contemporary scene, a text written prior to and published immediately prior to Hitler's assumption to power in January 1933 by the (American) Southern Baptist Sunday School Board contains the following but reveals, perhaps, the already darkening clouds looming over Europe:

His blood be upon us and upon our children. These solemn words do show a consciousness that the Jewish people recognized their guilt and were even proud of it. There was guilt enough for Judas, for Caiaphas and for all the Sanhedrin both Sadducees and Pharisees, for the Jewish people as a whole, and for Pilate. At the bottom the sins of all of us nailed Jesus to the Cross. This language is no excuse for race hatred today, but it helps explain the sensitiveness between Jews and Christians on this subject. And Jews today approach the subject of the Cross with a certain amount of prejudice.[8]

The *Baker Commentary on the Bible*, a one-volume commentary published in 1989 and used in the more traditionally conservative Christian communities, does not reflect this ambivalence, however:

The Jews sentenced Jesus to death (v 1), but Romans alone could execute the sentence (John 18:31), so now Jesus appears before Pilate (27:11–26).... By insisting on Jesus' death, the people fall under judgment and indeed invoke judgment on themselves (v. 25).[9]

An equally conservative commentary attempts to "explain" the Matthean comment by understanding it to be little or not at all different from those condemnations offered to Israel by their own prophets, in this case specifically likening it to that of Jeremiah:

To Pilate's words, "all the people" answer, "Let his blood be on us and on

> our children!" The idiom is familiar (2Sa 1:16; 3:28; Ac 18:6; 20:26).... Many say that by "all the people" Matthew is saying that *the Jews as a whole* reject Jesus. To them v. 25 becomes a prophecy of the destruction of Jerusalem and the nation; and a new people, the church, would take over. *There is some truth in this view, but it needs qualification.* Matthew certainly knows that *all* the first disciples were Jews. Thus the gospel's denunciations of the Jews are not more severe than those of many OT prophets, and in both instances it is understood that a faithful remnant remains. So what Matthew actually says cannot be judged as a general anti-Semitic comment, certainly not any more than Jeremiah's prediction of the destruction of Jerusalem and the Exile can.[10]

A seemingly noble effort to contextualize the Matthean passage, ultimately it "misses the mark." For the question is not whether the author of the text was or was not antisemitic; rather, it is whether a text that purports to be the words of God by a God-inspired author are historically accurate in their presentation (i.e., that the Jews themselves gathered in Pilate's presence did in fact utter these horrible words), and, by extension, how such a text is understood not only by those who preach it and comment upon it but by those who hear it and study it in the aftermath of the Holocaust/Shoah, and the countless generations of Christians who preceded them prior to the Second World War.

A modern Roman Catholic commentary, like the earlier Protestant commentaries examined, simply accepts the literal truth and historical accuracy of the text as it presents itself:

> **27:11–26. The trial and sentencing of Jesus...** The account of Jesus' questioning and sentencing by Pilate places the responsibility for Jesus' death on the Jewish leaders. The chief priests and elders manipulate the Roman governor (v. 12).... Given the choice of Jesus or Barabbas, the chief priests and elders manipulate the crowd to have Pilate free Barabbas and crucify Jesus (vv. 15–18, 20:23) ... the Jewish leaders are charged with acting out of jealousy at Jesus' popularity (v. 18).... Pilate declares Jesus to be innocent and places the responsibility on the crowd for the death of Jesus (vv. 24–25). The crowd accepts the responsibility.... The episode as a whole (vv. 11–26) stresses that the Roman governor allowed Jesus to be crucified, not because he was guilty of a crime, but rather because the crowd, incited by the chief priests, forced him into it.[11]

Although acknowledging the fact that the portrayal of Pilate as "weak and indecisive" is not consistent with other understandings of him as "inflexible, merciless, and obstinate," this commentary, too, places both primary blame and responsibility on the Jews, especially its religious leadership, and accords the latter more power that is historically justified.

A last Christian commentary example, although one somewhat uncomfortable for this author, is that published by David Stern, a "Jew for Jesus" or so-called "Hebrew-Christian" or "Messianic Jew" living today in Israel. He writes:

> **25 His blood is on us and on our children.** Or: "His blood be on us. . . ." This verse has been used to justify persecution of Jews throughout the centuries by Christians who presumed that the Jewish people had invoked a curse on themselves and on their posterity, and willingly accepted responsibility for "deicide." But a mob cannot speak in an official capacity for anyone, let alone for a people. Nor, in light of Ezekiel 18, can anyone invoke a curse on unborn generations. Moreover, even were the curse effectual, Yeshua prayed, "Father, forgive them, for they do not know what they are doing" (Luke 23:24).
>
> Besides, if the Jews were the only ones who killed him; then he didn't die for anyone else. But he died for all, not just for Jews: the righteous Messiah died for everyone who is unrighteous, which is to day, for everyone. Everyone, Jew and Gentile alike, is a sinner. *By sinning, everyone, Jew and Gentile alike, killed him. Therefore, everyone, Jew and Gentile alike, is guilty of Yeshua's death.*[12]

Again, the nobility of the effort to contextualize the understanding of Matthew 27:25, and the theological necessity of "bringing the Jews to see the light of the Christ" as applicable to a Jewish understanding of *m'shichut*/messianism, are hesitatingly appreciated although dwarfed by the question of whether such is affirmed as historically accurate, and whether Jewish complicity or primary responsibility for the death of the Christ is a sin tainting subsequent generations, and whether all subsequent so-called "punishments," including the Holocaust/Shoah, are directly related to the Christ's death.

A Jewish Response to Saint Matthew

The question, then, remains: How are Jews to respond, initially to the passage itself, and, subsequently, to its (in)applicability and/or (ir)relevance in this post-Holocaust/Shoah era?

From an historical perspective, Jews simply cannot affirm the accuracy of Matthew 27:25. A religious tradition that continues to assert the sanctity of the family as the basic unit and building block of society, and primacy of children to make that family whole, cannot abide a verse and scenario that not only degrades those Jews who were questionably present, but puts into their mouths a curse upon their own children, their children's children, and all the generations to come. Even granting that there were those Jews possibly in league with the Romans and those duplicitous Jewish leaders interested in cozying up to their Roman oppressors, the announcement is itself so horrendous as to defy credibility, and must, therefore, be rejected as a true depiction of events. Instead, it must be attributed to a negative embellishment on the part of the unknown author of the Matthean text, who himself may or may not have believed it to be true, but whose own orientation was to portray the Jews as primarily responsible for the death of the Christ.

Far more serious, however, is the fact that for 2000 years, this verse has been preached as truth to its Christian adherents with disastrous results to its Jewish recipients. Truly understood to be the "enemies of Christ," and constantly affirmed and reaffirmed by generations of Church leaders, Jews have paid dearly throughout Europe for their supposed sin of deicide. Thus, Hitler was able to draw upon generations of antisemitic and anti-Jewish feelings and worse, and present to audiences hungry for a scapegoat the very personification of all that was wrong with their world and offer them a "Final Resolution" dependent upon annihilation and extermination. Thus, there is no other credible solution but to accept the New Testament's partial responsibility, specifically verses such as Matthew 27:25, as part of the aforementioned foundational complicity for the Holocaust/Shoah.

From a Jewish perspective, therefore, what is required is, first, this recognition of foundational complicity for this "teaching of contempt," as the late Jules Isaac so poignantly reminds us. In addition to understanding the text in its own historical context, present and future generations of committed Christians—in churches, parochial schools, colleges, universities, and seminaries—must also be taught through as yet undeveloped and unwritten curricula the damage that has been done to the Jews in subsequent years because of texts such as this. Christian lectionary traditions must be rethought and reorganized to *exclude* such passages from their annual reading cycles. Indeed, after the Holocaust/Shoah, committed Christians interested in bridge building between themselves and Jews must now be prepared to read their sacred New Testament text in the presence of Jews, *and Jews must be prepared to read it with them.* It will not now suffice, nor should it ever, for Jews simply to confront and condemn the sins of others for the past without instrumentally involving themselves in helping to create the present and prepare for the future.

Each of these pointed suggestions will be expanded upon *ad seriatim.*

The recognition of the foundational complicity of the New Testament text in helping to pave the way for what would ultimately become the Holocaust/Shoah after centuries of anti-Jewish preachments by its authoritative interpreters and spokespersons, and activities by those all-too-willing recipients, is not easy—either for Jews to broach or for Christians to accept. That verses such as Matthew

27:25—and there are others—have played a significant part in conditioning Western civilizational attitudes toward Jews must not be understated but accepted. As scholars of Judaism and Christianity and the Holocaust/Shoah, and the relationship between these three, continually examine and reexamine such texts in concert with those representing both faith traditions, what continues to emerge is a rethinking of *how* to read Holy Scripture in light of this history, its relationship to this history, and present and future implications because of this history.

I have been personally and instrumentally involved in one such example for now almost a decade. At the Annual Scholars Conference on the Holocaust and the Churches, founded by Franklin Littell and Hubert Locke in 1970, the oldest such conference on the Holocaust/Shoah in the United States, four scholars—Zev Garber, Henry Knight, James Moore, and the author—present *in a public forum* a rereading of selected passages of both the Hebrew Bible and the New Testament, and reflect on their contemporary relevance in light of the Holocaust/Shoah. One such collection of these commentaries has already been published with more to come.[13] What began as a small workshop/panel presentation has now grown to a full plenary session with more than 150 persons attending, with the first out-of-conference presentation being held at Aurora University, Aurora, IL, in March 2001. Such dialogical modeling, a coming together of Jews and Christians over sacred texts *because* of the Holocaust/Shoah, may yet serve as a new paradigm of post-Holocaust/Shoah awareness for all concerned. It starts, however, with the recognition of the pain caused to Jews because of this text sacred to Christians.

Second, curricula need to be developed among all segments of the Christian denominational community in all institutional settings over which these segments have both responsibility and authority that do far more than contemporize the positive relationship that seemingly presently exists between Jews and Christians on the subject of Jews and *religious* Judaism and less so on the State of Israel. What needs be taught—dare we say *mandated*?—is the historical relationship that has existed between Jews and Christians for the past 2000 years in all of its positivity and negativity, including the Holocaust/Shoah. Courses in Jewish/Christian relations at all academic levels—from small children in primary parochial school classes to postcollege/university and graduate school adults in church-related settings to seminarians at both the beginning and then ending of their formal training—must become core parts of the instructional process of religiously committed Christians in their evolving bridge-building construction with Jews and Jewish communities. Jews themselves, perhaps as never before, must likewise avail themselves of the possibilities already resident in various communities and academic environments to further this dialogical process, between rabbis and Christian clergy, academics, and congregations, and look for "teachable moments" as they present themselves, to the point of involving themselves *upon invitation* in the design of such curricula.

A cautionary note: Such curricula will not be easy to write on any level. The topic is pain filled and difficult, but necessary nonetheless if Jews and Christians—and others—are to move forward after the horrific events of the Holocaust/Shoah. But working in concert, and that is truly the only way such curricula can be constructed, will go far to lessen the heaviness of such an educational endeavor.

In addition, it is not only for Christians that such materials must be developed and taught. Jews, too, in concert with caring Christians, must develop curricula that address these same concerns but whose potential audience is Jews in their own educational settings, from primary and parochial schools through congregational school, adult education programs, and seminaries and *y'shivot* to college and university campuses.

One such notable example is that of the Jewish Chautauqua Society, an arm of the (Reform) National Federation of Temple Brotherhoods, which places academically qualified *rabbis* on college campuses and endows some professorships and visiting lectureships to teach non-Jews about Judaism and related subjects. Such a program must, therefore, be expanded and embraced by all wings of the American and Canadian Jewish communities.

Third, lectionary cycles in both Protestant and Catholic communities, again in concert with Jewish scholars, obviously at the highest levels of churchly authorities, must be revisited and reexamined to *exclude* those passages that have caused harm to Jews throughout the centuries. Such an effort, however, is much more difficult and problematic than that of the curricula, for it addresses frontally the whole notion of the sacredness of the New Testament texts, their Divine inspirational foundation as the very Words of God, and the historical veracity and accuracy of those texts. Positively, however, it does open up a whole new avenue of Biblical scholarship: that of religiously committed Christian scholars working with those outside their own faith communities to learn, understand, and reflect upon their own traditions and extrapolations and implications.

Such an approach, however, should not be totally one sided. Not only should Jews be willing to engage in serious learning and scholarship with regard to the New Testament together with those in the Christian communities, they should also reexamine their own lectionary traditions with regard to the Hebrew Bible and those passages that potentially cause grievous harm to others—such as, for example, the supposedly Divine mandate to genocidally destroy all manner of Canaanite persons and living possessions. Then, too, those biblical passages that address both the election of Israel and the self-perception of Israel as God's chosen people must be studied anew *in the presence of Christians* together with their rabbinic commentaries in the aftermath of the Holocaust/Shoah. A painful beginning for Jews, also, to be sure, but a necessary beginning nonetheless.

Conclusion: The Past as Future

Yesterday is no guarantor of tomorrow. The tragic history of the past, including the Holocaust/Shoah, is filled with horrible and painful lessons to be learned by both Christians and Jews, but such lessons do not by definition mandate a repetition of that past. If yesterday is to be approached honestly and openly, with all of the difficulties inherent in its study—including the study of texts sacred to both Christians and Jews, no matter how onerous—then tomorrow, too, must be approached in that same spirit of honesty and openness. Christians must learn from Jews and Jews must learn from Christians; indeed, the ongoing dialogue between God and humanity on the part of the one must take place in the presence of the other. The events of fifty years ago in the "century of genocide" will forever remain a stain on Western civilization. How we Christians and Jews choose to deal with our knowledge of this past both today and tomorrow will, most assuredly, determine how we will be perceived—for good or ill—by the generations who will succeed us.

NOTES

1. Doris L. Bergen, "Between God and Hitler: German Military Chaplains and the Crimes of the Third Reich," in *In God's Name: Genocide and Religion in the Twentieth Century*, eds. Omer Bartov and Phyllis Mack (New York: Bergahn Books, 2001), 128–129. Her own reference for this incident is Gordian Landwehr, OP, "So sah ich sie sterben," in *Priester in Uniform: Seelsorger, Ordensleute und Theologen als Soldaten im Zweiten Weltkreig*, ed. Hans Jurgen Brandt (Augsburg: Fortress, 1994), 349–350 (emphasis not in Bergen's citation).
2. Helen Fein, *Accounting for Genocide* (Rutherford, NJ: Farleigh Dickinson University Press, 1979).
3. The question itself is somewhat problematic for two reasons: The name "Barabbas" is understood as "Son of the Father," the paternal reference of which is itself unclear. Second, by whom is Jesus called "the Messiah?" Certainly not the Roman overlords; certainly not the Jewish community, other than, perhaps, his own immediate followers. Perhaps what we are dealing with here is an editorial gloss by the author of the Matthean text rather than an accurate historical comment?
4. Here, too, a problem suggests itself: The implication of Pilate's suggestions "see to it yourselves" would somehow imply that the Jews had responsibility for the implementation of the death penalty, when such was in fact not the case. Under Roman jurisdiction, Jews had little if any civil authority over their own affairs, much less criminal authority. All such punishments were meted out according to Roman rather than Jewish law.
5. The *New John Gill's Exposition of the Entire Bible* modernized and adapted for the computer by Larry Pierce of *Online Bible*. Gill's understanding of these five Talmudic citations is wrong: Nowhere do they imply any association whatsoever with children nor any extension whatsoever beyond the person or persons referenced therein to succeeding generations.
6. *Matthew Henry's Commentary on the New Testament*, QuickVerse 7.0 CD-Rom Edition (Hiawatha, IA: Parson Technology, n.d.). Emphases not in original text.

7. Indeed, Richard L. Rubenstein's powerful essay, "The Dean and the Chosen People," makes just such a claim: Dean Heinrich Gruber of the Evangelical Free Church of Berlin, himself an ardent anti-Nazi and imprisoned by them for his oppositional views, understands the Holocaust/Shoah to be God's condemnation upon the Jewish People for their collective failure, historically and contemporarily, to embrace the Christ and accept the truth of Christianity. See Richard L. Rubenstein, "The Dean and the Chosen People," in *After Auschwitz: Radical Theology and Contemporary Judaism* (Indianapolis, IN: Bobbs-Merrill Company, 1966), 46–58.
8. *The Robertson's Word Pictures of the New Testament* (Online Edition; Nashville, TN: Broadman Press, 1932). Emphases not in original text.
9. Walter A. Elwell, ed., *Baker's Commentary on the Bible* (Grand Rapids, MI: Baker Books, 1989), 757.
10. Kenneth L. Baker and John Kohlenberger III, eds., *Zondervan NIV Bible Commentary: Volume 2: New Testament*; an abridgment of *The Expositor's Bible Commentary* (Grand Rapids, MI: Zondervan Publishing House, 1994), 127.
11. Robert J. Karris, O.F.M., ed., *The Collegeville Bible Commentary Based on the New American Bible* (Collegeville, MN: The Liturgical Press, 1992), 900–901.
12. David H. Stern, *Jewish New Testament: A Translation That Expresses Its Jewishness* (CD-Rom Edition; Clarksville, MD/Jerusalem: Jewish New Testament Publications, 1979).
13. James F. Moore, ed., *Shofar: An Interdisciplinary Journal of Jewish Studies* 15 (1996): 1–118.

CHAPTER 6

The Apostle and the Seed of Abraham

RICHARD L. RUBENSTEIN

In the twentieth century Jewish students of the New Testament such as Martin Buber, Leo Baeck, and Hans Joachim Schoeps have sought to revise the negative evaluation that characterized the age-old Jewish attitude toward Jesus of Nazareth. These scholars have tended to regard Jesus as a representative of the prophetic tradition. Buber even referred to Jesus as a brother. Nevertheless, as Günther Bornkamm has observed, Paul is still regarded as a stranger standing outside of the mainstream of Jewish life of his time.[1] Whether Paul is seen as a Hellenistic Jew alien to the authentic traditions of the Palestinian heartland or as more pagan than Jewish, he is usually regarded as one of the personalities most responsible for the Judeo-Christian split. There is also a very strong tendency to ascribe to Paul a large measure of responsibility for the religiously inspired anti-semitism that has brought so much sorrow to the Jewish people. "Jesus, yes; Paul, never!" would seem to be the watchword of much of the thoughtful Jewish New Testament scholarship in modern times.

I have never been able entirely to share that judgment. It seems to me that the issues to which Paul addressed himself arose almost entirely *within* the religious and symbolic universe of the Judaism of his time and that he never ceased to regard himself as a believing, faithful Jew rather than as an apostate. The fundamental issues dividing Paul from the Pharisees were the questions of whether Jesus was in fact Israel's Messiah and whether his resurrection had ushered in that period known as the "Days of the Messiah." Paul had no doubt that the Messianic Age had commenced. His argument with his own people revolved around the question of how one ought to live in the new age. He did not reject the belief that God had made known His will to the prophets, teachers, and sages of Israel. Without belief in God's revelation in Scripture, his theology would have been meaningless. Paul's quarrel was over the question of God's timetable for the salvation of humanity. He was convinced that the redemption his people had longed for had begun and that what they had seen obscurely could finally he understood clearly in the light of the Messiah's redemptive activity.

Apostle of the Messiah or Turncoat?

Paul was a Jewish messianist, not an antisemite.[2] Unfortunately, when people dwell in radically different "worlds" or symbolic universes they are likely to regard each other with great hostility.[3] Each correctly perceives the other's "world" as a challenge to the integrity of his own. When brothers find themselves in such opposing spheres, as did Paul and the Pharisees, fraternal feelings are likely to become fratricidal. Paul wrote some very harsh things about his fellow Jews after they ceased to share a common world. His harshness was not unlike that of the members of the Community of the Dead Sea Scrolls.[4] When Paul wrote that his fellow Jews had proven faithless to their God, he was speaking of his own kin in what he regarded as a family dispute. Things are often said within the family that have a very different meaning when repeated by outsiders. *It was not Paul but some of his spiritual heirs who interpreted his writings so that they contributed toward the climate of opinion that permitted Auschwitz.*[5] Paul could not have anticipated the development of antisemitism, nor can he be held responsible for it.

Paul never ceased to love his people in his own way. When he declared: "For I would willingly be *anathema* and cut off from Christ if it could help my brothers of Israel, my own flesh and blood" (Romans 9:3), he expressed his concern for what he honestly believed to be Israel's salvation. Admittedly, Paul's conception of what constituted Israel's salvation was not one that most of his Jewish contemporaries would have accepted. Nevertheless, there is no hint of malice in his attitude. He is impatient, harsh, at times furiously angry, but his negative feelings are based upon his inability to understand why his fellow Jews cannot see what he has seen and believe what he has come to believe: that God has redeemed both Israel and the Gentiles through the death and resurrection of Jesus of Nazareth. We must not confuse Paul's impatience and anger with the degrading attempts to force conversion upon the Jews in the Middle Ages. Paul did not betray his own people, as did the apostates of a later time, by joining a larger, more powerful community. He left a stronger Jewish community to join a fragile, persecuted sect that made claims for itself that the civilized world, when it deigned to take notice, regarded as folly.[6]

To this day, it is difficult for thoughtful Jews to see Paul as other than an apostate, applying to him the kind of animus Jews have understandably felt toward members of their community who became Christian in medieval and modern times, and who often became malevolent persecutors of their own people. When Rabbi Solomon Ha-Levi (Saul) converted (c. 1390) and ultimately became Don Pablo de Santa Maria (Paul), bishop of his native city, Burgos, he proved to be one of the most hostile antisemites in all of Spanish history. The experience of the Jewish community with turncoats has been exceedingly bitter. Jews have tended to interpret Paul's conversion in that light.

Understandable as such feelings may be, they do not do justice to Paul. The Apostle can be judged only against the religious and cultural background of his own rather than a later time. In Paul's time the Jewish world was divided into a number of sects, each of which claimed that it alone was faithful to God's word as revealed in Sacred Writ. Today, the heirs of the Pharisees have won the spiritual battle within Judaism; their interpretation of Judaism is regarded as authentic and normative. The Pharisees were already exceedingly influential in Paul's day, but they were by no means unchallenged. In Paul's time, rejection of Pharisaism was not equivalent to rejection of Judaism. Other groups, including the followers of Jesus, considered themselves loyal and faithful Israelites, although they offered competing interpretations of God's covenant with Israel. Paul offered one such interpretation.

Though the competing sects possessed irreconcilable differences, they did start out from certain common assumptions about God's dealings with Israel. Paul, the Pharisees, the Sadducees, the Community of the Scrolls, and the Jerusalem Church shared a common religious world based upon the biblical theology of covenant and election. Paul did not reject that theology either before or after his conversion. After his conversion, he gave a radically novel interpretation of what was meant by Israel's election and God's redemptive activity. Just as the Community of the Scrolls believed that only those faithful to its norms were the truly elect community, Paul and his fellow Christians were convinced that the people of God now consisted solely of those who were "in Christ." Paul's exclusivism paralleled that of the Community of the Scrolls. Paul did not reject the Scripture as the vessel of God's word to his people, but be did insist that it had to be interpreted in the light of the Messiah's death and resurrection.

Even in his radical reinterpretation of Scripture, Paul was indebted to his rabbinic teachers. His belief that Scripture could be understood only in light of the Messiah's career was in some respects derived from the rabbinic doctrine of the twofold Law. According to the Pharisees, the true meaning of the *written text* of Scripture could be apprehended only in light of their own interpretative traditions, which they designated as the *oral Law*. They insisted that the written and the oral Law were completely in harmony. However, they were frequently at odds with the Sadducees, who contended that the written text alone yielded an authoritative understanding of God's will. Thus the Sadducees rejected the doctrine of the resurrection of the dead because they saw no evidence for it in Scripture. By contrast, the Pharisees interpreted the Law by means of their oral traditions so that it yielded the doctrine of resurrection although one searches Scriptures in vain for explicit evidence of this belief. When Paul contrasted the "letter" and the "Spirit" of the Law (II Corinthians 3:6), he was pursuing an interpretative strategy that had been suggested by his rabbinic teachers.

By interpreting Scripture in the light of their own experience, the Pharisees made it a living document for their community while preserving a sense of continuity with the past. *This is exactly what Paul, the former Pharisee, did in light of his own experience.* Paul's vision of the Risen Christ became the prism through which all of life took on new meaning. He never asserted, "I reject the Law and the covenant because of Jesus Christ." The sacred traditions of his people never ceased to be divinely inspired for the Apostle. His problem was that of harmonizing a tradition he regarded as holy with his own experience. Things would have been very different had Paul really thought of himself as an apostate or believed that he was creating a new religion. He did what any other religious Jew at the time might have done had he been similarly affected. Admittedly, Paul's experience entailed so radical an alteration in his spiritual cosmos that the new meanings he ascribed to Scripture seemed to his former peers and their successors to be a total rejection of Israel's sacred traditions.

Both Paul's fidelity to his Damascus experience and the Jewish claim that the Apostle was deluded exemplify one of the most difficult problems faced by any religion of revelation. When men and women believe that God reveals his will to them, a potential conflict is introduced between those religious institutions that claim a monopoly of interpretative authority and those charismatic individuals who claim that God has bypassed the institutions to reveal his will directly. Established institutions tend to limit God's revelation to the distant past. They look with the gravest suspicion on "latter-day saints" and personalities such as Paul. Nevertheless, there is absolutely no reason why God's revelation must be confined to any time, place, or person. Nor are there irrefutable criteria by which a claim such as Paul's can be judged to be less credible than the claim of Moses or Isaiah, There are, of course, practical reasons why institutions are compelled to reject latter-day revelations. Once charisma has become routinized, to use Max Weber's phrase, it can only regard the bearer of a new revelation as a disturber of the peace.

Paul was such a disturber of the peace. He understood the profound contrast between his revelatory experience and the traditions of the Pharisees.[7] Ironically, he felt compelled to be faithful to his encounter with the Risen Christ because of the very conception of a revealing God that he had received from his Jewish teachers. After Paul's time, and perhaps in reaction to him, the rabbis expressed the direst warnings about heeding "heavenly voices."[8] They also were to insist that prophecy had long since departed from Israel.[9] In Paul's time, however, the situation still retained a measure of fluidity. Because God had made known his will to other Israelites before him, Paul may have asked himself whether there was any possible basis for rejecting what had been so overwhelmingly revealed to him. He resolved the conflict between tradition and experience in favor of his own experience.

An echo of Paul's conflict may be discerned in II Corinthians: "Not that we are capable, of ourselves to put anything to our credit; for *our qualification comes from God.* He it is who empowered us to be *Servants of a new covenant,* not of the letter, but of the Spirit. For the letter kills, but the Spirit gives life."[10]

Paul understood the encounter with Christ on the road to Damascus, as well as his subsequent revelations to be gifts of the Holy Spirit. They had completely transformed his understanding of God's covenant with Israel, so much so that it had become "a new covenant." When he asserted "the letter kills, but the Spirit gives life," there was an implied biographical reference. By "letter" Paul undoubtedly meant Scripture as interpreted by the Pharisees in spite of their doctrine of the twofold Law. Before Damascus, Paul had known only the "letter" as his fundamental religious guide; after Damascus, his understanding of Scripture had been radically transformed by the gift of the Spirit, his vision of the resurrected Messiah.

Nevertheless, Paul did not at any time question the Law's abiding holiness. Even his negative comparison of Moses with himself was not inconsistent with his view of the Law. To traditional Jews, Paul's assertion of his own superiority over Moses has the aura of arrogance if not blasphemy, yet Paul was moved by no such intent. He wrote to the Corinthians: "Now if the ministry *of death, engraven letter by letter on tablets of stone* appeared surrounded by such glory that the children of Israel could not fix their gaze upon Moses' face because of its glory (although it was only transient) how much more glorious will be the ministry of the Spirit. . . . for if the transient ministry had its time of glory, how much more is the enduring ministration glorious!"[11]

No Jew can read Paul's characterization of Moses' leadership as a "ministry of death" without initial offense. The characterization became even more offensive when these words were later used by non-Jews to foster antisemitic violence. In fairness to Paul, we must recognize that his harsh words were motivated by his belief that the God who appeared to Moses had revealed himself more completely to the Apostle. Paul was convinced that Christ as Messiah had placed the giving of the Law in proper perspective. He saw Moses as having presented a version of God's revelation that could not bring salvation without proper interpretation. He did not disagree with the Pharisees on this issue. He was, however, convinced that he, not they, was empowered properly to interpret Scripture, declaring that those who remained faithful to the old understanding were blind to Scripture's true import:

> We do not act as Moses did, who put a veil over his face (so that the people of Israel could not perceive the ultimate significance of that which was to be abolished). But their minds became hardened (and that is why) the same veil remains drawn, even today (in spite of everything) at the reading of the Old Covenant. But until today, every time that Moses is read, a veil lies over their minds. It cannot be removed because it is only through Christ that it is abolished.[12]

The text is difficult, the imagery rich. Paul contended that what had been veiled over in premessianic Judaism had been unveiled by faith in Christ. This would accord with the psychoanalytic conception, which I accept, that the Christian religious revolution brought to the surface unconscious feelings about divine-human figures that had been repressed or sublimated in Judaism.

In any event, Paul wanted to contrast the old and his new way of understanding God's Law. That is very different from rejecting the Law entirely. Furthermore, although Paul strenuously objected to the circumcision of non-Jewish Christians, he did not normally object to the observance of the Law by Jews or Jewish Christians.[13] Paul himself apparently remained to a degree an observant Jew. He claims to have submitted five times to the punishment of thirty-nine stripes inflicted upon him by Jewish officials.[14] Had he really broken with his people he would not have submitted to this punishment. The extent of Paul's observance of traditional Jewish Law remains a matter of scholarly debate, but he apparently maintained a semblance of observance when among Jews: "to the Jews I was like a Jew, to gain the Jews. To those who live under the Law, as if I were under the Law—although I am not under the Law—to gain those who live under the Law."[15] Of course, no Pharisee could have written that he lived "*as if* I were under the Law . . . to gain those who live under the Law," but the fundamental issue was where men stood in the divine timetable. Paul behaved "as if" he were under the Law because he did not wish to give initial offense to religiously compliant Jews. His ultimate object in dealing with them was to reveal the Good News of the coming of the Messiah.

Those who minimize the break between established Judaism and the primitive Church tend to interpret Paul's relations with the Church, and especially with Peter, in terms of mutual antipathy.[16] The Jerusalem Church has been depicted as committed to circumcision and the observance of the Law as preconditions for entry into the new community. It was supposed to have sent out emissaries to discredit Paul's work among the Gentiles, especially his opposition to the circumcision of Gentile converts to Christianity. Paul's "Judaizing" opponents are pictured as Jews zealous for the Law, whether or not they were actually emissaries of Jerusalem. *What is at stake in this interpretation is the question of Paul's relations with his own people.* Those who stress his hostility to those Jewish Christians who insisted on circumcision as a precondition to entry into their community usually picture him as turning his back on his own kin and creating a rival Gentile religion that was destined to maintain an antagonistic posture not only toward Judaism but toward Jewish Christianity as well. This view is consistent with the image of Paul as the turncoat and founder of Christian anti-semitism. In all probability, the conflict between Paul and the Jerusalem Church and between Paul and Peter has been exaggerated. On Paul's first visit to Jerusalem three years after his conversion, he stayed with Peter for fifteen days [Galatians (Gal.) 1:18]. We have no record of their discussions, but it is difficult to imagine them ignoring the Christian religious revolution and they must have compared ideas. At a later date, Paul recognized Peter's mission to the Jews as somehow paralleling his own mission to the Gentiles (Gal. 2:27). There is reason to believe that Peter shared Paul's conviction that Christ was the "end of the Law." Peter is known to have dispensed with the dietary laws in his encounter with Cornelius the Roman centurion (Acts 10:1–48) and at the church at Antioch (Gal. 2:12).[17] Although it is true that Paul bitterly criticized Peter for having withdrawn from table fellowship with Gentile Christians when "certain friends of James" arrived on the scene, the basis of Paul's criticism was that Peter was acting out of expediency rather than principle (Gal. 2:12–14). Paul does not suggest that there were theological differences between them either in Galatians or in Corinthians.[18] Furthermore, at the Apostolic Council described in Acts 15:7–11, Peter is pictured as taking a position similar to Paul's with regard to the sufficiency of baptism without circumcision for the admission of Gentile converts. There is no need to draw too great a contrast between Paul and Peter.

Similarly, the contrast between the Jerusalem Christians and Paul has probably been overdrawn.[19] Paul was insistent upon his independence from the Jerusalem Church, but independence must not be seen as opposition. Paul's autonomy vis-à-vis the Jerusalem Church was based on the same conviction that motivated his independence from the Pharisees. Paul believed that he had received both his commission as an Apostle and the content of his Gospel "through a revelation of Jesus Christ" (Gal. 1:12). At the Apostolic Council he was anxious not to cause a breach in the unity of the Church of Christ, but there is little doubt that he would have done so had the leaders rejected his position on the mission to the Gentiles. Even when Paul wrote that the leaders of the Church had accepted his position, he quickly added that it was of little consequence to him that the "pillars" were regarded as leaders "since God has no favorites" (Gal. 2:6). The fundamental issue for Paul at the time of conversion and in the presence of the Jerusalem leaders was the word of God versus the word of man. No worldly preeminence could give any man the authority to add or detract from what God had revealed to Paul.

Although Paul insisted on his independence of all human authority, his account of the Apostolic Council in Galatians emphasized the Council's agreement that "the Gospel of the uncircumcision" was committed to him. Paul described that accord: "And when they perceived the grace that was given to me, James and Cephas and John, who were reputed to be pillars, gave to me and Barnabbas the right hand of fellowship, that we should go to the Gentiles and they to the circumcised" (Gal. 2:9). There are some differences between the meeting described in Acts 15 and the one Paul described as an eyewitness in Galatians 2. It is possible that we have the record of two meetings rather than one.[20] In any event, both Acts and Galatians agree that Paul and the leaders of the Jerusalem Church arrived at a viable accord after a serious discussion of the issues between them. When Paul prepared to return to Jerusalem at the conclusion of his final missionary journey, he regarded that agreement as still binding (Romans 15).

We know, of course, that Paul met with bitter opposition throughout his career. Some of it came, understandably enough, from the leaders of the Jewish mainstream. Much of it may also have come from overzealous Gentile converts. According to Johannes Munck, the "Judaizing" antagonists at Galatia, who demanded the circumcision of Gentile converts, were not Jewish Christians but Gentiles who had become overly zealous for the observance of the traditions of the "old" Israel after they had entered the "new" Israel.[21] We need not dwell at length on Munck's arguments; they have been debated by scholars since their publication.[22] What is significant is Munck's contention that there was a far smaller gulf between Paul and the Jerusalem Christians than most scholars had previously conceded. There was, of course, a major difference in emphasis. The Jerusalem Church was primarily interested in bringing the Gospel to Israel; Paul's concern, at least initially, was to proclaim the Good News of Israel's Messiah to the Gentiles. Although this placed him in a very different sphere of activity, neither Paul's letters nor Acts suggest that Paul and the "pillars" of the Jerusalem Church were at odds on this division of labor or on the requirements for entry into the Church.

There were probably practical reasons for the division of labor. For one thing, Paul may have been an embarrassment and a danger to the primitive Church. The Church's situation was precarious enough without Paul's theological radicalism, as the stoning of Stephen had demonstrated. The party of the Pharisees in Jerusalem could hardly have felt well disposed toward a man they regarded as a turncoat. According to Walther Schmithals, the Jerusalem Church was as convinced as Paul that the Law was no longer necessary for salvation even for Jews.[23] However, they were compelled to maintain at least the appearance of being observant Jews. Living in Jerusalem, the leaders of the Church realized that they could not challenge the observance of the Law by Jews and remain free from persecution. Their attitude was probably similar to Paul's when he testified that he lived "as if" under the Law in order to win people to the Gospel (I Corinthians 9:20). They too lived "as if" under the Law. They had little choice if they were to remain in Jerusalem.

Perhaps the hest way to describe the attitude shared by Paul and the Jerusalem Church concerning the Law is that both were indifferent to its observance by Jews or Jewish Christians as long as those who observed it understood that salvation came from Christ, not the Law. Paul wrote to the Corinthians urging both the circumcised and the uncircumcised to "remain in the state in which he was when he was called."[24] He argued that "circumcision is nothing and uncircumcision is nothing" (7:19), by which he meant that there was nothing either good or bad in observing or failing to observe the details of the Law. The Law was no longer the path to salvation. Whether it was observed or not in the Age of the Messiah was a practical rather than a religious matter. For the Christians of Jerusalem, observance was a matter of prudence. Such considerations could be justified theologically. The Church could not have been free to win souls for Christ in Jerusalem had it openly challenged the Law. Nevertheless, both Paul and the leaders of the Church agreed that outside of Palestine Gentile converts need not accept the Law. Paul's counsel that both the circumcised and the uncircumcised ought to continue as they were before conversion was relevant to the situation of the Church. It is also evidence that he understood and approved of the stand of the Jerusalem Christians on the Law; it is very likely that they also understood and approved of Paul's doctrine that Christ was the *telos* of the Law.

Israel's Conversion and Humanity's Salvation

In spite of the agreement at the Apostolic Council that Peter would "preach to the circumcised" and Paul to the "uncircumcised," Paul never ceased to hope that his own kin would accept Jesus as their Messiah. Although Paul regarded the mission to the Gentiles as his distinctive calling, his desire to bring about the conversion of the Jews was at least as powerful as that of the Jerusalem Christians. Some Pauline scholars have suggested that the Apostle had his own plan for Israel's conversion that differed radically from the more direct methods of proclaiming the Christian message used by the Jerusalem Church. Apparently, Paul believed that the success of his mission was a precondition for the conversion of the Jews, who would accept Christ only after the conversion of the Gentiles. Thus Paul's conception of himself as Apostle to the Gentiles involved his hopes for his kin as well. Paul's description of his call to be Apostle to the Gentiles (Gal. 1:15) was reminiscent of similar calls to Isaiah (49:1–6) and Jeremiah

(1:4) in which God is depicted as designating his servant from the womb to be his messenger unto the nations: "Then God, who had specially *chosen* me, while I was *still* in my *mother's womb* called me through his grace and chose to reveal his Son in me, so that I might preach the Good News about him to the Gentiles" (Gal. 1:15–16). The italicized words are apparently quoted from Isaiah 49:1. Jeremiah had a somewhat similar conception of his own commission: "Now the word of the Lord came unto me saying 'Before I formed you in the belly I knew you and before you came forth out of the womb, I sanctified you and appointed you a prophet to the nations'" (Jeremiah 1:4). Not only did Paul regard himself as greater than Moses, but he saw God's call to the prophets as an anticipation of his own commission as Apostle. There were, of course, differences in the message, the time, and the manner of delivery. Nevertheless, Paul regarded himself as God's "Chosen instrument" to carry Christ's name before the Gentiles.[25]

Paul's claim that he had been designated for his role from his mother's womb is an example of his rich symbolic consciousness. Paul was intuitively aware of some of the archaic emotional forces that had impelled him to his vocation. Long before psychoanalysis gave conceptual expression to the idea that unconscious forces having their inception in the history of the race begin to express themselves in the individual *in utero*. One might argue that Paul's use of the phrase was stylistic and dependent upon the older imagery of the prophets. There are, however, too many instances in which we have found Paul's symbolic consciousness at work for it to be likely that he was merely resorting to a literary convention. On the contrary, it is more likely that he used the symbolic conventions of his time to express the intuition that the forces that had impelled him to his role were at least as old as he was. One wonders whether this was one of the passages Freud had in mind when he referred to the "dark traces of the past" that lay ready to break forth into consciousness in Paul's soul.

According to Munck, Paul was convinced that Christ would not return to complete the work of salvation until the Apostle had first completed his labor of carrying the Gospel to the Gentiles and thereafter bringing about the conversion of the Jews.[26] Paul thus regarded his commission as Apostle to the Gentiles as part of a greater work, the redemption of both Jew and Gentile in Christ. If Munck is correct, Paul believed that the final consummation of the Messiah's labors depended upon him!

Paul's dream of a unified mankind in which tribal and creedal differences would finally be obliterated was consistent with a compelling strain in Jewish thought that has persisted from the days of the prophets to our own time. Nowhere is Paul more prototypically Jewish than in his strenuous pursuit of this ideal. Perhaps the very stringency of Judaism's definition of itself in opposition to the "Gentiles" helped to generate the vision of a unified mankind. When carried to an extreme, any particularism flies in the face of the yearning for union and community that has frequently moved men. That yearning may be utopian, but it remains powerful to this day and it was probably especially intense in Paul.

It is also likely that Paul's upbringing in Tarsus influenced his desire for humanity unified in Christ. Living as a member of a minority community in a predominantly non-Jewish city, Paul was probably more sensitive to the problems of ethnic and religious division than he would have been had he been reared in Jerusalem. Diaspora communities depend on the sufferance of the host community, a fact that conditions their social and economic status, their behavior, and even their self-perceptions. It would be stretching the point to suggest that Paul shared many of the complex psychological attitudes that have conditioned diaspora Jewish identity in modern times. Nevertheless, Paul's overriding concern for the ultimate unity of Jew and Gentile has had historical parallels among those diaspora Jews who dreamed of the unification of humanity as a way out of their own isolation as Jews.

Paul's dream of the unity of humanity "in Christ" was not one that the majority of his kinsmen shared. Acts is full of reports of Jewish opposition to his missionary work.[27] Usually when Paul came to a new community, he preached in the local synagogue. With predictable regularity the synagogue authorities became hostile and compelled him to establish his own churches. In some communities the traditionalists sought to kill him; in others they incited the populace and the authorities against him.

A typical incident is depicted in Acts 17. After Paul and Silas arrived in Thessalonika, he preached in the synagogue for "three consecutive sabbaths," developing his arguments "from Scripture . . . proving how it was ordained that the Christ should suffer and rise from the dead" (17:2–3). Some Jews were convinced, as were some Greeks. Paul's success and the controversial character of his preaching soon impelled the Jewish authorities to stir up the populace against him. As recorded in Acts, their complaint has a ring of truth about it: "The people who have been turning the whole world upside down have come down here. . . . They have broken every one of Caesar's edicts by claiming that there is another King, Jesus" (17:6–7). To the extent that the special circumstances of Paul's startling conversion became known, the opposition of the Jewish community must have been further aggravated.

The hostility between Paul and his kinsmen was mutual. Perhaps the most savage expression of Paul's anger is to be found in Thessalonians. Paul wrote to the Church at Thessalonika, apparently at a time of persecution:

> For you my brothers, have been like the churches of God in Christ Jesus which are in Judaea, in suffering the same treatment from your countrymen as they have suffered from the Jews, the people who put the Lord Jesus to death and the prophets too. And now they have been persecuting

> us, and acting in a way that cannot please God and makes them *enemies of the whole human race*, because they are hindering us from preaching to the Gentiles and trying to save them . . . but retribution is overtaking them at last. (I Thessalonians 2:14–16)

In a later generation Jews were to be regarded by antisemites as "enemies of the whole human race" without qualification. In Paul's outburst, their enmity consisted in impeding his mission to the Gentiles. Because Paul was convinced that nothing less than the salvation of humanity was at stake, it is not surprising that he regarded *any* opposition to his work as enmity against humankind.

Paul's bitter condemnation of his own people in I Thessalonians lacks any moderating qualification. In fairness to Paul, we must remember that his hostility was entirely consistent with his people's way of handling religious conflict at the time.[28] The same methods often continue to be employed today by those who are convinced that their distinctive tradition alone, whatever it may be, expresses the word of God.

Nevertheless, Paul's anger reveals only one aspect of Paul's complex feelings toward his kinsmen. In spite of that anger, Paul fully expected "Israel after the flesh" to be converted to faith in Christ. Moreover, Paul expected to play a crucial role in their conversion. To understand Paul's role as he anticipated it, we must consider the significance he ascribed to the collection of money he had gathered from the churches of Greece and Asia Minor to present to the Church in Jerusalem. Romans 15 was written by Paul after he had gathered the collection from the Gentile churches but before he set out from Greece, presumably from Corinth, to journey to Jerusalem. He wrote that he expected to present the collection upon arriving in Jerusalem on behalf of the "poor among the saints" (Romans 15:26) (i.e., the "saints" within the Church). This chapter is one of our best sources for understanding Paul's preoccupations immediately before he set out with the all-important gift for the Jerusalem Church.

It is evident from the text that Paul feared for his own safety in Jerusalem. He asked his readers to pray that he might "escape the unbelievers in Judaea." He also asked that they pray that the gifts he brought be "accepted by the saints" (Romans 15:31). Paul was well aware of the hazards of his enterprise. In view of the variety of interests Paul had challenged, as well as the unfortunate example of the stoning of Stephen, the visit to Jerusalem was indeed a precarious venture. Nevertheless, Paul felt compelled to make the journey because of the importance he ascribed to collection. Both Nickle and Munck emphasize the fact that Paul did not regard the collection as a gift of earthly valuables. *It was to be Paul's proof to all in Jerusalem, Christian and non-Christian alike, that the Gentiles had found salvation in Christ.* Paul had gathered the collection with difficulty over a period of several years. The venture had met with opposition in Corinth and perhaps in Galatia.[29] According to Acts, Paul was accompanied by at least eight companions representing the Gentile Churches (20:4f.). Munck held that the presence of so large a delegation was Paul's way of making the delivery of the collection "an unconcealable public affair."[30] Paul wanted all Jerusalem to learn of the mighty deeds wrought by Christ for the humanity's salvation by the conversion of the Gentile world.

Both Munck and Nickle argue that Paul believed that the presentation of the collection would be one of the culminating acts in the drama of salvation preceding Christ's glorious return. Paul believed that the Messiah had appeared in Jerusalem. Even after conversion the city remained for him what it was for his rabbinic contemporaries, the *omphalos*, the navel of the universe, the very center of the cosmos.[31] It was in Jerusalem that the final acts in the drama of salvation were expected to unfold. As Isaiah and Micah had prophesied, it was to Jerusalem that the nations would come in the last days and it was from Jerusalem that the word of the Lord would finally flow (Isaiah 2:2f.; Micah 4.1f.).

Although the Munck–Nickle hypothesis has been challenged by some very distinguished scholars, over the years I have regarded it as very plausible because it rings true psychologically. Consider Paul's postconversion situation: He had turned his back on everything he had previously believed. He was undoubtedly regarded by his former teachers and colleagues as either a madman or an apostate. Even his new colleagues were less than unanimous in their praise. Many rejected his claim to be an Apostle. Others offered a host of ungenerous comments about him. Even the leaders of the Jerusalem Church were probably more comfortable with him in faraway Greece and Asia Minor than in Judaea, Paul's extraordinary sensitivity to the underlying dynamics of the Jewish religious world was paralleled by his awareness of the way others reacted to him. His apologia in II Corinthians 10:1–13:10 exhibits his acute sensitivity to the opinions of others. Only one conviction permitted him to transcend that sensitivity: He believed his authority came directly from Christ.[32] He also believed that it had been used to "build up" rather than "pull down" his followers (II Corinthians 10: 8). Even if the entire world rejected his message, Paul would have persevered.

Nevertheless, no one who worked as tirelessly for the conversion of others—literally for the conversion of all of humanity—could have been without hope of vindication. Paul may have anticipated that the delivery of the collection would be the occasion of his final vindication. One psychoanalyst views the journey to Jerusalem with its predictable perils as evidence of Paul's masochism, but there is no reason to regard the enterprise as unduly masochistic.[33] Paul's quest for vindication and his conviction that he would ultimately achieve it are enough to explain why he not only ignored the dangers awaiting him but spent so much time assembling the collection and preparing to return to Jerusalem.

At first glance, Paul's expectation that the presence of non-Jewish Christians laden with gifts would bring about Israel's conversion seems overly optimistic, especially in view of the fact that neither Jesus nor the preaching of the "saints" had achieved this end. Objectively, Paul was mistaken, but, as we shall see, his expectation was not without a certain psychological plausibility. The key to Paul's optimism can be found in his conception of the conflict between the Church and the Synagogue: The imagery that Paul utilized to describe that conflict is that of fraternal *strife*.

Paul introduced the theme of fraternal conflict in Romans 9–11 after expressing his sorrow that Christ had been rejected by his own "flesh and blood" (Romans 9:5). He held that God would bestow salvation only on those who are truly worthy to be reckoned among Abraham's seed. Nevertheless, Paul argued that physical descent from Abraham by itself is insufficient for inclusion among those chosen by God for salvation. Paul used a series of Christian *midrashim* or homilies to make his point. He cited the examples of Isaac and Jacob to reinforce the idea that physical descent from the first patriarch by itself is insufficient for membership in God's elect community. Both patriarchs were *chosen by God* to be "true" descendants of Abraham, although each had a brother who might have inherited Abraham's blessings. In Paul's homilies, Isaac and Jacob become prototypes of the Church, whereas the rejected brothers, Ishmael and Esau, become prototypes of the Synagogue. For Paul the Church was the chosen brother; the Synagogue was the rejected brother (Romans 9:6–13).

Paul marveled at what he believed to be God's choice of the Gentile Christians to become the true "Israel." He saw it as a fulfillment of Hosea's prophecy: "I will say unto them that were not my people, 'Thou art my people' and they shall say, 'Thou art my God'" (Hosea 2:23; see Romans 9:25–26). For Paul, the people who "were not my people" were the non-Jews who by their faith in Christ said "Thou art my God." According to Paul they were called "Children of the living God" (Romans 9:26). Thus election has passed from Abraham's descendants "according to the flesh" to those who were his spiritual descendants (see Romans 4:13–17). For Paul Christians alone were spiritual descendants of Abraham and, as such, the favored sons. The "unbelieving" Jews were, of course, the rejected offspring.

Because of its enormous emotional power, Paul's image of Israel as the unfaithful brother rejected by God has strongly influenced both the Church's self-understanding and her interpretation of her relationship to Judaism. *One of the most depressing aspects of my research on Paul has been the dreary regularity with which even well-meaning Christian commentators, following in the spirit of Paul's interpretation of the conflict, have seen Israel's inability to accept Jesus as the Messiah as deliberate, willful offense against God.* Thus C. K. Barrett wrote of Israel's "defection," calling Israel "an apostate people."[34] As a Jew who has remained faithful to my own tradition, I hardly appreciate being characterized by Barrett as mired in "Jewish apostasy."[35] The same bias is found in Munck, who wrote of Israel's "guilt" and "impenitence" in rejecting Christ.[36] The examples could be endlessly multiplied, although it is true that in recent scholarship the trend has begun to lessen. Unfortunately, the refusal to accept Judaism as other than an apostate form of Christianity has had direst consequences for Jews throughout their history and, most especially, in the response of the pre-Vatican II Christian Church to the destruction of the European Jews during World War II. As the history of the Inquisition has demonstrated, the Church has been infinitely more hostile to those it regarded as apostates and heretics than to unbelievers.

This unfortunate, but almost inevitable, interpretation of Judaism is *a direct consequence of Paul's insistence that the Church is the true Israel and that the "old" Israel could be saved only by conversion to faith in Christ.* The effect of this interpretation has been to widen immeasurably the gulf between Christianity and Judaism. To be a Jew faithful to the traditions of the Pharisees and rabbis, the religion of the Jewish mainstream, was for Paul and his spiritual heirs to be in willful enmity, rebellion, and apostasy against God. Nevertheless, we must remember that Paul wrote as a member of a competing Jewish sect seeking to discredit its rivals, not as an outsider. Unfortunately, when Christianity became an independent, overwhelmingly non-Jewish religious tradition, it carried over Paul's harsh critique and refused to acknowledge Judaism as an authentic religious tradition with an integrity that is in no sense dependent on any other tradition.

In fairness to Paul, I must repeat that there was no special malice involved in his critique. When, for example, Paul likened Israel to Sodom and Gomorrah in Romans 9:29, he merely quoted Isaiah 1:9, in which the prophet offered a comparable denunciation of Israel in his own time (Romans 9:29). On the contrary, Paul was trying to be as generous toward his spiritual adversaries as the logic of a supersessionary religion of revelation would permit. My own dissent from that kind of religious ideology, especially after Auschwitz, is motivated by my conviction that there are no false gods, that all gods are true, at least in the sense that the sacred traditions of mankind are functional expressions of the life and values of the peoples who maintain them. This position arises very largely out of my emphatic rejection of the exclusivism embedded in a literal reading of biblical religion.

However, Paul's insistence that the "old" Israel has become like Ishmael (Romans 9:6–9; see Gal. 4:21–31) can also be seen as yet another example of the working of Paul's symbolic consciousness. The idea that the conflict of the "descendants" of Isaac and Ishmael or Jacob and Esau is largely a matter of fraternal rivalry was already implicit in the original biblical narratives. In rabbinic Judaism the conflict between Rome and Judaea was often depicted symbolically in terms of the strife between Jacob, the studious, contemplative brother, and Esau, the ruddy, violent hunter.[37] The interpretation of religious strife in terms of sibling rivalry is by no means the only component in the age-old Judeo-Christian conflict, but it is an important one, particularly when the conflict is focused, as it was for Paul, on the question of who is God's favored child. At a later date, the psychological power of these images was immensely strengthened when the Crucifixion came to be regarded as a deicide. Jews in every generation were then accused of being veritable murderers of God. There is no comparable defamation of one religious tradition by another. Behind the twin assertions that the Church was the true Israel and that the "Old" Israel had been cast of as Christ-killers lay the implied assertion, "*We Christians are the Father's favorites, You Jews have been rejected by the Father. You tried to murder Him by murdering His Son.*"

We can now understand why there was a certain psychological plausibility to Paul's belief that the conversion of the Jews would begin in earnest when he arrived in Jerusalem with the collection. Paul believed that by stirring his own kinsmen to envy the Gentile Christians he would move them to adopt the new faith. Paul asserted that God's ultimate purpose in making him Apostle to the Gentiles was to make the Jews jealous of the "new" Israel and thereby to move some to conversion. Thus, Paul saw his mission to the Gentiles as the prelude to his culminating task, that of winning over the Jews. According to Paul, God's purposes would not he fulfilled until Jew and Christian became one people of God. He expressed his purpose as Apostle to the Gentiles: "I have been sent to the Gentiles as their Apostle, and I am proud of being sent, but *the purpose of it is to make my own people jealous of you, and in this way save some of them*" (Romans 11:14; italics added).

Envy or jealousy hardly seems an appropriate motive for religious conversion until one reflects on the extent to which Paul interpreted the Church–Synagogue conflict in terms of fraternal strife. The source of fraternal rivalry is almost always envy lest the parents bestow a greater measure of love on the rival sibling. Paul's plan to stir his kinsmen to jealousy was psychologically consistent with his underlying intuition of what the rivalry between Church and Synagogue was all about. Although we lack any way of validating the conjecture, it is reasonable to assume that Paul's perception of the nature of the conflict reflected his own experience. We know that he had a sister living in Jerusalem (Acts 23:16). Although we have few other details concerning his family background, it is possible that as a Pharisee, Paul experienced the very same kind of envy of Christians, perhaps subliminally, that as a Christian he hoped to stir up in his kinsmen.

Mutual envy probably plays an important role in the Judeo-Christian encounter to this day. In spite of their insistence on the unique destiny of Israel before God, traditional Jews often envy non-Jews their greater security and liberation from nonfunctional behavioral constraint. It would also seem that non-Jews often envy Jews by taking seriously Israel's pathetic claim to be God's favored child, yet claiming that the election has passed to the Christian Church. Hannah Arendt has observed that both the Pan-Slav and the Pan-German forms of tribal nationalism that flourished in the first decades of the twentieth century claimed that God had elected their respective tribes and had ordained the tribe's right to dominate its neighbors. Arendt claimed that much of the extraordinary virulence of the Pan movements' antisemitism was due to their envy and fury at Israel's older claim to be the elect of God.[38] Paul's apparently naive desire to move his kin to jealousy is fully consistent with the Apostle's intuitive psychological depth manifest elsewhere in his letters.

Paul was also convinced that conversion would lead to the general resurrection and the final salvation of mankind: "Since their rejection meant the reconciliation of the world, do you know what their acceptance will mean? Nothing less than life from the dead!" (Romans 11:15). Thus, *Paul saw Israel's conversion as the supreme event within God's redemptive plan.* Once Israel was "saved," at least representationally, the final sequence of eschatological events would commence: Christ would return. The dead would be resurrected and Christ would then hand over the kingdom to God the Father, "having done away with every sovereignty, authority and power" (I Corinthians 15:25).

It should be obvious that whatever the merits of Paul's eschatological vision, it was not the expression of an apostate's malice. Rightly or wrongly, Paul regarded himself as playing a role in the redemption of both his own people and mankind second only to Jesus. If this interpretation of Paul's conception of his role and Israel's place in the divine economy has merit, one must ask whether there was not something inflated and grandiose in Paul's extraordinary understanding of himself and what he believed he could accomplish. It is possible that Paul's identification with Christ was so complete that he willingly set in motion the chain of events leading to his own martyrdom.[39] In any event, things did not turn out as Paul had anticipated. When he arrived in Jerusalem, his kinsmen were stirred to anger rather than jealousy and conversion. He was attacked in the Temple and taken into custody for his own safety by Roman soldiers, thereby initiating the events leading to his eventual death.

Paul's mission to convert his own people ended in failure. Nevertheless, the Apostle cannot he regarded as a deluded visionary whose pretensions were finally destroyed by a contemptuous world. In light of history, Paul's perception of himself as Apostle to the Gentiles proved correct to a degree that far exceeded his most grandiose expectations. No other figure in the history of the Church has been as influential in interpreting the meaning of the Christian message from generation to generation. Nor is it likely that Christendom will ever again know an interpreter of comparable authority and influence. Ironically, *Paul's rabbinic teachers provided their pupil with much of the training he used to argue so persuasively against them.* The Pharisees were Judaism's foremost interpreters of Scripture and they taught Paul the interpreter's skills and methods. Paul's spiritual gifts, especially his symbolic consciousness and his ability to make manifest the unmanifest, were, of course, his own. Where the Pharisees taught Paul how to unveil the deeper meanings embedded in the text of Scripture, he sought to uncover the deeper meanings to be discerned in the life, death, and resurrection of the one he believed to be Israel's Messiah. In any event, Paul could only build on what he had received.

Fraternity and Fratricide

This essay is a revision of a chapter in a book I wrote thirty years ago entitled *My Brother Paul.*[40] In that work, I remarked that I had called the book *My Brother Paul* with considerable sadness. I recognize Paul as a brother; I concur in his judgment that the Judeo-Christian encounter is fraternal. Regrettably, I cannot pretend that I find fraternity devoid of fratricide. There has always been a fratricidal element in the meeting of Church and Synagogue. I find no malice in Paul's identification of the Synagogue as the wayward, unfaithful brother. Nevertheless, I believe the identification has had predictable results from which Paul might have shrunk in horror. Paul's insistence that before God men are divided into collectivities of faithful and are perfidious brothers, an insight he had perhaps acquired from his rabbinic teachers and the biblical doctrine of Israel's election, helped to release fratricidal emotions that everntually became regnant in Judeo-Christian relations.

The sorry story of Christian violence and Jewish contempt (for Christian violence reinforced the negative opinion Jews had of their brother religion as well as their own sense of chosenness) ultimately derived from the fact that human beings are born incomplete and seek throughout life to replicate the protective enclaves they knew in infancy. Men and women apparently find it difficult ever to leave entirely behind the loves and hatreds of the world of childhood. Paradoxically, it was Paul's genius that he repressed that world less than did his former peers among the Pharisees. Where men find no familial relationships, they must apparently create them lest they be stricken with the terrifying sense of their own hopeless solitude in an unfeeling cosmos. They project the image of a Heavenly Father who chooses among brothers as the protective capacities of their earthly fathers diminish in credibility. They turn their fellows into brothers so that they can war over the illusory patrimony of earthly or heavenly progenitors. In every age they repeat the tale of Cain and Abel, Isaac and Ishmael, Jacob and Esau, and Joseph and his brothers. Even the sacrificial death of Jesus may contain an element of fratricide. After all, Paul described him as "the first born of many brothers" who must endure death's perils so that the younger brothers may live.

Was Paul's dream of one humanity united in Christ a hopeless illusion? Not entirely. Paul maintained that the final end to fraternal strife was inseparable from overcoming suffering and mortality. Like most apocalyptic visionaries, Paul's dream was based on a thoroughly realistic assessment of the existential limitations of the world he lived in. He was, of course, far more optimistic about the imminent abolition of the world of the Old Adam than the evidence of history would seem to justify. Two thousand years after the Apostle's career, the world of suffering and mortality continues to hold sway. Furthermore, fraternal strife exists within the "body of Christ" as well as between the Church and other religious communities. Nevertheless, I believe Paul was correct in believing that fraternal discord would cease when the drama of human history was terminated, when death was overcome, and when God would become "all in all." Before strife and suffering can come to an end, the Old Adam must give way to the new. Thus Paul was indeed correct in his insight that fratricidal strife would last as long as humanity as we know it endures.

NOTES

1. Günther Bornkamm, *Paul*, trans. D. M. G. Stalker (New York: Harper & Row, 1971).
2. See Markus Barth, "Was Paul an Anti-Semite?" *Journal of Ecumenical Studies* 5 (1968): 78–104; and Krister Stendahl, "Judaism and Christianity," *Harvard Divinity School Bulletin* 28 (October 1963): 1–9.
3. See Peter Berger, *The Sacred Canopy* (Garden City, NY: Anchor Books, 1969), 3–51, for this insight.
4. See I Thessalonians 2:14–16.
5. See Richard L. Rubenstein, *After Auschwitz*, 2nd ed. (Baltimore: Johns Hopkins University Press, 1992), 29–61.
6. I Corinthians 1:18–29.
7. See I Corinthians 1:18–28.
8. The classic rabbinic tradition is the story of how Rabbi Eliezer tried to validate his opinion in a discussion with Rabbi Joshua by invoking a heavenly voice (*bat qol*). The heavenly voice did indeed declare that the Law (*Halakhah*) is in accord with the opinion of Rabbi Eliezer, but Rabbi Joshua rejected this opinion, declaring, "It is not in heaven" (Deuteronomy 30:12). Rabbi Jeremiah, who flourished two generations later, interpreted Rabbi Joshua's position: "The Law was given to us from Sinai. [Since then] we pay no attention to heavenly voices . . ." *(Baba Mezia*, 59b).
9. There was a tradition that after the death of Haggai, Zechariah, and Malachi, "the Holy Spirit ceased from Israel." Israel was nevertheless granted the privilege of hearing heavenly voices, but as we have seen, they had less authority by far than the rabbis. See *Tosefta Sotah*, 13, 2; *Sanhedrin* 11a; *Sotah* 48b; *Yoma* 9b.
10. II Corinthians 3:5, 6 (italics added).
11. II Corinthians 3:7–11 (italics added).

12. II Corinthians 3:13–15.
13. See I Corinthians 7:18–22.
14. II Corinthians 11:24.
15. I Corinthians 9:20.
16. This problem has been discussed by Johannes Munck, *Paul and the Salvation of Mankind* trans. F. Clarke (London: SCM. 1959), 69–86. He has shown that under the leadership of F. C. Baur, the Tübingen school's hypothesis dominated the interpretation of Paul's relations with the Jerusalem Church and his own people.
17. This view has been challenged by John Bligh, who believes that the tradition that Peter was instructed by God in the vision of the sailcloth to eat without regard to the Jewish dietary laws (Acts 10:9–16) is misplaced. According to Bligh, Paul rather than Peter had the vision. Bligh stressed the antagonism between Peter and Paul, but at the expense of the integrity of the received text. See John Bligh, *Galatians* (London: St. Paul Publications, 1969), 104–106.
18. See I Corinthians 1:12ff.
19. This is, of course, Munck's thesis, which I accept. For a strong argument against Munck, see Bligh, *Galatians*, 31ff.
20. In Acts 15, the Apostolic Council ruled that all that was necessary for Gentile converts was to abstain from "anything polluted by idols, from fornication, from the meat of strangled animals and from blood" (Acts 15:20). In Galatians the agreement that Paul had been commissioned to preach to the "uncircumcised" and Peter to the "circumcised" is stressed. Nevertheless, the fact that the two accounts differ does not mean that there were two meetings. See Bligh, *Galatians*, 144ff.
21. Munck, *Paul*, 88–134.
22. See W. D. Davies, "A New View of Paul—J. Munck, 'Paulus und Heilsgeschicte,'" in *Christian Origins and Judaism: A Collection of New Testament Studies* (London: Darton, Longman & Todd, 1962); Bligh, *Galatians*, 32ff. Walter Schmithals, *Paul and James*, trans. Dorothy M. Barton (London: SCM Press, 1965), 13–15. Also Rudolph Bultmann, "Eine Neues Paulus Verständnis?," *Theologische Literaturzeitung* 84 (1959).
23. Schmithals, *Paul and James*, 38–62.
24. I Corinthians 7:18–20.
25. See Acts 9:15f.; 22:14f.; 26:16–18.
26. Munck, *Paul*, 116–143.
27. See Acts 9:22–25, 29; 13:50; 14:2, 4–6, 19; 17:5–10; 18:4, 6; 18:12–17; 19:8–9; 20:18–35.
28. For example, the Dead Sea Scroll community was convinced that it alone constituted "the Children of Light." All the rest of Israel, not to say the rest of humanity, were thought of as dwelling in moral and spiritual darkness. See Geza Vermes, *An Introduction to the Complete Dead Sea Scrolls* (Minneapolis: Fortress Press, 1999).
29. See II Corinthians 8:1–9:15; I Corinthians 16:1; Galatians 2:10.
30. Johannes Munck, *Christ and Israel*, 11; Keith Nickle, *The Collection: A Study in Paul's Strategy* (London: SCM Press, 1966).
31. Davies, *Christian Origins and Judaism*, 259.
32. Galatians 1:1; see also, I Corinthians 1:1; II Corinthians 1:1; Romans 1:1.
33. See Sidney Tarachow, "St. Paul and Early Christianity," in *Psychoanalysis and the Social Sciences*, Vol. 4, eds. Werner Muensterberg and Sidney Axelrad (New York: International Universities Press, 1955).
34. See C. K. Barrett, *A Commentary on the Epistle to the Romans* (New York: Harper & Row, 1957), 180, 194.
35. Barrett, *Romans*, 213.

36. Munck, *Paul and the Salvation of Mankind*, 300; *Christ and Israel*, 89. The same inability to accept the integrity of Judaism is to be found, among very many others, in E. Käsemann, "Paul and Israel," in *New Testament Questions of Today*, trans. W. J. Montague (Philadelphia: Fortress Press, 1969), 183–187.
37. See C. G. Montefiore and H. Loewe, *A Rabbinic Anthology* (Philadelphia: Jewish Publication Society, 1960).
38. Hannah Arendt, *The Origins of Totalitarianism* (New York: Harcourt Brace, 1951), 221–266.
39. See II Corinthians 5:8ff.; 12:10f.; Philippians 1:21–26.
40. Richard L. Rubenstein, *My Brother Paul* (New York: Harper & Row, 1972).

CHAPTER 7

Double Bind

Sacrifice in the Epistle to the Hebrews

JENNIFER L. KOOSED

I was having trouble with the class I was teaching. They had proven to be resistant to certain critical, interpretative strategies. The trouble began as early as the conquest narratives in Joshua and Judges, but was fully manifested in our discussion of Isaiah 7:14—was it "virgin" or "young woman"? Then, the day in which we discussed the servant songs in Isaiah, my fellow teaching assistant Grace Imathiu (an ordained Methodist minister and New Testament scholar) took over my class. She spent an hour arguing about the identification of the servant with Jesus. Grace's point was the same as mine: this text meant something quite different to its original audience and that meaning is legitimate, then and now. In addition to this, there are details in the songs that do not correspond to Jesus at all. The suffering servant is ambiguous, open to a variety of interpretations, unable to rest comfortably in any one reading. After class, Grace and I were standing in the hall comparing notes. We were approached by a woman in my class. She thanked Grace for leading the discussion group and then said, "You know, when Jennifer says things like that I don't believe her, but since you said it, I guess it must be true."

This story raises two questions. First, is it legitimate exegetically for Christians to read the Hebrew Scriptures as the "Old Testament"? In other words, is it legitimate for Christians to read them as scriptures that predict and are then completed by the New Testament? And second, what are or have been the real-world effects of such a hermeneutic? The resistance from my students (as opposed to the students in Grace's group who were more willing to entertain different possibilities) to reading the Hebrew Bible as separate from and other than their Old Testament stemmed from one aspect of identity that marked me as different—different from Grace Imathiu, from Dr. Renita Weems (the professor for this class), and from the students. I am Jewish. They simply refused to hear certain things from me about "their" Bible.

Interpreting the Jewish Scriptures through a christological lens is evident already in the earliest strata of New Testament writing. This essay will refract the question of hermeneutical validity and ethical responsibility of such an exegetical lens through the Epistle to the Hebrews. Specifically, it will look at Hebrews 4:14–5:10 and 7:1–29, which present an interpretation of the enigmatic figure of Melchizedek found in Genesis 14:17–20 and Psalm 110:4.

I

The Epistle of the Hebrews marks a pivotal stage in the self-definition of the nascent Christian church. In this text, the Jewish Scriptures are read as a shadow of the perfection enacted by Jesus as the Christ. The Epistle is concerned with demonstrating both continuity with and superiority to the Scriptures in order to establish both legitimacy and difference; in fact, the text seeks to establish a "legitimate difference."[1] For example, in the Melchizedek passages, Jesus becomes both the eternal high priest and the perfect sacrifice.

The Epistle to the Hebrews was not penned by Paul, nor is it a letter. Rather, scholars classify it as a "word of exhortation" (13:22), a sermon. And, in the words of Origen of Alexandria in the third century: "As for who has written it, only God knows." The precise historical situation of the community also proves difficult to determine. There are no concrete political or geographic references within the text that would allow an interpreter to link it to a particular setting. However, the strong rhetoric throughout the epistle enables the reader to reconstruct the social situation of the community addressed.

Judging from the admonishments throughout the text, the audience was a persecuted community, experiencing pressure from both Gentile and Jewish neighbors (10:32–34, 12:4). Specifically, as John Dunnill argues, they were a Jewish sectarian group: "Christians for whom Judaism offers the natural alternative identity-base, and who are vulnerable to theoretical and social pressures to turn back, or turn aside, to that alternative."[2] These Jewish Christians and Gentile converts would have felt the distinction between themselves and Judaism keenly. Separating themselves from Judaism through proclamation of the Christ, they were "excluded from their community as betrayers of their race, culture and religion."[3] As such, they clung to the outsider traditions within the Jewish Scriptures. Like the early Hebrews, the hearers of the Epistle to the Hebrews are exiles, strangers in a strange land. Without Jewish identity to exempt them legally, persecution at the hands of the Romans may have been a result of their refusal to participate in the state cult.[4] The author was therefore attempting to establish continuity with Judaism in order to quell outside criticism, while at the same time proving superiority to Judaism in order to prevent internal backsliding. Reaffirmation of the traditions, rituals, and communities of Judaism would have shielded them from state persecution, as well as returned them to family and friends who were probably at best mystified, at worst enraged by this new sect.

Outside, the social pressure of the Jewish and Gentile world was threatening group identity and cohesion. Inside, there may have also been a weakening of faith due to the delayed *parousia* (the expected return of Jesus Christ).[5] The text emphasizes the coming judgment (2:2–3, 6:8, 10:25, 29–31, 12:18–24, 26–29) and Christ's final role (2:8, 10:13). There is a balance between a realized eschatology and a futuristically oriented eschatology that would reassure the community of its present moment, as well as keep it hopefully anticipating the End Time.

The author and the audience of the Epistle to the Hebrews were faced with a pressing question, one that resonates even today: What is the relationship between Judaism and Christianity? As a text that addresses Jewish Christians caught between Jewish and Gentile social pressures, as well as tensions within their own burgeoning theology, Hebrews is entirely dependent upon the Jewish Scriptures. Richard Longenecker identifies thirty-eight citations and fifty-five allusions to Scripture in the Epistle.[6] Most of these are taken from the psalter (33), the Pentateuch (26), and the prophetic canon (20).[7] There is no one scriptural verse or passage that dominates. However, what does dominate is the theological notion of Jesus as both High Priest and perfect sacrifice. This idea is the organizing principle behind the Epistle and its use of the Jewish Scripture.[8]

Although we may be able to understand such a hermeneutical move in the social and historical context of a struggling new religious community, what happens when these same texts are read from the position of a powerful dominant religion? What does this type of appropriation of Scripture mean now after the Holocaust? Is it appropriate and is it responsible? Does it carry the same meaning now as it did then? What are the limits of such a hermeneutic and what are the ethical categories that can be used to judge?

In Hebrews 4:14–5:10 and 7:1–29, Jesus is portrayed as the ultimate High Priest, the one who atones for all sins for all time. Melchizedek is the focal point for this argument, serving as the figure who propels Jesus to heights that surpass the Levitical priesthood. Melchizedek is as enigmatic a character in the Jewish Scriptures as he is in the Epistle to the Hebrews. He makes only two brief appearances. His introduction comes in Genesis 14:18–20:[9]

> And King Melchizedek of Salem brought out bread and wine; he was priest of God Most High. He blessed him and said, "Blessed be Abram by

> God Most High, maker of heaven and earth; and blessed be God Most High, who has delivered your enemies into your hand!" And Abram gave him one-tenth of everything.

Building, presumably, from this passage, Psalm 110 mentions an order of priests according to Melchizedek:

> The Lord says to my lord,
> "Sit at my right hand
> until I make your enemies your footstool."
> The Lord sends out from Zion your mighty scepter.
> Rule in the midst of your foes.
> Your people will offer themselves willingly
> on the day you lead your forces on the holy mountains
> From the womb of the morning,
> like dew, your youth will come to you.
> The Lord has sworn
> and will not change his mind,
> "You are a priest forever
> according to the order of Melchizedek."
> The Lord is at your right hand;
> he will shatter kings on the day of his wrath,
> He will execute judgment among the nations,
> filling them with corpses;
> he will shatter heads
> over the wide earth.
> He will drink from the stream by the path;
> therefore he will lift up his head.

This is the full extent of reference to Melchizedek in the Hebrew Bible. Melchizedek does, however, roam outside of the canon. He appears in a Qumran scroll (11QMelchizedek) and figures prominently in the apocalyptic 2nd Enoch. In these other traditions, Melchizedek transforms into a heavenly being. Contrary to a heavenly portrayal, Hebrews relies upon an earthly priest as a prototype to the heavenly Jesus. As such it is an independent parallel tradition to the others; it is not reliant upon them. Hebrews remains firmly fixed within the two canonical passages quoted above.

The appearance of Melchizedek in Genesis 14 is explicated in Hebrews 7. First, his name, office, and home are interpreted: "His name, in the first place, means 'king of righteousness'; next he is also king of Salem, that is, 'king of peace'" (Hebrews 7:2). This argument depends upon knowledge of Hebrew even though the author of Hebrews, like most of the New Testament authors, uses the Greek text of the Bible. Jesus is also known as the "king of righteousness" and the "king of peace."

The author of Hebrews goes on to note the absence of a genealogy for Melchizedek in Genesis. Although it is true that most characters in Genesis are introduced with a full genealogy, Hebrews elevates this unusual though not necessarily unique aspect to a metaphysical model for the future preexistent Christ: "Without father, without mother, without genealogy, having neither beginning of days nor end of life, but resembling the Son of God, he remains a priest forever" (Hebrews 7:3). The latter phrase, "a priest forever," connects the Genesis 14 account with Psalm 110:4, which is quoted or alluded to seven times in the passages concerning Melchizedek. The Psalm links a Davidic messiah with a priestly function, and this provides the textual basis for the "unique Hight-Priest Christology of Hebrews."[10] It is asserted in these verses that Melchizedek resembles Jesus in name, and eternality of office. Melchizedek is the Old Testament shadow of the New Testament Christ.

Hebrews 7 continues in its argument that Melchizedek is higher than the Levites. This claim hinges on the fact that Abraham gave tithes to Melchizedek and was blessed by him. The full passage reads:

> See how great he is! Even Abraham the patriarch gave him a tenth of the spoils. And those descendants of Levi who receive the priestly office have a commandment in the law to collect tithes from the people, that is, from their kindred, though these also are descended from Abraham. But this man, who does not belong to their ancestry, collected tithes from Abraham and blessed him who had received the promised. It is beyond dispute that the inferior is blessed by the superior. . . . One might even say that Levi himself, who receives tithes, paid tithes through Abraham, for he was still in the loins of his ancestor when Melchizedek met him. (Hebrews 7:4–7, 9)

Because Melchizedek is more exalted than Abraham and thus more exalted than Levi who was carried in Abraham's loins, and because Melchizedek is a foreshadowing of Jesus the Christ, it follows that Jesus is higher than Abraham and Levi, and therefore higher than the entire Levitical priesthood, the covenant they uphold, and the ritual function they fulfill.

In their exegesis of Genesis 14, by calling Christ "high priest," these passages in Hebrews are also anticipating and incorporating the Levitical priesthood as described in Leviticus and Numbers:

> For it was fitting that we should have such a high priest, holy, blameless, undefiled, separated from sinners, and exalted above the heavens. Unlike

> the other high priests, he has no need to offer sacrifices day after day, first, for his own sins, and then for those of the people; this he did once for all when he offered himself. For the law appoints as high priests those who are subject to weakness, but the word of the oath, which came later than the law, appoints a Son who has been made perfect forever. (Hebrews 7:26–28)

This is, to say the least, creative exegesis.[11]

Behind the Epistle's interpretation of the Levitical system, the operative assumption is that blood sacrifice is the most essential and efficacious mechanism for entering into the presence of the divine.[12] This theological dictum is not challenged nor is it explained; it is simply assumed to be true. Hebrews does employ interpretive methods based upon Hellenistic philosophy: the heavenly realm is real and the earthly world is but its shadow. Yet, Jesus' blood is not just a metaphor for death. The actual blood, red and sticky, is what makes the death by crucifixion an efficacious sacrifice for the cleansing of sins. There is a continuity in the physical reality of the blood between the Jewish scriptural sacrifices and those in the Epistle to the Hebrews. The blood is the earthly component of the heavenly realm, and that which makes the heavenly realm possible. The blood remains the same, but the type of blood and the method of its spilling are radically transformed. The "old" system has failed to fulfill its intended end. Jesus is the perfect sacrifice because he is perfect in every other way as well.

Donelson traces out the tensions and the contradictions within Hebrews about this very issue. At first, he notes, the tension between the old and the new is positive—the old is good but the new is better. But the tension between the old and the new that creates this nice Christology is not as gentle as this. The old does not fall naturally into the new. Jesus is not simply an extension, a perfection, of the old. This tension includes real conflict, even incompatibility. On the one hand, the author of Hebrews carefully applies the positive functions of the old priesthood to Jesus, and this application assumes some value in the old. On the other hand, the replacement of the old with the new includes the notion that the old never worked at all.[13]

In the end, the Old Testament priesthood is shown to have always been flawed and therefore insufficient. Temple sacrifice has no real power to affect the inner person—it cannot take away sin, or cleanse the person, or effect real change. We all need Jesus for this. In the words of John Scholer: "What the old covenant priesthood ignorantly presumed itself to achieve and accomplish, i.e. access to God, is realized only by priests under the new covenant establishment in Christ."[14]

Jesus is strong. For Hebrews, he is superior to everything in every way: Christ is superior to the prophets (1:1–3), superior to the angels (1:4–11, 2:5–18), superior to Moses (3:1–6), superior to Joshua (4:1–11), and superior to the Jewish priesthood (4:14–5:10, 7:1–29). Christ is minister of a superior covenant (8:1–13) and minister in a superior tabernacle (9:1–28). Christ makes a superior sacrifice (10:1–18). The Old Testament is to the New Testament as prophecy is to fulfillment and Judaism is to Christianity as the foreshadow is to the real. When the old covenant is labeled "obsolete" (8:13) it is only a small shift to imagine the old covenant people as "obsolete" as well.

II

There are many similarities between the interpretive moves in Hebrews and other forms of exegesis in first-century Judaism. Philo had already employed spiritual exegesis, allegory, and typology to reinterpret the Hebrew Scriptures in light of Hellenistic philosophy. The *pesherim* from Qumran display the same type of reorienting of ancient texts, line-by-line, to speak to contemporary situations. And rabbinic midrash is always looking to uncover the meanings that lie in the gaps found in scripture. There is one major difference however: never do these exegetical romps render obsolete the text they interpret. Never do they erase the other meanings of the texts, nor do they ever annul the validity of the original. But in the very act of reinterpreting the Jewish scriptures, Hebrews repudiates them.

Christianity without Judaism is nothing but a few dirty tatters. Christianity with Judaism fully intact is nothing but another Jewish sect that would have been reabsorbed into the mainstream. This is the double bind. Early Christians had to affirm the Jewish scriptures, laws, and rituals while at the same time demonstrating that they are invalidated, surpassed, superseded. They needed to demonstrate "legitimate difference."

The relationship between the anti-Judaism expressed in New Testament texts and the virulent antisemitism of Europe in the early twentieth century is not a one-to-one correspondence. But neither is there a radical break between the two.[15] The struggle to define the community over and against both Jews and pagans, and the desire to avoid state persecution as well as social ostracism resulted in the various portraits of Jews and Judaism within the New Testament. Throughout the early centuries of theological formulation and continued political struggles, these scriptural portraits were drawn upon and incorporated into the Christian world view. Soteriologically, as the unique incarnation of the divine on Earth, Jesus suffered and died for human sins. In this model, it is important that Jesus was rejected and murdered by his own people, because this makes total his abjection. His suffering had to be extreme for the sacrifice to break the hold of evil on humanity. And, using the terminology of Hebrews, the more extreme Jesus' suffering, the more perfect his sacrifice. The Jews, as a whole people, became responsible for his death not only because of the evidence culled from the Gospel accounts, but also because they continued to reject the salvation Jesus offered.

Since the rejection of Jesus and his consequent suffering and sacrifice were extreme and therefore perfect, this sacrifice becomes one that is efficacious for everyone. Christian universalism stresses the insignificance of political and ethnic boundaries. However, this universalism includes an exclusive component, namely, that one must believe in Jesus as the Christ in order to enter into this universal family. Thus, those who are outside of Christianity are those who chose to remain outside of Christianity and this bespeaks a moral perversion.[16] The Jews are the worst of this lot since their remaining within their own religion is perceived as an obstinate misreading of their own scriptures. The Jews blindly and ignorantly cling to their superseded covenant. The Epistle to the Hebrews demonstrates more thoroughly than any other New Testament document the christocentric interpretation of the Jewish Bible used as evidence of the obstinacy, and therefore moral turpitude of the Jewish people.

By the Middle Ages, hatred of Jews was not just about negative sentiments toward the religion they practiced. True, an individual Jew may escape this prejudice through baptism, but as a people, the Jewish murder of Jesus and the continuing rejection of Christianity reached metaphysical status. They were in league with the devil in the cosmic battle between good and evil. At this time, such fantastic accusations as blood libel and ritual murder emerged. The scientific mentality of the nineteenth century picked up the metaphysical differences ascribed to Jews in the Middle Ages and renamed them biological.

Although Hitler was not himself a Christian, and even advocated anti-Christian policies, he did employ the rhetoric of nearly 2000 years of Christian theological anti-Judaism and antisemitism to formulate and propagate his final solution to the "Jewish problem." In his investigations of Nazi Germany, Saul Friedlander asks whether the antisemitism of this period was just an extreme form of a "general threat of otherness," or did it "carry peculiar characteristics?" He concludes the latter:

> Whereas in general the Other's most threatening aspect seems to reside in an identifiable difference, the most ominous aspect of the Jewish threat appeared as related to sameness. The Jews adaptability seemed to effect all boundaries and to subvert the possibilities of natural confrontation. The Jew was the inner enemy par excellence. It is this mimetic ability which, as we shall see, will open the way for the most extreme phantasms.[17]

The Other within is always more threatening than the Other outside who can be readily identified and contained. The Jews in Germany were among the most assimilated and acculturated Jews in the world. And it is precisely here where the most horrific manifestation of antisemitism emerged: the systematic murder of six million Jewish men, women, and children. The Epistle to the Hebrews incorporates Judaism into its theology in a way that lays the foundation for the threatening internal Other.

Early Christianity was a diverse religious movement that engaged in vociferous debates about the nature of Jesus, the relationship between the new sect and the old religion, and the interpretation and place of the Jewish scriptures and rituals. Two of the poles are represented by Jewish Christians and Marcionite Christians.

Jewish Christians believed that Jesus represented continuity with the tradition and the scriptures. He was a righteous man, adopted by God to be God's son at his baptism. This adoption empowered Jesus to perform wondrous deeds. But he was not born of a virgin, he was not divine, he was not preexistent. There was only one God, and to see Jesus as this God did not accord to monotheistic belief; instead, it was blasphemous. To be a Christian, one first had to be Jewish—therefore, Gentile men had to be circumcised and women and men had to keep kashrut and the sabbath. This sect used a version of Matthew's Gospel (without the infancy narrative), and completely rejected Paul as an arch-heretic.

The other pole was the Marcionite Christians, followers of the second-century scholar Marcion. They completely rejected the Jewish heritage of Christianity. Rather than being a Jew, continuous with his tradition, Jesus came to save humanity from the Jewish Law. And Paul was his truest apostle. According to Marcion, Paul urged everyone to give up the Law alltogether. The God of the Old Testament is a God of justice and wrath, whereas the God of the New Testament is one of mercy and forgiveness. Jesus was not actually born, not a human. Marcionites used a gospel closest to Luke, and all ten of Paul's letters (all of the canonical letters except I and II Timothy and Titus), with any positive reference to the law and the God of the Hebrew Bible expunged.

What became orthodox Christianity ended up taking a middle road between these two extreme positions. They affirmed continuity: the Hebrew Bible is authoritative scripture, the God of the Jews and the God of the Christians is the same god. Yet, they also preached discontinuity: the Law was fulfilled and therefore adherence to the law such as circumcision, kashrut, and sabbath was no longer necessary. Jesus is both fully human and fully divine. But this tension may be precisely what has made the continuing presence of Jews in the world intolerable. Because Jews are the Other within, the virulent antisemitism can be resolved only by destroying the Jews and destroying all traces of that destruction—an erasure so complete that it has forgotten what is forgotten.[18]

If the first road not taken had been taken, in other words, if the theology of the Jewish Christians had become orthodox, it is quite possible that Jewish Christians would have been gradually reabsorbed into the Jewish community, as many of them perhaps were. Then there would have been no Jewish Christian problem (and hence no antisemitism) in the history of the Western world because there would have been no Christianity. If the second road not taken had been taken, in other words, if the theology of the Marcionites had become Orthodox, perhaps the threat would have dissipated as well. The anti-Jewish thrust of Marcion's work is obvious and undeniable. But after the initial prejudice, it takes Judaism entirely out of the equation. The Other within is sometimes the most frightening other of all—it is the one that is necessary to the definition of the community, yet constantly threatens to destabilize that very definition.

Christianity needs Judaism at the same time it repudiates Judaism. By remaining simultaneously within and without, the Jews become the target of a particularly virulent hatred. Could the history of anti-Judaism and antisemitism been avoided if Christianity would have made a clean break with its parent religion, thus mitigating the threat of the Other within, by excluding it wholly?

III

Since the Holocaust, Christians have begun to reexamine their theologies, scriptures, and traditions for anti-Judaism and antisemitism.[19] In this is a move toward responsibility for the tragedy and a desire to prevent it from ever happening again by understanding, then eradicating the root causes. One recent trend in biblical scholarship is to argue that the New Testament cannot be antisemitic, and sometimes not even anti-Jewish, since Jesus, Mary, all of the disciples, Paul, and most of the writers of the New Testament were Jewish. Any anti-Jewish or antisemitic readings of the texts are misreadings. Steven McKenzie (following Raymond Brown), in speaking of the Epistle to the Hebrews, takes this position:

> In referring to the old covenant's being ineffective and even obsolete, the author of Hebrews does not mean that God's moral law has been abolished. Indeed, the author's point is that the old covenant was an imperfect version of the heavenly prototype. This is, admittedly, a kind supersessionism. But it is only the ceremonial laws of the Hebrew Bible that have been superseded.[20]

Despite the begrudging admission of "a kind of supersessionism," McKenzie ends up reading Hebrews as a counter to supersessionism:

> The careful consideration of the meaning of covenant in the New Testament passages provides an important counter against the problem of supersessionism. When the New Testament is read carefully, especially with the Hebrew Bible as its background, it becomes clear that the "new

> covenant" of Christianity stands squarely in the heritage of ancient Israel and its series of covenants with God. Indeed, the earliest Christians were all Jews, and their "new" religion was regarded as a sect of Judaism.[21]

After all, he then goes on to note, the sacrificial system that Hebrews believes Christ has superseded is no longer practiced by Jews anyway: "When Hebrews uses the term obsolete (8:13) it is referring to the sacrificial ritual, it does not apply to a Judaism without sacrifice, which is what Judaism is today." McKenzie argues in conclusion that "supersessionism, then, is unwarranted and is not endorsed by the New Testament."[22] So now Christians have been reading their scriptures incorrectly for 2000 years? This is not a viable solution to the problem.

Another recent book on Hebrews, Lewis Donelson's *From Hebrews to Revelation*, addresses the "creative" and "clever" exegetical methods of Hebrews and questions their legitimacy. However, this is done without reference to the supersessionism inherent in hermeneutic employed in Hebrews. Rather, he concludes that the "theology of Hebrews emerges at least in part, from a respectful encounter with the syntax of these [Jewish] texts."[23] He also concludes that this is a model for the modern reader: "the task of reading must be taken up again by us, with a fidelity both to ourselves and to the text equal to what we find in Hebrews."[24]

Perhaps this is a solution of sorts. By the fourth century the situation of the early Church had completely changed. Christianity was then the religion in power, the religion of the Empire. The situation had changed (and remains changed) but the incendiary rhetoric of a minority trying to survive in a hostile environment remained (and remains). The content no longer fits the context and must change as well.

Using the language of Emmanuel Levinas, Jesus is the Other and his face in its nakedness says "do not kill me." If Christians cannot recognize the vulnerability in the face of their Jewish neighbors, they should at least be able to see the vulnerability in the face of the Jewish Jesus as he hangs upon the cross. He was one of the poor, one of the oppressed, and he was crushed by an imperialist occupying power, a powerful state-sponsored killing machine. By doing violence to the Other, especially to the Jewish Other, Christians continue the very same violence that resulted in the death of their founder. The Christian mythological and cosmic view of Jesus has proven dangerous for people outside of the Christian community. The outsider language and theology of the Epistle to the Hebrews are the very foundations for this type of thinking, even though neither the author nor the communities that first received the text had the power to implement violent measures against anyone. Is it legitimate for Christians to read the Hebrew Bible as the Old Testament? The Hebrew Bible is part of their scriptural tradition now, and as an outsider to that tradition I would not want to dictate how it should be read. But I can point out the damage this type of reading has done and continues to do, even in the small ways exhibited in my classroom experience of teaching these texts. And I can point out the tensions within the hermeneutic, tensions that remain unstable and therefore always in danger of erupting into violence.

NOTES

1. I would like to thank Melissa C. Stewart for her acute readings of this article. I owe this phrase to her.
2. John Dunnill, *Covenant and Sacrifice in the Letter to the Hebrews* (Cambridge, England: Cambridge University Press, 1992), 24. Dunnill uses the sociological methods of both Bryan Wilson and Gerd Theissen to draw his conclusions.
3. Ibid., 29.
4. Victor C. Pfitzner, *Hebrews* (Abingdon New Testament Commentaries; Nashville: Abingdon Press, 1997), 29.
5. Charles A. Gieschen, "The Different Functions of a Similar Melchizedek Tradition in 2 Enoch and the Epistle to the Hebrews," in *Early Christain Interpretation of the Scriptures of Israel: Investigations and Proposals*, eds. Craig A. Evens and James A. Sanders (Sheffield: Sheffield Academic Press, 1997), 372.
6. Richard Longenecker, *Biblical Exegesis in the Apostolic Period* (Grand Rapids, MI: Eerdmans, 1975), 164–167, as quoted in Marie E. Isaacs, "Hebrews," in *Early Christian Thought in Its Jewish Context*, eds. John Barclay and John Sweet (New York: Cambridge University Press, 1996), 154–155.
7. The Scriptures used by the author of Hebrews are the Greek versions. Only six of the ninety-three citations and allusions do not agree with either LXXA (Codex Alexandrinus) or LXXB (Codex Vaticanus). Sometimes the argument even relies upon the septuagintal translation, and would not be possible through the Hebrew Masoretic Text.
8. Lewis R. Donelson, *From Hebrews to Revelation: A Theological Introduction* (Louisville: Westminster John Knox Press, 2001), 10.
9. All biblical quotations are from the NRSV.
10. Gieschen, 375.
11. Donelson calls Hebrews' exegesis of Genesis 14 both "very creative" (23) and "pretty clever" (24). Gieschen also uses the phrase "creative exegesis" (375).
12. See Pfitzner, 42; Isaacs, 152; and Donelson, 11.
13. Donelson, 12–13.
14. John M. Scholer, *Proleptic Priests: Priesthood in the Epistle to the Hebrews* (Sheffield: Sheffield Academic Press, 1991), 205.
15. In the nineteenth and twentieth centuries, traditional prejudices based upon religious ideologies were updated to fit the new secular and scientific mentality of modernity. See Jacob Katz, *From Prejudice to Destruction: Anti-Semitism, 1700–1933* (Cambridge, MA: Harvard University Press, 1980) for a detailed analysis of this transformation. See also Robert S. Wistrich, "The Devil, the Jews, and Hatred of the 'Other,'" in *Demonizing the Other: Antisemitism, Racism and Xenophobia*, ed. Robert S. Wistrich (Amsterdam: Harwood Academic Press, 1999), 1–15, for a description of Medieval Christianity's "virulent phobias" and the ways in which they both correspond to and differ from Nazi Germany's antisemitism.

16. Henri Zukier, "Transformation of Hatred: Antisemitism as a Struggle for Group Identity," in Wistrich (ed.), *Demonizing the Other*, 123–125.
17. Saul Friedlander, "'Europe's Inner Demons': The 'Other' as Threat in Early Twentieth-Century European Culture," in Wistrich, *Demonizing the Other*, 213.
18. See Jean-François Lyotard, *Heidegger and 'the Jews'* (Minneapolis: University of Minnesota Press, 1990), for this aspect of the Holocaust.
19. This had even begun before the Holocaust. An Anglican priest and church historian by the name of James Parkes wrote a history condemning antisemitism in Christian teaching, *The Conflict of Church and Synagogue* (New York: Atheneum, 1977 [London, 1934]).
20. Steven L. McKenzie, *Covenant* (St. Louis: Chalice Press, 2000), 118.
21. Ibid., 119.
22. Ibid., 120–121.
23. Donelson, 32.
24. Ibid., 26.

PART III

Reading as Christians

CHAPTER 8

Reading from the Day "In Between"

WALTER BRUEGGEMANN

Christians living through and now beyond the twentieth century have discovered that the Shoah, evil *in extremis*, poses new questions about our most trusted affirmations and our most familiar mantras. In attempting to respond to such questions, we may discover too that the freightedness of familiar Christian rhetoric is heavy and deep, and admits of readings and hearings that are heavier and deeper than we had yet been pressed to notice. The following discussion considers the way in which the reality of the Shoah disrupts the rhythm of even the most elemental claims of Christian faith, in particular the decisive liturgical and theological move from the Cross on Good Friday to the Resurrection on Easter Sunday. In between these two days lies Saturday, the second day. This day in between is a day of death, and a day of interminable waiting. Thinking about the implications of the Shoah for Christian life and faith has led me to rethink also the importance of this day.

I

The church, from its inception, organized its imagination, its liturgy, and its life around the memory and significance of the Triduum of Good Friday—Saturday—Easter Sunday. In the durable study of C. H. Dodd, the recited tradition of I Corinthians 15:3–6 has been taken as the defining historical–theological signature of Christian confession:[1]

> For I handed on to you as of first importance what I in turn had received: that Christ died for our sins in accordance with the scriptures, and that he

was buried, and that he was raised on the third day in accordance with the scriptures. . . .

The three-day sequence moves from "Christ died and was buried" to "raised on the third day"; both claims, moreover, are "in accordance with scripture." This recital surely voices the main claims of the early church. The *day of death* and the *day of resurrection* are taken as undoubtedly "historical," even though the "historicality" of Easter is exceedingly difficult to formulate adequately.[2] These two days of death and resurrection, moreover, are the most theologically freighted and theologically defining moments in the account of the Gospel and in the life of the Gospel community.

Paul of course has given articulation to these matters that has proven to be normative in the church. Of the first day, Paul has written, "We preach Christ crucified" (I Corinthians 1:23); "For I decided to know nothing among you except Jesus Christ and him crucified" (I Corinthians 2:2). The defining marks of faith are Friday-ridden. It is this cross-marked claim that produced this critical judgment of Martin Kähler that "one could call the Gospels passion narratives with extended introductions."[3] Conversely, Paul has also asserted in his vigorous affirmation of resurrection, "if Christ has not been raised, then our proclamation has been in vain and your faith has been in vain" (I Corinthians 15:14). The *Friday* and *Sunday* claims are pivotal and indispensable for the faith and life of the church.

II

In the "kerygma" of I Corinthians 15:3–6, Paul skillfully claims for both the Friday and Sunday of Jesus that the days happened "in accordance with scripture," thereby making a major interpretive maneuver: the testimony of the Old Testament is brought into the service of these defining claims.[4] The connection made by Paul opens out the claim of the Triduum so that it can be more broadly considered by an Old Testament student.

It is not clear what Paul's reference is in "the scriptures." The most obvious candidate is of course Hosea 6:2:

> After two days he will revive us
> on the third day he will raise us up,
> that we may live before him.

In this text, the poet affirms that it is in the faithful character of the God of Israel both to "smite" and to "raise up." This is presented as God's characteristic way of working, and that characteristic way of working is ground for the specific hope in the crisis addressed by the poet. What is characteristic will be done here and now. In such a stylized usage, "the third day" surely means "in a short time" and is not to be taken with chronological literalness. We may entertain the thought that Paul's formation, although it may or may not appeal to this particular text, intends to assert that God's characteristic fidelity is decisively and manifestly operative in these twin moments in the life of Jesus. Although the text of Hosea 6:2 seems a good connection, Hans Walter Wolff observes that in no early church document is this text cited until the usage of Tertullian, late indeed.[5] If Paul's allusion is more generically to the Old Testament and not text specific, we are at liberty to consider other textual materials that might illumine Paul's usage.

I have of late given close attention to the so-called Ark Narrative of I Samuel 4:1–7:1.[6] It has struck me with immense force, as a Christian, that this narrative is also a three-day drama:

> *Day 1*:The defeat of YHWH[7] by the Philistines and the humiliating exhibit of YHWH in the Ashdod shrine of Dagon (4:19–22).
>
> *Day 2*: The struggle in the night with Dagon and the first humiliation of Dagon on the second morning (5:1–2).
>
> *Day 3*: The total disarming of Dagon by YHWH, discovered early on the third day (5:4).

This three-day drama presents YHWH moving from humiliating capture and defeat to triumph and emancipation. Moreover, the action is all in the dark of the night, unseen by the Ashdodites who come "early in the morning" to observe only the consequences of the combat of the night. The three-day drama accomplished a complete repositioning of YHWH to which testimony is given in the narrative, even though the turn was completely hidden in the night, hidden from the Israelite narrator as from the Ashdodites.

In my study of the so-called Ark Narrative, I became aware of the remarkable parallels in the patterned claims in Isaiah 40–55 concerning the power of the others gods, the victory of YHWH, the return of YHWH's glory, and the triumphant homecoming to Israel with YHWH in joy. It is not said that the drama was conducted in three days, no doubt because that poetry must address an historical crisis stretching over two generations. Nonetheless, the parallel between the Ark Narrative about the *defeat and triumph* of YHWH and the pattern of *exile and homecoming* in Second Isaiah is enough to suggest that the three-day drama—whatever may be made of the concrete time—offers a dramatic sequence concerning defeat and victory for YHWH with enormous implications for YHWH's people, their defeat and victory. The drama of three "moments" in the life of YHWH is made more dramatic by the reality that the turns are hidden. They are hidden in Ashdod; they are in parallel fashion hidden in Babylon. Nobody sees anything. Only on the "third day" is the consequence of the turn visible, when the people of YHWH embrace all the joy that belongs to freedom and homecoming. I suggest that although Hosea 6:2 may give us a specific reference point to "the third day," that "according to the scriptures" the three days concern the defeat, the hidden struggle, and the victory of YHWH. Paul's appeal in I Corinthians 15 may be specific, but it also reflects the characteristic way Israel narrated its sense of God's own life.

III

It is to be noticed, and for our purposes important, that the church has had very little to say about the "second day," so that in effect the drama is reduced to a two-day sequence. The two-day accent is evident in the kerygma of I Corinthians 15:3–6 that has no comment on the "second day" and in the contemporary, widely shared formula:

> Christ has died,
> Christ is risen,
> Christ will come again.

To be sure, from early on the church asserted that "he descended into Sheol."[8] Such a formula accounts for the second day of course, but the familiar formula has been left largely undeveloped in subsequent theological interpretation. That brief formulation, cast in mythological language, is fluid and open enough that it admits of a great deal of interpretive possibility, even though the matter has remained largely unexplored. The characteristic silence of the church concerning the formula has not made much of it, given the church's readiness to pass as quickly as possible to the "third day" and the Easter victory of Christ.

In seeking to make something of the "second day" and the "descent into Sheol," we can clearly identify three possible perspectives. First, it is sensible to understand the second day as an extension of the first day: "he died and was buried." Thus the second day represents a verdict of "still dead," and the dead spend their vacuous time in Sheol. Karl Barth has proposed that the term "buried' carries all the freight that needs to be carried, for buried signifies dead, powerless, nullified, empty, humiliated:

> It is another reminder of the true *humanity* of Christ. . . . To say that He was buried is the most unambiguous way in which it is possible to stamp a being as true actual man. . . . The deepest most ultimate meaning of "He emptied Himself, taking the form of a servant" (Phil. ii 7) is expressed by the *sepultus*.[9]

All Barth has to say of the phrase"descended into Sheol" is that it is a synonym for burial and indicates self-surrender.[10] At the most, the additional clause serves only to reenforce, underscore, or intensify what has already been said in "buried."

A second option for dealing with the "second day" that received great attention in the early church is to push the second day toward the third, so that it is already one arena of the victory of Christ to become visible "early on the third day." A primary impetus in this inclination is offered in I Peter 3:19–29; 4:6:

> in which also he went and made a proclamation to the spirits in prison, who in former times did not obey, when God waited patiently in the days of Noah. . . . For this is the reason the gospel was proclaimed even to the dead, so that, even though they had been judged in the flesh as everyone is judged, they might live in the spirit as God does.

Already on the second day Christ is at his effective ministry, doing for those in Sheol what he also has done by his effective death on earth. One aspect of this cosmic victory (to be locally disclosed on the third day) is to provide salvific relief for the generation of Noah, all those who had died before Christ. This interpretive tendency does not linger over the dread reality of *kenosis*, but portrays Christ already on the second day filled with victorious power. In this trajectory there is no question of

> a victory obtained by means of a descent, but a triumphant making known of a victory already won. There is no question but that the First Letter of Peter, like the rest of the New Testament, is thinking here of the death of the Cross and the Resurrection of Christ.[11]

This hastening to the third day is dramatized in the liturgic temptation of "Easter vigils" that seek to begin Easter affirmation earlier and earlier, so that the distinctiveness of the second day is eroded if not nullified completely.

Thus interpretive possibility may collapse the second day into the first as *an extended deadness*, or collapse the second day into the third as *an already begun victory*. The third alternative is to maintain the discreteness of the second day as bearing its own theological and liturgic import. In my own reading on the subject, John Calvin most carefully and precisely delineates the second day discretely.[12] He explicitly rejects the thought that the phrase "descended into Sheol" is only a synonym for "buried," refusing to reduce the second day to the first. And although he recognizes the force of I Peter 3:19, he refuses to link the second day to the victory of the third. Calvin insists on going deep into the dread of the second day and, I suggest, articulates the deep tension that is intrinsic in evangelical claims for the second day. On the one hand, Calvin not surprisingly links the second day to the saving work of Christ. On the second day, "it was expedient at the same time for him to undergo the severity of God's vengeance, to appease his wrath and satisfy his just judgment."[13] That is, the second day is the outcome when Christ savingly takes on God's wrath, thereby effecting rescue for those who merit that wrath. The substitutionary effect leads to a citation of Isaiah 53:5.

At the same time, however, Calvin's salvific concern does not tone down his recognition of the wretchedness of the second day, for the wretchedness is fundamental to its salvific outcome. Calvin answers his critics who accuse him of attributing "to the Son of God a despair contrary to faith," "something evil of itself."[14] Even though Calvin wants to claim the second day as salvific and so tilts it to the third day, he unflinchingly insists on the ultimate death of Christ, not "only a bodily death" but a complete separation and alienation from God that perforce evokes a citation of Psalm 22:1 in Matthew 27:46. Calvin the theologian sees this wretchedness as an answer to and refutation of the temptation of the Apollinarians and Monothelites who want Christ in his death to be not utterly human. Calvin, the evangelical pastor of salvation, will never forego the salvific dimension of the second day; but to do so he must give voice to the utter abandonment of Jesus on the second day, even to the very depth of nullity. The phrase "descended into hell" admits of no simple decoding and does not intend to be decoded. We may appreciate Calvin's decisive protection of the second day from collapse, a necessity to show the depth and reality of the kenosis that lies at the center of the narrative.

IV

It is my simple suggestion that the Shoah—and perhaps other unbearable brutalities may qualify alongside the Shoah—requires Christian faith and liturgy to pause long and deeply on the second day . . . very long indeed, so long that the joyous acclamation of the third day is sobered in the extreme and delayed a long while. First, there is, even in Calvin, a scent of victory on the second day, if not yet in effect then already on the way and legitimately anticipated. The Shoah may suggest that such an anticipatory scent is much too soon, much too premature, for the stench of the ovens does not yet let us notice the better fragrance of rescue. The protection of the second day as a deep moment in God's life, as Calvin seems to recognize, serves to retard an all too ready Christian triumphalism when on the ground there is in fact no visible triumph. I understand, of course, that one way the church has conceded the lack of triumph on the ground is to acknowledge—post Easter—that Christians must await the "second coming," because the third day has not been sufficient. That may be an adequate acknowledgment of the deathly facts on the ground. I incline to think, however, that the Shoah requires that such facts must come to Christian voice already on the second day and not on the "fourth day," for fourth day acknowledgments of minds us that a great deal remains "unrealized" in any "realized eschatology."[23] Indeed, realized eschatology characteristically is the claim of those who do not look far beyond themselves in their well-being. To acknowledge the continuingly "unrealized" on the third day is to stake a great deal more on "Christ will come again."[24] Such an acknowledgment, moreover, transforms the interplay of Day Two and Day Three into an act of hope that is as realistic on the ground as it is buoyant about the promises.

Steiner concludes that it belongs to humanity to have an immensity of waiting that is funded by "metaphysical imagining." This immensity of waiting is what is left for us in the Day Two–Day Three reality, waiting that is buoyant and not filled with despair, but only waiting.[25] Steiner asks, "How could we be patient?" Day Three mandates patience because of the buoyancy. But Day Two in its concreteness and wretchedness invites impatience about the facts on the ground. The church's patience surely must be sobered and called to account by a body-rooted impatience.

5. Steiner calls this hard-held hope "Sabbatarian," always *rooted to Saturday* and not yet to Sunday. It remains unexplored, but surely important, that the second day of Christian faith coincides with the Jewish Sabbath. If Sabbath means to cede control of one's life over to God, then perhaps the second day of wretchedness is the recognition that control is ceded at great risk.[26] The sabbath enacts a decisive caesura in human control. It is that caesura that requires Christians to disrupt buoyancy that is too sure when not yet in hand.

This convergence of themes—Jewishness, this-worldly, less triumphal, waiting, sabbatarian—invites a rereading by Christians that may more readily be done alongside Jews who also wait in faith. This shared rereading and shared waiting are much illuminated by Martin Buber's notion of the ways in which Jews and Christians hope differently and the way we engage in an immense waiting together. The waiting for Christians is concretely shaped by the third-day, resurrected Jesus. But that concretely shaped waiting is fueled by older promises as well and by expectation that "he will come again." In the end, the wait is for the one accused of abandonment on the second day (Matthew 27:46). Of the waiting Buber offered the following assurance:

> What is the difference between Jews and Christians? We all await the Messiah. You believe He has already come and gone, while we do not. I therefore propose that we await Him together. And when He appears, we can ask Him: were You here before?". . . I hope that at that moment I will be close enough to whisper in his ear, "For the love of heaven, don't answer."[27]

facts on the ground continue to offer hints of unreality concerning those facts.

The second critique that may be voiced is that much of Christian interpretation of this odd, loaded phrase, "he descended into Sheol," has been so preoccupied with Christological precision that it mostly has not gotten around to the lived reality of people in the world. Interpreters regularly insist that whereas such imagery of "descent into hell" is located in mythical phrasing, it is in fact not mythical. And of course we can readily assert that every Christological formulation has as its implicit and unspoken counterpoint the reality of the world, implied by the *fleshed reality* of the entire drama. The case, however, is that the reality of the world characteristically remains implicit and unspoken, or the reality of the world is understood in such sweeping, salvific theological dimension that matters never come down to socioeconomic–political issues of abandonment, wretchedness, and rescue.[15] In and odd and undeveloped phrase, Calvin quotes Hilary of Pontiers who asserts, "The cross, death, hell—these are our life." Calvin, moreover claims Hilary's assertion as his own.[16] That acknowledgment, however, is followed by another line from Hilary of which Calvin approves: "The Son of God is in hell, but man is borne up to heaven."[17] That is, to be sure, an unexceptional evangelical claim. Except that if "our life" were not understood in sweeping and cosmic terms of salvation but with socioeconomic and political specificity, the last half of the proposition would need often to be transposed as "Humanity continues to endure death and hell in the world." I do not say this to deny the salvific effect of Christ's descent, but to resist any excessive salvific claim on the second day, so that when the church comes to the joy of the third day, its acclamation of victory is sobered and less triumphal because of the durable wretchedness evident on the ground.

All of which is to say that the Shoah does indeed stand as a deep question to the deepest evangelical claims of the church. Moreover, the question admits of no easy response. The church must and will continue its Easter declaration or it ceases to be the church. But the Shoah, so it seems to me, is uncompromising in its insistence that the second day looms larger, deeper, and more seriously than we had noticed in the drama we Christians regularly confess and claim. The rush to the third day must be profoundly slowed. In part the rush now is a contemporary temptation of consumer Christianity that cannot abide the second day and in liturgical practice has nearly gotten free of the first day as well. Beyond that contemporary reality, however, the triumphalism of the church is very old and even defining. Easter, it may turn out amidst the wretchedness, may be more sign than event, more hope than accomplishment.

V

Thus Saturday looms on the ground and therefore inescapably in our theology and liturgy. The victory of Christ is situated in a wretchedness still visible, still powerful, still bleeding and burning and smelling in its deathliness. Any reader who has followed my previous work will have guessed that I have been led to these awarenesses by the stunning paragraph of George Steiner at the end of his book in which he meditates on the loss and absence of God in a waning world:[18]

> There is one particular day in Western history about which neither historical record nor myth nor Scripture make report. It is a Saturday. And it has become the longest of days. We know of Good Friday which Christianity holds to have been that of the Cross. But the non-Christian, the atheist, knows of it as well. That is to say that he knows of the injustice, of the interminable suffering, of the waste, of the brute enigma of ending, which so largely make up not only the historical dimension of the human condition, but the everyday fabric of our personal lives. We know, ineluctable, of the pain, of the failure of love, of the solitude which are our history and private fate. We also know about Sunday. To the Christian, that day signifies an intimation, both assured and precarious, both evident and beyond comprehension, of resurrection, of a justice and love that have conquered death. If we are non-Christians or non-believers, we know of that Sunday in precisely analogous terms. We conceive of it as the day of liberation from inhumanity and servitude. We look to resolutions, be they therapeutic or political, be they social or messianic. The lineaments of that Sunday carry the name of hope (there is no word less deconstructible).
>
> But ours is the long day's journey of the Saturday. Between suffering, aloneness, unutterable waste on the one hand and the drama of liberation, of rebirth on the other. In the face of the torture of a child, of the death of love which is Friday, even the greatest art and poetry are almost helpless. In the Utopia of the Sunday, the aesthetic will, presumably, no longer has logic or necessity. The apprehensions and figurations in the play of metaphysical imagining, in the poem and the music, which tell of pain and of hope, of the flesh which is said to taste of ash and of the spirit which is said to have the savour of fire, are always Sabbatarian. They have risen out of an immensity of waiting which is that of man. Without them, how could we be patient?[19]

Steiner frames his stunning conclusion by recognizing "Friday" and "Sunday" as peculiarly Christian and as commonly human. But "the second day"—Saturday—is almost unvoiced as it looms between suffering, aloneness, and unutterable waste on the one hand, and liberation and rebirth on the other. Steiner's concreteness concerning the torture of a child may at the same time be generically human in barbarism and specifically Jewish with regard to the Shoah.[20] In any case, Steiner settles for "the greatest art and poetry . . . the apprehensions and figurations in the play of metaphysical imagining" as a look to a Sabbatarian

future. That, on any Christian reading, is not enough. In any Christian re there is more. The question is how the "more" is to be sensed liturgical theologically with the Saturday stench all around us and the flames stoked with shameless regularity. It is the great wonderment, I believe, tha now reoccupy a Christian reader concerning our most elemental claims.

In pursuit of that wonderment, the following five notes strike me as tant:

1. The refusal to flinch in the realm of Saturday is so *characteristicall* Jewish theological interpretive tradition refuses to cover over the c ness in any floating, euphemistic form that protects the Almight tians who know about Friday anguish might ponder why we C need to be instructed by Jews, why we have long been resistant to struction, and what now must be done to be in a genuinely recep ture for such instruction.
2. The Saturday stench summons Christians away from every mytho metaphysical escapism into *socioeconomic, political realities* on the have mentioned Calvin's citation about hell and death as being Christians of course know about the facts on the ground; but very familiar cadences of Christian rhetoric suggest a "superworld" th a docetic denial of the intransigence of the bodily.[21] How odd th bodied, "incarnational" faith should be endlessly tempted in th way. The Shoah is the quintessential alert of human bodies tha truth not to be explained away. Indeed the body of Jesus as Chri is in anguished, abandoned solidarity with all these bodies who into hell. A "bodily resurrection"—bodies terrestrial?—eases n terrible concreteness that lingers in ashes and in unbearable sm tality.[22]
3. The effect of a concrete this-worldly engagement with the sec vites the church, in its Easter proclamation, to be *less triumpha* joy. Indeed, it is the triumphal pageantry of the church that h disregard of the second day. The reality of the second day— concretely on the ground—suggests that the victory of East modest, because the cruel demands of death are alive and well do not think we know how Easter claims can now be rearticu theologically or liturgically; but that they must be rearticulate dent. Unless they are, the church runs the risk of reciting a my above the pain so palpable on the ground.
4. The implication of the rearticulation of the third day in light day taken seriously is to reformulate the *delicate relationship victory and the Final Victory* in the Second Coming. The se

NOTES

1. C. H. Dodd, *The Apostolic Preaching and Its Developments* (New York: Harper and Brothers, n.d.), 7–35.
2. The peculiar claims and practices of "historical reason" are explored by Richard R. Niebuhr, *Resurrection and Historical Reason: A Study of Theological Method* (New York: Scribner's, 1957), and more broadly by W. B. Gallie, "The Historical Understanding," *History and Theory,* ed. George H. Nadel (Middletown, CT: Wesleyan University Press, 1977), 149–202.
3. Martin Kähler, *The So-Called Historical Jesus and the Historic, Biblical Christ* (Philadelphia: Fortress Press, 1964), 80, n. 11. I am grateful to my colleague, Charles Cousar, for helping me locate this specific reference.
4. See Richard B. Hays, *Echoes of Scripture in the Letters of Paul* (New Haven: Yale University Press, 1989), 84 and *passim.*
5. Hans Walter Wolff, *Hosea* (Hermeneia; Philadelphia: Fortress Press, 1974), 118.
6. Walter Brueggemann, *Ichabod Toward Home* (Grand Rapids: Eerdmans, 2002).
7. "YHWH," or the Tetragrammaton ("four letters"), is the personal name of Israel's God in the Hebrew Bible. It is traditionally left unpronounced, and is usually translated into English as "the LORD."
8. On the history of the phrase, see J. N. D. Kelly, *Early Christian Creeds,* 3rd ed. (London: Longman, 1972), 378–383.
9. Karl Barth, *Credo: A Presentation of the Chief Problems of Dogmatics with Reference to the Apostle's Creed* (London: Hodder & Stoughton, 1936), 84–87.
10. *Ibid.,* 88–91. Christoph Barth, *Die Errettung vom Tode: Leben und Tod in den Klage—und Dankliedern des Alten Testaments,* 2nd ed. (Berlin: Kohlhammer, 1997), 153, makes the same point. See his discussion of the phrase "descended into hell" with reference to biblical antecedents (pp. 145–153).
11. The statement is from W. Bieder, quoted by Hans Urs von Balthasar, *Mysterium Paschale: The Mystery of Easter* (Grand Rapids, MI: Eerdmans, 1990), 159. I am glad to acknowledge that it is von Balthasar's luminous book that has helped me the most in understanding the Triduum.
12. John Calvin, *Institutes of the Christian Religion II XVI 7–12* (The Library of Christian Classics XX; Philadelphia: Westminster Press, 1960), 511–520.
13. Ibid., 515. So Christoph Barth, *Die Errettung vom Tode* 152, concludes: "Der Zustatz *descensus ad inferos* im Apostolischen Symbol bestätigt also das neutestamentliche, durch das Alte Testament bereitgestellte und von daher übernommene Verständnis des Todes Jesu als 'Höllenfahrt,' d.h. als Gericht."
14. Ibid., 517–518.
15. Thus writing of von Balthasar's work, Ben Quash, "The Drama and the Ends of Modernity," in *Balthasar at the End of Modernity,* eds. Lucy Gardner et al. (Edinburgh: T & T Clark, 1999), 167, can write:

    > We must be disappointed that even in that most innovative area of his theology—the meditation (with Adrienne) on the descent into Hell—Balthasar tries to control the dazzling darkness with strategies that mitigate the drama. The Hell of Balthasar's theology is *outside* and *beyond* our own time. It is narrated in "epic" time, which is to say . . . it is "fundamentally different and totally remote." The irony of Balthasar's theology is that the moment when it aims most concretely to concern itself with struggle, suffering, and death, it also becomes most mythological. The Hell of Balthasar's theology of holy Saturday is *outside* and *beyond* our own time: it is, in effect, "totally remote." This has led Gerard O'Hanlon to remark that "from one who is so conscious of the reality of evil there is a curious

lack of engagement with the great modern structural evils." Balthasar misses his opportunity to conceive the search for justice as a project, "something with respect to which each of us has obligations in the immediate future of our lives." Instead, we find the same urge to concentrate on intuiting the wholeness and integrity (the *resolved* dramatic shape) of the Christ-form—a form which is now confidently seen to stretch to include even that which is utterly contrary to God.

While this stricture pertains first of all to von Balthasar, the same point in general can be made about the characteristic attempts at "Saturday" in Christian theological interpretation. It is plausible that a mythological propensity was greatly reinforced by Dante's *Inferno.*

16. Calvin, *Institutes,* 517.
17. Ibid.
18. Walter Brueggemann, *Theology of the Old Testament: Testimony, Dispute, Advocacy* (Minneapolis: Fortress Press, 1997), 312, 402.
19. George Steiner, *Real Presences* (Chicago: University of Chicago Press, 1989), 231–232.
20. Steiner's usage of "taste of ash" must clearly be a reference to the ovens of the Shoah. See also Tod Linafelt, ed., *Strange Fire: Reading the Bible after the Holocaust* (New York: New York University Press; Sheffield: Sheffield Academic Press, 2000).
21. Two matters on the body are crucial. First, Michael Polanyi, *The Tacit Dimension* (Anchor Books; Garden City; Doubleday and Co., 1967) has made the case about the ways in which the body knows. That is, no theoretical escape can deceive the body. Second, the body finally bears the costs and rescue must be bodily. On the latter point, see further Elaine Scarry, *The Body in Pain: The Making and Unmaking of the World* (Oxford: Oxford University Press, 1985).
22. See William T. Cavanaugh, *Torture & Eucharist: Politics and the Body of Christ* (Oxford: Blackwell Publishers, 1998).
23. Gerd Theissen and Annette Merz, *The Historical Jesus: A Comprehensive Guide* (Minneapolis: Fortress Press, 1998) 240–280, have reviewed the pertinent data and the critical discussion.
24. Oscar Cullman, *Christ and Time: The Primitive Christian Conception of Time and History* (Revised edition; Philadelphia: Westminster Press, 1964), 141, has offered the best known and influential attempt to relate in a faithful way what is "realized" and what is "awaited."
25. See II Corinthians 4:8-10. It is noteworthy that Paul's formulation of hope against despair is characterized as: " . . . always carrying in *the body the death* of Jesus, so that the life of Jesus may also be made visible in our bodies."
26. Matitiahu Tsevat, "The Basic Meaning of the Sabbath," *The Meaning of the Book of Job and Other Biblical Studies: Essays on the Literature and Religion of the Hebrew Bible* (New York: KTAV Publishing House, 1980), 48, remarks of the Sabbath, "Every seventh day the Israelite renounces his autonomy and affirms God's dominion over him." Of course in this comment Tsevat is not concerned with the Shoah. It occurs to me, nonetheless, that the "renunciation of autonomy" is what the church means to confess about the second day, and that in the Saturday of Shoah that renunciation reached its most acute form.
27. The conversation is reported by Elie Wiesel, *Memoirs: All Rivers Run to the Sea* (New York: Knopf, 1995), 354–355.

CHAPTER 9

Woman as Witness in a Post-Holocaust Perspective

MARGIE TOLSTOY

One of the most poignant moments in the gospel of John occurs on Easter morning when Mary Magdalen arrives at the place where Jesus had been buried and she finds the tomb empty. The angels ask why she is weeping and she answers, "because they have taken away my Lord and I do not know where they have laid him" (20:13). "Saying this, she turned around and saw Jesus standing, but she did not know it was Jesus" (20:14). Only after Jesus called out her name did she recognize him and said in Hebrew "Rabboni!" (20:16). For Mary Magdalen that restoration of vision is a moment of truth and glory. Woman as witness. She receives the protophany of the risen Jesus and announces the Easter kerygma. Mary Magdalen, "the primary and foundational apostolic figure in the Johannine community."[1] It is important for Christians to stay with that moment for awhile and to ask what it signifies to know Jesus, after Auschwitz. How does it manifest itself practically, politically, and spiritually to say like Mary Magdalen "I have seen the Lord"? Why has this extraordinary gift of grace been turned into an anti-Judaic polemic? Are Christians still standing at the empty tomb not knowing?

What is it about Christianity that allows a sensible and pious twentieth-century theologian to write "the Church of Christ has never lost sight of the thought that the 'chosen people,' who nailed the redeemer of the world to the cross, must bear the curse for its action through a long history of suffering."[2] This question has preoccupied many theologians. Situating the question in its historical context provides some plausible answers, but leaving the historical debates aside I want to bring in Carter Heyward's contribution that may shed some light on the matter. She suggests that "the hatred of Jews by Christians reflects a massive failure among Christians to accept the unfinished, ongoing character of salvation."[3] As Jesus is believed to represent the completion of God's saving work in history, salvation is available only to those who believe in him. Apart from the fact that the concept is quite unintelligible it may also, according to Carter Heyward, fall into the category of "theological fantasizing."

> from the very beginning of the church, we Christians have had great difficulty living as participants in an unfinished, imperfect creation. . . . Our difficulty with this participatory way of living in the Spirit has produced a number of terrible theological misunderstandings, including the misleading, only partially true, notion that *God became fully human in one person,* JESUS, *and him alone* (the basis of most doctrines of the incarnation) and an equally distorted assumption that *our salvation was accomplished through this brother's death on the cross* (in later theological developments, the basis of a doctrine of atonement) . . . such assumptions diminish, rather than strengthen, the power of God in us.[4]

The dynamic of this theological understanding that places Jesus *above* people rather than alongside requires a relationship of obedience and Jesus himself is considered to be the primary and ultimate example of living in total obedience to the will of the Father. Within a patriarchal context, this is the standard portrayal of conventional morality. It is well to remember that Jesus (as if) the obedient son of a patriarchal God is the product of a patriarchal religious imagination and does not reflect an objective God given reality. Scripture and tradition are historically ambiguous.[5]

Today obedience is no longer an adequate way to describe one's response to the love of God. Obedience is a misleading metaphor, suggesting "God is a power *over* us more than a Spirit *with* us; that God speaks *down* to us more than God yearns for our companionship; and that God needs *obedient children*" more than responsible adults.[6] Heyward wisely suggests that "*mutuality*, rather than obedience, is the basis of life in the Spirit and that learning to share our power in mutual relation is the most redemptive response we can make to the problem of evil."[7] In his life and ministry, Jesus as a Jew lives out the covenant and is an active participant as well as a "critical witness to the ongoing struggle to create more justice-loving, people-loving, creation-loving, God-loving societies."[8] The understanding that an all-powerful Being will come to the rescue and sort out oppressive social structures and prevent terrible things from happening to good people is a figment of the patriarchal imagination. Perhaps it was no coincidence that a woman turned away from the empty tomb and first witnessed the transformation. She alerted the disciples to an alternative reality. Later, the disciples received the message from Jesus himself behind closed doors: "Peace be with you. As the Father has sent me, even so I send you" (John 20:19). As if proof was needed, Jesus showed them his wounded hands and side. His work was accomplished, not theirs.

The doors had been shut "for fear of the Jews" when Jesus came and stood among them (John 20:19). The empty tomb and the closed doors are powerful symbols of loss and disorientation. This is not a finished story . . . but a new beginning. Unfortunately it is also the beginning of the "historical task of Christians to maintain perpetually the despised status of the Jews as a proof of their divine reprobation."[9] After Auschwitz it is imperative that Christians denounce these theological references within their sacred scripture that give credence to the demonic myth of the Jew. To ignore it is to perpetuate an empty tomb theology—a theology without vision.

I

Melissa Raphael, in her *Notes Towards a Jewish Feminist Theology of the Holocaust*, suggests that "Nazism represented a demonic but logical conclusion of the patriarchal worldview which objectifies all things as disposable means to power."[10] It was "a patriarchal model of God, not God in God's self, that failed Israel during the Holocaust."[11] Like Carter Heyward, she offers a post-Holocaust feminist theology of relation—of mutuality—that affirms the redemptive presence of God even in Auschwitz, or perhaps especially in Auschwitz. As an example she cites witness accounts of Jewish women's support groups in the camps where through mutual care and kindness Shekhinah is made present (the traditional female image of the holy presence of God) in the very abyss of profanity.[12] A different form of religious imagination is in place here. It does not demand supernatural solutions or answers to impossible questions. A moving account of a camp sisterhood that was formed in the spring of 1943 in the Plaszow labor camp in Poland by women between the ages of 16 and 26 illustrates the point. Rivka Englard, an Orthodox member of the group, was reported to have said that "life in Plaszow and Auschwitz was a test of our willingness to 'sanctify God' by adhering to our faith, by assisting as many Jews as possible and by remaining decent human beings."[13]

Raphael suggests that the medieval kabbalistic redemptive myths that gave comfort and courage to Jewish women in the camps can also serve as a structuring metaphor for woman as witness in post-Holocaust perspective. Each act of female *hesed*, of kindness, is like lighting the Sabbath candles, inviting the Shekhinah to enter the home. And each act of *hesed* then brings the divine image into the life of another person. The oral tradition of the Kabbalah furthermore holds the pragmatic belief that God brought the world into existence because "God wished to behold God."[14] So through *hesed* God is able to behold God.

That is a powerful and imaginative way of interrelating, a sensible prescription for human relationships as well as a perfectly convincing creation story. And it has the power to move mountains or at least to inform and transform. That brings us back to the Bible in which every story on every page tries to do just that. Living in relative prosperity, one tends to forget that sacred scripture is not some version of the good life. It is about transformation, moving away from self-centeredness to God-centeredness, to an active life with the living God. It is a process of transcending and of healing, of bridging the gap between what we are and—God willing—what we have in us to be.

It is understandable that people have lost faith after Auschwitz and have experienced the cruel reality of utter hopelessness as the absence of God. Yet absence and presence are connected. The redemptive power of forgiveness, that constructively engages with anger and hate, needs to find a place in our relation to God as well as to those who have inflicted pain. Tod Breyfogle is a wise teacher when he attacks the frail theology that promotes the notion that forgiveness has to be earned by the sinner through expressions of remorse when the truly hard work has to be done by those who are hurt. The work of forgiveness takes place as a disposition of love on the part of the injured person and is offered in proportion to the wrong incurred, not in relation to the repentance expressed. "Forgiveness is ultimately not an act of forgetting, but rather an even more intense remembering—a remembering of truth transformed in love in which the demands of justice give way to mercy."[15] That is the true nature of witness in post-Holocaust perspective: a return to a vision that has the power to transform. A return to that moment when Mary Magdalen turned around and said "Rabboni!"

II

How many Christians today still stand at the empty tomb not knowing? Once the Holocaust has become the window through which to view the world, not knowing may turn into lament: "Where was God at Auschwitz?" or "Where was Jesus Christ at Auschwitz?" Rabbi Irving Greenberg drives the question home:

> The Holocaust poses the most radical counter-testimony to both Judaism and Christianity. . . . The cruelty and the killing raise the question whether even those who believe after such an event dare to talk about a God who loves and cares without making a mockery of those who suffered.[16]

We must ask therefore on what piety, belief in God, is based. Is a theology habitable only if the affirmation of belief depends on the tangibility of God's love?[17] Has a hermeneutics of suspicion, after Auschwitz, permanently affected our relationship with God and with scripture? Perhaps, a paradigm shift is necessary; a shift in the theological as well as the ethical perspective, so that the question is not just how can God abide evil in the world, but particularly how can God be affirmed meaningfully in a world where evil enjoys such dominion.[18] There is an urgency in this task. A preliminary investigation may be needed concerning not just the question of meaning but also the understanding and accessibility of truth at a time of mistrust in final comprehensive explanations, which give our hold on reality a particular tentativeness. There is no meaningful homecoming in a world of contingent truths and the historical reality of the Holocaust stops all talk about meaning dead in its tracks. This naturally affects theology.

> After Auschwitz and Kolyma, all claims that everything does, in the end, make sense, are suspect. Nor is it by any means, only God that seems difficult to understand. Human beings are hardly more intelligible. A certain careless atheism supposes that it is "religious" truth that has been called in question. But in what "secular" story would all our killing fields find mention as but unfortunate episodes in an otherwise satisfactory tale? In those dark forests, it is the sense not simply of religion but of everything . . . that risks unraveling.[19]

It entirely justifies a crisis of faith. And a crisis of faith is closely linked to a loss of faith in the power of rationality, in the accessibility of unambiguous meaning in our everyday lives. And anyway, how adequate is reason to its own principles? Is it adequate to the rational principles of coherence and simplicity, to objectivity and impartiality?[20] The confidence, for example, of John Locke in the God-given power of reason seems to belong to a time of innocence, so entirely different and distant from our own. It is still worthwhile revisiting, if only as a reminder. In *An Essay Concerning Human Understanding* Locke wrote:

> I think it may not be amiss to take notice, that, however faith be opposed to reason, faith is nothing but a firm assent of the mind: which, if it be regulated, as is our duty, cannot be afforded to anything, but upon good reason; and so cannot be opposite to it. He that believes, without having any reason for believing, may be in love with his own fancies; but neither seeks truth as he ought, nor pays obedience due to his Maker, who would have him use those discerning faculties he has given him, to keep out of mistake and error. (IV, 17, 24)[21]

A footnote advises that we must always be regulated in the last resort by reasonableness. This is equally true of "revelation," experience of God seemingly unmediated by reason. Locke's outspoken dislike of "enthusiasm" of any kind obliges him to stop that particular route of escape from the necessary discipline of reason.

> *Reason* is *natural revelation*, whereby the eternal Father of light and fountain of all knowledge, communicates to mankind that portion of truth which he has laid within the reach of their natural faculties: *revelation* is *natural reason enlarged* by a new set of discoveries communicated by God immediately; which reason vouches the truth of, by the testimony and proofs it gives that they come from God. So that he that takes away reason to make way for revelation, puts out the light of both, and does much what the same as if he would persuade a man to put out his eyes, the better to receive the remote light of an invisible star by telescope. (IV, 19, 4)[22]

> *Reason must be our last judge and guide in everything.* (VI, 19, 14)[23]

Locke assumes the rationality of both God and man (exclusive language is appropriate). Mediated through a particular and specific embodiment of reason—testimony and proof—he seeks to prove the existence of an independent form of universal reason and thereby give legitimacy to his own rational duty and his own creator.[24] Locke is neither objective nor impartial in his desire to present *The Reasonableness of Christianity*. At that time he did not want to leave a secular conception of the natural law at the mercy of human convenience and so he tried his very best to rest human duties and rights directly on the revealed doctrines of Christianity.

This "natural" theology is no longer habitable after Auschwitz. The propositional truths that Locke is after are dislocated by the godforsakenness of the Holocaust. The revealed doctrines of Christianity lost credibility. The question still goes begging after the empiricist search for evidence in the world is rejected as "to what sort of deity one is rationally justified in giving devotion?"[25] This is no optional extra for Christians. An awareness of anti-Judaism in the gospels is deeply disturbing and raises questions of a very fundamental nature. All Christians may concur with Walter Brueggemann when he says "as I learn, I am aware of how much unlearning I have to do."[26] Questioning the rationality of religious belief is evidently not a redundant activity, but it can no longer be justified as the dominant mode of investigating religious truth. Different voices need to be heard and it is important that women contribute, not necessarily with an opposing perspective but with a new and alternative vision. The oppositional mode of reasoning is often unhelpful as well as misleading. Our thinking in and about the world is frequently shaped by an understanding within the dynamic of oppositional forces: faith and reason, life and death, order and disorder, rich and poor, unity and separation, good and evil, contingent and necessary truths, them and us, and so on. So much of theology is preoccupied with the paradigm of opposition. Lyn Bechtel draws attention to a fundamental flaw in that form of reasoning. She admits that life or creation exists within the complex, creative interfacing of oppositional forces. "Although these forces are oppositional and differentiated, they are unified in one continuous progress—a differentiated unity and because of that basic unity, the elimination of one oppositional force also eliminates the other—that is, if death is eliminated, so is life. Death is critical to life."[27] Similarly, Michele Le Doeuff pointed out that "the alternative between a hegemonic reason and a revolt of unreason can be seen as mythical, a connivance or complicity between forms which present themselves as opposites."[28] Lyn Bechtel notes that theologians tend to treat these oppositional forces in a reactionary manner in order to establish an ethic of control. The most obvious example is God, who must be completely disassociated from differentiated unity and only associated with goodness, power, and control. Bechtel remarks that although theology projects control onto God, in actuality it is humans who are in control.[29] A familiar patriarchal pattern remains in place. Hence the assumed coherence of the question of why a good God allows evil to exist in the world.

III

Where was God at Auschwitz? The theodicy question can never be answered satisfactorily. "Anyone who works out a rational way to integrate evil and radical suffering in an ordered fashion into a total intellectual system of which God is part, thereby justifies it."[30] The question "Where was God in Auschwitz?" is a lament, an expression of extreme anguish, and a cry for help. As a demand for theological explanation it is a dead end. The theology is uninhabitable. The poetic notion of a "suffering God" is often extracted from the ruins of that theology because it may have "the capacity to unleash human compassion, responsibility and hope."[31] Elizabeth Johnson's defense of the use of this image is sensitive and discerning:

> Only when set carefully and consistently within the context of a God who is utterly committed to the *humanum*, whose glory is the human being . . . fully alive, does the symbol of the suffering God release its empowering power. Then it signifies the power of suffering love to resist and create anew. In no way is this theological speech intended to yield a literal description of God. The rule of analogical language applies here in full strength. Even less does it attempt even remotely to reconcile the mystery of suffering and evil with the holy mystery of God. Such a conceptual solution is not possible. Speaking about the suffering God . . . is valid only if accompanied by the struggle to change the conditions in the direction of a new heaven and a new earth.[32]

Similarly, the question "Where was Jesus Christ at Auschwitz?" cannot be answered meaningfully in terms of a theological explanation. Nicholas de Lange posed the question for a Christian audience, in order to, like Elizabeth Johnson, unleash human compassion and a sense both of repentance and responsibility. He does not mince his words and the accusation has the power of revelation.

> Where was Jesus Christ at Auschwitz? The answer to this frightening question cannot be clear or straightforward. There has never been anything clear or straightforward about the relationship between Jesus Christ and his own people, that Jewish people which he so loved and so castigated, in true prophetic fashion. I do not turn my back on the image of Christ recrucified in the Shoah, but as a Jew I have to say that my prior concern must be with the image of Christ crucifying his own people.
>
> It is painful to contemplate the thought of those pierced hands dripping with the spilt blood of so many innocent victims.[33]

This image must haunt every Christian; making "Jesus Christ an accomplice in the crucifixion of his own people by his devotees."[34] It casts a long shadow over the Easter narrative. It focuses the mind on the work that needs to be done like no other. It is not enough to consider the deicide question as something from the past that has now been dealt with,[35] because the text supporting the accusation is unambiguous and has the status of sacred scripture. De Lange puts the Christian accusation of deicide on its head and each anti-Judaic remark in the Christian Bible is a chilling reminder of the consequences of this unpleasant and at times vicious polemic.[36] Christians cannot go on living with this. It is shameful and embarrassing. The suggestion that it is possible to reread the Gospel as post-Holocaust literature is helpful.[37] After all, the gospels were written at a time when people were forcefully reminded of the first destruction (the *Churban*) of the Temple while anticipating or indeed experiencing the catastrophe of the second. In John 2:19–21, Jesus identifies himself with the Temple. The charge of deicide parallels the destruction of the Temple and the simple explanation *mipnei hataeinu*, "because of our sins" was applied to both. For the followers of Jesus, however, that accusation now concerned only "unconverted" Jews who refused to follow Jesus and recognize him as the Messiah.

Nearly 2000 years later, after Auschwitz, Christians have to find an alternative home for their story of salvation. Ignaz Maybaum speaks of Auschwitz as the twentieth-century Calvary of the Jewish people.[38] Providing a stark Jewish perspective Maybaum writes that Christianity presented the man on the cross as a glorified persecuted tragic hero and obscured the fact that he was a Jew hanging on a Roman gallows. And to add insult to injury, "Christianity made this pagan and cruel monstrosity respectable, representing it through the symbol of the

Cross as the Christian tragedy."[39] The symbolic significance of the crucifixion is of course powerful enough without the anti-Judaic rhetoric. William Klassen's study of Judas makes an important and challenging contribution to post-Holocaust Christology when he argues convincingly that the incident of the "betrayal" by Judas is based on a mistranslation.[40] Christianity is an orphaned religion unless it returns to the Judaism of Jesus and reconnects with contemporary Judaism and Jewish scholarship.[41]

The question as to what sort of deity one is rationally justified in giving devotion remains as relevant as ever. Reading the gospel as post-Holocaust literature is indeed helpful and not an attempt to deny its sacred nature. On the contrary, it allows one to join the gospel writers in their passionate search for ways in which God can be affirmed in a world in which evil enjoys such dominion without deifying the text. Theology at the beginning of the twenty-first century has no choice but to take on board the fierce critics of religion who have been around for the last 200 years. Nietzsche's "Death of God" and Buber's "Eclipse of God" articulate a sense of the silence of God in a post-Holocaust world. The truly relevant question today is not so much, "Do you believe in God?" but the bolder question, "in what sort of God do you believe?" After Auschwitz, Christians stand with Mary Magdalen—woman as witness—at the empty tomb, waiting to turn around, waiting for the moment of transformation.

NOTES

1. Sandra M. Schneiders, *Written That You May Believe: Encountering Jesus in the Fourth Gospel* (New York: Herder and Herder, 1999), 215.
2. Dietrich Bonhoeffer, *No Rusty Swords: Letters, Lectures and Notes 1928–1936.* Collected Works, Vol. 1, ed. Edwin H. Robertson, trans. Edwin H. Robertson and John Bowden (London, New York: Harper & Row, 1965), 226.
3. Carter Heyward, *Saving Jesus From Those Who Are Right: Rethinking What it Means to Be a Christian* (Minneapolis: Fortress Press, 1999), 24.
4. Ibid., 25.
5. James Carroll writes, in *Constantine's Sword* (Boston: Houghton Mifflin Co., 2001), 172:

   > The great question for Christians is, How is Jesus God? It can come as no surprise to one for whom revelation is a profoundly human, and therefore time-bound, way of knowing to realize that the Jesus movement only gradually came to ask that question. It applied categories of divinity to him through the turmoil of argument, guesswork, estimation, imprecise language, and error far more than through sudden inspiration from above. For religious inspiration, like all things in history, evolves over time.

6. Heyward, *Saving Jesus*, 81.
7. Ibid., 82.
8. Ibid., 134.
9. Rosemary Radford Ruether, *To Change The World: Christology and Cultural Criticism* (London: SCM Press, 1981), 33.

10. Melissa Raphael, "When God beheld God: Notes Towards a Jewish Feminist Theology of the Holocaust," *Feminist Theology* 21 (1999): 61.
11. Ibid., 53
12. Ibid., 54.
13. Raphael, "When God Beheld God," 59, cited in Judith Tydor Baumel, "Social Interaction among Jewish Women in Crisis during the Holocaust," *Gender and History* 7 (1995): 79.
14. Z'ev ben Shimon Halevi, *Kabbalah: Tradition of Hidden Knowledge* (London: The Littman Foundation, 1993), 106; cited in Raphael, "When God Beheld God," 63.
15. Tod Breyfogle, "Forgiveness and Justice in a Secular Polity," *Reviews in Religion and Theology* 6:2 (1999): 134.
16. Rabbi Irving Greenberg, "Cloud of Smoke, Pillar of Fire," in *Holocaust: Religious and Philosophical Implications*, eds. John Roth and Michael Berenbaum (New York: Paragon House, 1989), 307–308.
17. My thanks to Prof. David Ford, who first mentioned the need for "a habitable theology" after Auschwitz in a lecture given for the "Jewish and Christian Responses to the Holocaust," Tripos paper in the Divinity Faculty of the University of Cambridge.
18. Arthur Cohen, *The Tremendum: A Theological Interpretation of the Holocaust* (New York: Continuum, 1981/1993), 34.
19. Nicholas Lash, "Among Strangers and Friends: Thinking of God in our Current Confusion," in *Finding God in All Things: Essays in Honor of Michael Buckley, S. J.*, eds. Michael J. Himes and Stephen J. Pope (New York: Crossword Publishing Company, 1996), 60.
20. Pamela Sue Anderson, *A Feminist Philosophy of Religion* (Oxford: Blackwell, 1998), 31.
21. John Locke, *An Essay Concerning Human Understanding*, Vol.2, collated and annotated by Alexander Campbell Fraser (New York: Dover Publications, 1959), 413.
22. Ibid., 431.
23. Ibid., 438.
24. Anderson, *Feminist Philosophy of Religion*, 34.
25. Ibid., 228.
26. Walter Brueggemann, "A Fissure Always Uncontained," in *Strange Fire: Reading the Bible after the Holocaust*, ed. Tod Linafelt (New York: New York University Press; Sheffield: Sheffield Academic Press, 2000), 37.
27. Lyn M. Bechtel, "A Feminist Approach to Job," in *A Feminist Companion to Wisdom Literature*, ed. Athaliah Brenner (Sheffield: Sheffield Academic Press, 1995), 225.
28. Michele Le Doeuff, *The Philosophical Imaginary*, trans. Colin Gordon (London: The Athlone Press, 1989), 118.
29. Bechtel, "A Feminist Approach to Job," 231.
30. Elizabeth A. Johnson, *She Who Is: The Mystery of God in Feminist Theological Discourse* (New York: Crossroad, 1992), 271.
31. Ibid., 271.
32. Ibid.
33. Nicholas de Lange, "Jesus Christ and Auschwitz," *New Blackfriars* (July/August 1997): 310–311.
34. Ibid., 310.
35. *Nostra Aetate*, 28 October1965:

    Even though the Jewish authorities and those who followed their lead pressed for the death of Christ (see John 19:6), neither all Jews indiscriminately at that time, nor Jews today, can be charged with the crimes committed during the passion. It is true that the church is the new people of God, yet the Jews should not be spoken of as rejected or accursed, as if this followed from holy scripture. Consequently, all must take care, lest in catechizing or in preaching the word of God, they teach anything which is not in accord with the truth of the Gospel message or the spirit of Christ.

36. See, e.g., John 8:44.
37. Nicholas de Lange, "Jesus Christ and Auschwitz," 313.
38. Ignaz Maybaum, *The Face of God After Auschwitz* (Amsterdam: Polak & van Gennep Ltd., 1965), 35.
39. Ibid., 48.
40. William Klassen, *Judas: Betrayer or Friend of Jesus?* (London: SCM Press, 1996).
41. Elizabeth Johnson in her Mary Ward Lecture for 1999, "Jesus-Sophia—Ramifications for Contemporary Theology," draws attention to the identification of Jesus with Holy Wisdom: "Jesus is the human being Sophia became."

CHAPTER 10

New Testament Theology after the Holocaust

Exegetical Responsibilities and Canonical Possibilities

LLOYD GASTON

I

We cannot say that we did not know. Jules Isaac published his *Jésus et Israël* in 1948, a work begun in 1943 after the arrest and murder of his wife and daughter and written in hiding and on the run.[1] In 1954 or 1955, when I first began my theological studies, my teacher Oscar Cullmann told me that it was a very important book that I must read. Later the last of Isaac's books on the subject but the first to be translated into English, *The Teaching of Contempt*, had a much broader effect.[2] It took some time to absorb how the long history of the church's "teaching of contempt" toward the Jewish people could lead to such monstrous results. It took some time for biblical exegetes to realize how their work contributed to such teaching and to begin to accept responsibility for it.

It was not difficult to give a name to the presupposition underlying such harmful exegesis: triumphalism, or replacement theology, or supersessionism. It was the idea that God had abandoned Plan A, the covenant with Israel, in favor of Plan B, a new covenant with the church. Continuing Israel then became at best theologically irrelevant or at worst punished for unbelief. Protestant Christians in particular have had difficulty with the concept of law or Torah and have tried to get rid of it, not thinking that there could eventually be a connection between legicide and genocide. Insofar as the historical-critical method means primarily the radical criticism of the assumptions of the interpreter, and insofar as unconscious assumptions in this area have had bad consequences, we ought to be very suspicious of all received wisdom concerning Christian views of Judaism. It is good to try to articulate what have been the assumptions underlying traditional interpretation to see if they have indeed been infected by supersessionist views. For example, although it is of course possible that Jesus contrasts his authority with that of Moses in Matthew 5 or that Paul contrasts his ministry with that of Moses in 2 Corinthians 3, one would need to scrutinize thoroughly the assumptions that underlie such a hermeneutic of antithesis.

The task was a familiar one: to search for instances of false interpretation and to seek to find a better explanation. There are of course many passages in which the supersessionism lies not in the interpretation but in the text itself. But historical criticism had the tools for that. When a text was multilayered and one could distinguish redaction from earlier sources and traditions, often the anti-Judaism could be confined to the final layer. Often it seemed that the supersessionism found in the New Testament was a consequence of reflection on the fall of Jerusalem in C.E. 70 and not to be found in earlier traditions. For people teaching ministerial students who were learning to use not whole books but single pericopes in their preaching, the task seemed all the easier. We thought we could simply define for our own purposes the text to be interpreted or in intractable cases avoid it altogether.[3] Thereby a major new problem was created and immediately hidden. Apart from good intentions, there was no criterion for determining which writing or which form of the text was more authoritative than the others. We shall return to this problem.

There is an additional factor to be considered. Since the Enlightenment there has been a temptation among the more "progressive" exegetes to think of their work as being scientific, based only on value-free objectivity. We need to become more modest. There is no exegesis without presuppositions, especially when they are unconscious. Specifically this is true when it is done in a church context. It is not the case that exegetes determine assured results for the theologians to receive and try to utilize for better or for worse. Although one hopes that exegesis of the Biblical texts will be a factor in theological reflection, it is also certainly true that theological presuppositions influence exegesis and probably true that only conscious theological considerations can exorcise bad Biblical interpretation. The relationship between exegetical study of the New Testament and Christian theology should be acknowledged to be complex.

The discipline of Biblical studies has recently entered a promising but unsettled experimental phase through interaction with many other disciplines besides theology. The majority of its practitioners today are not engaged in preparing candidates for service in churches or synagogues and may or may not have any theological interests. Nevertheless, the study of texts is important to all of us because of some ideological or practical agenda. No exegesis is without presuppositions, even if they are not explicitly theological. Not all dogma is theological, but all dogmatic posturing can be arrogant. Of the new methods being developed, I find reader-response criticism to be most helpful for present purposes, in that it locates meaning neither in the text nor in the reader but in the interchange between the two, where the text says something objective but different to each hearer and situation. That should mean paying attention to *Wirkungsgeschichte*, the long history of interpretation from text to present. Also, to restrict the text to its final written form seems to be to be perverse and simply inappropriate for most Biblical literature. But for purposes of responsibly reading the text after the Holocaust I think the solution must be sought where the problem arose, in the interaction between exegesis and Christian theology.[4]

Probably the most important Christian response to Isaac's second main theme in *The Teaching of Contempt*, the assumption of "the degenerate state of Judaism at the time of Jesus,"[5] is to be found neither in theology nor in exegesis proper but in the revised, improved understanding of the history of early Judaism. Historians have begun to write this history based not on hostile Christian sources but on Jewish sources, understood as far as possible from the perspective of those sources. It was simply the application of an old historiographic principle also to this area. The scholarly maxim is *ad fontes* (back to the original sources), and the Biblical commandment that applies is the prohibition not to bear false witness against the neighbor. Once the Wellhausen view of "late Judaism" as a degenerate and legalistic and unspiritual religion is replaced by a more positive picture, much of the supposed historical necessity for supersessionism is undermined. It also opens the possibility of a more appreciative approach to contemporary Judaism.

The opposite of supersessionism is affirmation of God's continuing covenant with the Jewish people. If the horrors of the Holocaust impelled Christians to take responsibility for their past exegesis and historiography and preaching and liturgy, an encounter with living Judaism can open up new challenges and opportunities. Christian–Jewish dialogue, through personal friendship or scholarly exchange, has enabled many participants to identify common concerns and to respect and appreciate differences.

Let me mention just a few areas in which Christians can and have learned from Jewish colleagues to respond more satisfactorily to analogous situations. The most urgent and agonizing is of course theodicy after Auschwitz.[6] We must learn to modify and reformulate if not the whole concept of providence then at least such absolute attributes as omnipotence.[7] All of these metaphysical abstractions, including also omniscience and perfection of being and immutability and impassability, seem quite incompatible with the God of the whole Bible. Christians have often had difficulties dealing with particularism and universalism and avoiding theological imperialism. We can learn from Judaism how to express passionate loyalty to our own particularity while affirming room for others to have an equally valid attachment to another particularity. The concept of covenant partnership with fidelity expected from both God and Israel can teach Christians how better to reconcile divine grace and human responsibility.[8] Christians can learn to see themselves not in antithesis to the Sinai covenant and the Torah and the Israel of God but in continuity with them. One place in which these questions and others raised earlier come together is in the understanding of Scripture and canon, and I offer a brief tentative discussion of a possible solution.

II

I begin with a brilliant, revolutionary, and surely controversial theological assertion by Walter Brueggemann. He states that God is to be encountered not behind the text in ontological categories and not apart from the text in causal intervention in history but exclusively "in, with, and under the text itself."[9] (The sacramental echoes are surely deliberate.) This represents a major shift from the old "Biblical theological movement," one of whose influential works spoke of "God who acts."[10] Now we encounter God as the "God who speaks" and who speaks in the language of Israel. This appears to be a theology that decisively rejects supersessionism and that provides a possible solution to the problem of theodicy. It also demands that theology be a theology exclusively of the Word of God and that we pay careful attention to the way a canon functions.

The most basic outline of how the church confesses its faith in creedal formulations and tells the story of humanity under God in a way that distorts canon has been forcefully presented by R. Kendall Soulen.[11] That faith and story involves three acts: creation by a gracious God, the fall of humanity into sin and death, and the solution to that problem in redemption through Jesus Christ, made available in the church. Such a story needs, in addition to the New Testament, also Genesis 1–2 (creation) and Genesis 3 (fall) but really nothing else. The rest of the Old Testament was read as a history of fallenness and as a promise of or allegory for the redemption. How can we restore the fullness of the canon of the Old Testament for Christian theology?

One could define the formation of canon (or Scripture) as the deliberate selection and collection of ancient traditions into a new authoritative group of writings that has a normative function for a community such that any other later normative writing or speaking must be seen in relation to it. That is clearly a very decisive event in the life of a religious community and one that probably can happen only once. The formation of Scripture of course establishes "stability," to use the terminology of James A. Sanders,[12] but if that were all, the community would soon die of arteriosclerosis. Canon must also be "adaptable for life," which means being open to midrash, to innovative interpretation in new situations. It is doubtful, however, if a second canon can be added to the first, for then the new canon becomes the real canon, to which the old must relate itself in order to establish its legitimacy, reversing the time sequence between Scripture and midrash. At least I believe that to have been the case in the Christian church, where the establishment of the New Testament as canon went hand in hand with the demotion of the Old Testament to subordinate status.

Was such a Scripture created in Israel? In a now classic statement, D. N. Freedman argued that it was. According to him, a radically new redaction and reordering of old traditions occurred during the exile (580–550 B.C.E.) to produce Torah, Former Prophets, and Latter Prophets, as "public documents, for which the highest religious authority was claimed, promulgated by an official . . . group in the Jewish community."[13] A generation or so later (c. 500 B.C.E.) extensive additions were made to the corpus of the Latter Prophets. The Writings, most of which were in existence at the time, were not at first part of the Scripture, and when they were later collected and edited, it was in conscious relation to Scripture, a "canon-conscious" inner-biblical exegesis and redaction and midrash. They might be called "deuterocanonical" from a Jewish perspective if "canon" were a Jewish word. In any case, the existence of Scripture, including at least many of the Writings, can be assumed as authoritative documents by at least some groups certainly by the beginning of the first century B.C.E. One of the reasons for saying this is that if Scripture produces midrash, then conversely midrash presupposes Scripture, and as Vermes says, "in exegetical writings of the second century BC the main haggadic themes are already fully developed."[14] There never was a church council at Jamnia, and the Rabbis did not seriously debate inclusion or exclusion. What they did do was to produce an extensive authoritative corpus of writings in conscious (Halakhic Midrash) or unexpressed (Mishnah, later "oral Torah") relationship to Scripture.

III

To come now to the formation of the New Testament canon,[15] it seems to have been shifted from the end of the second to the end of the fourth century, at least partly because of a new dating of the Muratorian fragment.[16] It is not a literary unity, not did it occur at a brief, crucial time in the life of the church. It is rather a miscellaneous collection of various occasional writings. Its boundaries have no self-evident validity, and every criterion mentioned—apostolicity, catholicity, orthodoxy, traditional usage—has important exceptions both of inclusion and exclusion. In particular, inspiration was never adduced as a criterion for canonicity in the early church, because the Spirit was held to be given to the whole church. None of the writings in the New Testament claims canonical authority for itself (Revelation claims apocalyptic authority), and most refer specifically to Scripture outside themselves. No one has ever been able to find a unity in the New Testament canon[17] (as there is in Freedman's Old Testament scripture), but instead we have learned to speak of the varieties of New Testament religion.[18] Two phenomena that were of great embarrassment to the early church, the plurality of the gospels and the particularity of the Pauline epistles,[19] lie at the very heart of contemporary understanding of these texts. It is true that "the New Testament is the Church's book" not only in that the church created the canon in the fourth and fifth centuries but also with respect to the composition of the individual writings in the first and second centuries. Nevertheless, we need to find some extrinsic perspective against which the traditions of the church can be measured and to ask how it can help in the interpretation of the New Testament writings.

In response to the theological question of identifying an authority that is not a product of but transcendent over the church, the answer within a Christian context seems at first to be clear. But if it seems obvious that Jesus Christ is the canonical principle, it is not at all obvious how one can understand that statement as anything other than a purely formal principle. We can look at two classic attempts to put flesh on the principle. First is the hierarchical concept of the ancient church, which says that authority runs as follows: God → Christ → apostles → bishops → church. This can be seen, e.g., in I Clement 42:

> The apostles received the gospel for us from the Lord Jesus. Jesus Christ was sent from God. Thus Christ is from God and the apostles are from Christ. In both instances the orderly procedure proceeds from God's will, . . . and the apostles after preaching in country and city appointed their first converts to be bishops and deacons of future believers. And this was no novelty, . . . since Scripture says, "I will appoint your bishops in righteousness and your deacons in faith." (Isaiah 60:17)

Again, in Justin, 1 Apology 39,

> The Spirit of prophecy speaks . . . in this way: "For out of Zion shall go forth the law and the word of the Lord from Jerusalem . . ." (etc. Isaiah 2:3). For from Jerusalem there went out into the world men, twelve in number and these illiterate, of no ability in speaking, but by the power of God they proclaimed to every race of men that they were sent by Christ to teach to all the word of God.

Note how both Justin and Clement base their argument on Scripture! This theory of apostolic succession was popular in the ancient church, and its effects are still very much with us today. It is only this theory that justifies the position of the gospels first in the New Testament and the special liturgical honor given to the gospels in certain church tradition. The problem is that it is manifestly untrue! The only apostle to have contributed any writing to the New Testament, Paul, hardly ever passes on tradition received from Jesus and may even boast that he never knew him (II Corinthians 5:16). It was a nice theory, but here surely theology has no historical or Biblical basis on which to build whatsoever.

The modern attempt to base revelation on tradition stemming from Jesus has had no greater success. Again, it seems at first quite reasonable to ascribe to Jesus greater authority than the gospels that report it, perhaps even to print his words in red ink. But it is perhaps significant that the church never thought to preserve the teaching of Jesus in the language in which he spoke it. Here the *Leben Jesu* movement founders on the phenomenon that already worried the ancient church: the plurality of the gospels. Quite apart from any modern judgments about the authenticity of individual sayings, the gospels seen synoptically show that the gospel writers were prepared to alter the Jesus tradition rather freely to address their own particular situations. The teaching of Jesus is not a given but must be reconstituted. The problem is that no two reconstructions are the same, and they all show evidence of selectivity based on modern religious desires. The quest for the historical Jesus finally dug its own grave, for the more it tried to recover the teaching of Jesus the more it became apparent how much that teaching differs from the Jesus figure liberal theology wanted to find. It is not that I am uninterested in current reconstructions of the historical Jesus, it is just that I do not find them helpful for systematic theology, apart from their important negative function of opposing a docetic and non-Jewish Jesus.

Is there another criterion that might stand above the church's list of authoritative writings? The Lutheran tradition in particular has been concerned with the question of the canon within the canon. Note how the word "canon" is being used in two senses, "criterion" and "list." The same ambiguity has plagued much of the discussion since ancient times.[20] Luther's classic statement is: "That is the true test by which to judge all books, when we see whether or not they promote Christ. . . . Whatever does not teach Christ is not yet apostolic, even though St. Peter or St. Paul does the teaching. Again, whatever preaches Christ would be apostolic, even if Judas, Annas, Pilate, and Herod were doing it."[21] Here is a way of putting Christ in the center, not as a link in passing revelation through apostolic succession but in terms of what God had done in Christ's death and resurrection. Here is a criterion above the church's canon, which effectively relativizes the individual writings under the center of the gospel. It is, however, much more seriously deficient in its subjectivity: if James does not promote Christ for some, that writing does for others. It is perhaps such considerations that have led E. Käsemann to propose a more specific and objective canon within the canon or "material center" (*Sachmitte*), namely the justification of the ungodly. This is perhaps a bit theological and certainly very Paul centered, but it is also not as objective as it seems. Although it is true that every church tradition and many individual Christians have their own canon within the canon, unconscious or acknowledged, there is no criterion to adjudicate their rival claims. As Käsemann argued, "the New Testament canon does not . . . constitute the foundation for the unity of the church."[22] But he can also give no compelling reason why that unity must be achieved on *his* terms, and the problem of the New Testament canon remains.

The canon of the New Testament is not a unity and cannot serve as a norm. That is true not only of the individual writings but also of the kerygmata they contain. Scholars as different as W. Bauer and J. D. G. Dunn agree that the early Christian movement began with a rich diversity of kerygmata and gospels and Christologies and theologies. That is only to be expected, since we are dealing after all with church traditions and both the communities that formulated them and the communities for which they were being adapted. Insofar as there is unity, it lies in the conviction that God has acted in Jesus Christ and that this God is the God of Israel and the Scriptures of Israel. The significant subtitle of C. H. Dodd's *According to the Scriptures* is *The Substructure of New Testament Theology*.[23] The Scripture of Israel is the criterion, the canon, to which the early Christians appealed, and it is definitely not the creation of the church. It seems then best not to speak of a canon of the New Testament at all but rather of *midrash* (J. A. Sanders) or *explicatio* (J. Calvin).[24] It really does make a difference when one recognizes, along with C. F. Evans, that "Christianity is unique among world religions in being born with a Bible in its cradle."[25]

As James Sanders's version of canonical criticism points out, the creation of a canon of Holy Scripture is a decisive step in the life of a community. It lies in the nature of a canon to provide stability. Although one can in theory or in practice neglect parts of it or reject the whole to start a new religion, no new canon can be added to canon once it is created. At the same time it lies in the nature of canon to be "adaptable for life," and if it is truly to function as Scripture it cries out for constant reinterpretation in the ongoing believing communities. A necessary counterpart to canonical criticism is "comparative midrash," which includes but is more than a history of interpretation. If it is true that once a canon is formed revelation is restricted to the canonical text, it must also be emphasized that revelation does occur again and again in the believing communities in their various situations, sometimes with radically new meaning. If the concept of inspiration (and thus of revelation in a postcanonical situation) is to be meaningful, it must refer not just to a private transaction in the past but to what God does in the present. Inspiration occurs whenever a community, in its own particular situation in time and space, within the continuity of the whole tradition of interpretation, is inspired to hear what God says to them in the words of Holy Scripture. "Every Scripture, whenever (from time to time) it is inspired by God, is profitable for teaching, reproof, correction, and training . . ." (II Timothy 3:16). "*Ubi et quando visum est deo*," as the Reformers said. As revelation is more authoritative than an ancient text, so midrash can be more authoritative for the community than the canon as such. There is a tension between the exegetical meaning of a text, which can more or less be established historically, and the homiletical, even inspired meaning, which is true for its time and place but is not authoritative for other situations in the same way as is the exegetical meaning. The canon remains as a control over interpretations that claim to be revelation but are not or are no longer such.

There were major problems involved when the church thought it had two canons, an Old Testament and a New Testament. The first problem lies in the adjectives "Old" and "New," insofar as they are held, consciously or unconsciously, to have any meaning at all. Again, I refer to the Babylonian captivity of Hebrew Scripture under the chains of the concept "Old Testament." The concept "New Testament" can and almost always has led interpreters of these documents into a hermeneutic of antithesis. In what follows, we shall look at some of the theological consequences that accrue from a hermeneutic of continuity, which depends (I think) on the concept of canonical Scripture and authoritative midrash.

It is clear that the teaching of Jesus is to be understood completely in Biblical categories and that none of it is intended to be in antithesis to them. His teaching can in particular be understood as authoritative midrash of the Scriptural passages proclaiming the Kingdom of God, saying that now they were about to be fulfilled. Jesus' teachings and his deeds are to be interpreted without remainder as part of the Judaism of his day, in continuity with Scripture and the tradition of its post-Biblical interpretation. That means that by incorporation into Jesus as the one in whom God has acted for their sake Gentiles have complete access to Jesus' Scripture (and its living interpretations) and to Jesus' God who speaks in them. The doctrine of the Trinity has logical priority over Christological doctrines, something obscured by too abstract formulations. What is said is that the "Father" to whom the "Son" relates is none other than the God of Abraham, Isaac, and Jacob, the God of Sarah and Rebekah and Rachel and Leah, the God of Moses and Jeremiah and Ezra and Esther. The doctrine of the Trinity formulates the fact that through the Son and the Holy Spirit this is the God Gentiles worship too.

Also Christology depends on Scripture, as an interpretation of it and not an addition to it. The oldest creedal formula in Paul's letters, in its shortest form, states that "Christ died in accordance with the Scriptures . . . was raised in accordance with the Scriptures" (I Corinthians 15:3–5). Even resurrection is not in itself revelatory but is an ambiguous event that is in itself mute. No church was ever founded on the basis of the resurrection of Lazarus or Jairus's daughter or the widow's son or Tabitha or Eutychus, or on the ascension of Enoch or Elijah or Moses or Mary. What makes Jesus' resurrection important and gives it revelatory force is that it was "according to the Scriptures." The risen Christ "beginning with Moses and all the prophets interpreted to them in all the Scriptures the things concerning himself" (Luke 24:27). Failure to recognize this could lead us to misunderstand, even to trivialize, the claims made by the Christology of the earliest Christians.

Paul claims that his gospel was "proclaimed beforehand to Abraham" because "Scripture knew beforehand that God would justify the Gentiles from faithfulness" (Galatians 3:8), that "the gospel of God concerning his Son was promised earlier through his prophets in Holy Scriptures" (Romans 1:2), and that "the Law and the Prophets testified to the righteousness of God through the faithfulness of Jesus Christ" (Romans 3:21f). It was expected that Scripture was the criterion for the truth of the gospel: those who received the word "examined the Scriptures daily to see if these things were so" (Acts 17:11). And yet this tends not to be sufficiently recognized by modern scholars. Vielhauer, for example, complains that Paul's interpretation of the "Old Testament" is completely arbitrary and need not be taken seriously.[26] All of this is because of the concepts of "New Testament" and "Old Testament," and the fact that the former seems not to relate very well to the latter. But if we begin with the concept of Holy Scripture, then we need to take seriously its living transmission in the midrash of subsequent communities. The task of the Pauline interpreter is then not to contrast Paul and the Old Testament itself but to try to reconstruct something of the history of interpretation of the text and to locate Paul with respect to these midrashic traditions. Insofar as this can be done, Paul's own midrash, although creative, is not at all arbitrary and outlandish. Here is a good example of how a change of concept might enrich exegesis and give more, not less, authority to the writings of the New Testament.

Finally, I appeal to the final work of Paul van Buren, *According to the Scriptures*, with which I am in substantial agreement. He points out that the new Christian gospel was first formulated when the old Scriptures were heard to speak directly to the shock of Jesus' death and the surprise of Jesus' resurrection. This opens up the canonical possibilities. The church may (and must) read the Old Testament as our story too, and this reading is greatly enriched when we hear the basic story being constantly given new dimensions in post-Biblical Jewish exegesis. When the New Testament is read in that context of ongoing living reinterpretation it becomes more understandable and, I believe, more authoritative in addressing the church today. The idea of comparative midrash also allows Christians to acknowledge modern Judaism and opens the possibility of learning from contemporary Jews. Our different situations allow each to hear different revelation from the same Scripture and for each to honor the hearing of the other. The new way of understanding canon also helps resolve the dilemma of our exegetical responsibilities after the Holocaust: "The indispensable role of the Old Testament in the formulation of the early gospel . . . argues that it could and should be used in the church to identify and correct anti-Judaic polemics in the New Testament."[27]

NOTES

1. Jules Isaac, *Jésus et Israël* (Paris: Fasquelle Éditeurs, 1948).
2. Jules Isaac, *The Teaching of Contempt: Christian Roots of Anti-Semitism* (New York: Holt, Rinehart & Winston, 1964).
3. See the useful survey by Norman A. Beck, *Mature Christianity: The Recognition and Repudiation of the Anti-Jewish Polemic of the New Testament* (Selinsgrove: Susquehanna University Press, 1985).
4. Two Christian theologians have explicitly embarked of a systematic reformulation of theology in the light of the Holocaust: Paul M. van Buren, *A Theology of the Jewish-Christian Reality: Part 1, Discerning the Way* (New York: Seabury, 1980); *Part 2, A Christian Theology of the People Israel* (New York: Seabury, 1983); *Part 3, Christ in Context* (San Francisco: Harper & Row, 1988); Clark M. Williamson, *A Guest in the House of Israel: Post-Holocaust Church Theology* (Louisville: Westminster/John Knox, 1993); *Way of Blessing, Way of Life: A Christian Theology* (St. Louis: Chalice, 1999). There have of course also been other fine contributions.
5. Isaac, *Contempt*, 74–108.
6. See most recently, Zachary Braiterman, *(God) after Auschwitz: Tradition and Change in Post-Holocaust Jewish Thought* (Princeton: Princeton University Press, 1998).
7. For different but also cogent reasons for abandoning the concept, see Langdon B. Gilkey, "Cosmology, Ontology, and the Travail of Biblical Language," *JR* 41 (1961): 194–205; and Maurice Wiles, *God's Action in the World: The Bampton Lectures for 1986* (London: SCM, 1986).
8. See, e.g., David Hartman, *A Living Covenant: The Innovative Spirit in Traditional Judaism* (New York: Macmillan, 1985).
9. Walter Brueggemann, *Theology of the Old Testament: Testimony, Dispute, Advocacy* (Minneapolis: Fortress, 1997), 19; cf. 714 and passim in between. It is my fervent hope that systematic theologians would take this point and many others in this remarkable book into intense consideration.
10. G. Ernest Wright, *God Who Acts: Biblical Theology as Recital* (London: SCM, 1952).
11. R. Kendall Soulen, *The God of Israel and Christian Theology* (Minneapolis: Fortress, 1996).
12. See especially *Canon and Community: A Guide to Canonical Criticism* (Philadelphia: Fortress, 1984); and *From Sacred Story to Sacred Text* (Philadelphia: Fortress, 1987).
13. D. N. Freedman, "The Law and the Prophets," *Supplements to Vetus Testamentum 9* (Leiden: Brill, 1962), 250–265, 251.
14. Géza Vermès, *Scripture and Tradition in Judaism: Haggadic Studies* (Leiden: Brill, 1973), 228.
15. See especially H. von Campenhausen, *The Formation of the Christian Bible* (London: Black, 1972); and H. Y. Gamble, *The New Testament Canon: Its Making and Meaning* (Philadelphia: Fortress, 1985).
16. See A. C. Sundberg, Jr., "Canon Muratori: A Fourth Century List," *HTR* 66 (1973): 1–41.
17. In dealing with the criteria in the early church for inclusion in the New Testament canon, "one can only speak of the principle of having no principles," K. Aland, *The Problem of the New Testament Canon* (London: Mowbray, 1962), 15.
18. See W. Bauer, *Orthodoxy and Heresy in Earliest Christianity* (Philadelphia: Fortress, 1971); and J. D. G. Dunn, *Unity and Diversity in the New Testament* (London: SCM, 1977).
19. See O. Cullmann, "The Plurality of the Gospels as a Theological Problem in Antiquity," in *The Early Church* (Philadelphia: Westminster, 1956), 39–54; and N. A. Dahl, "The Particularity of

the Pauline Epistles as a Problem in the Ancient Church," in *Neotestamentica et Patristica: eine Freundesgabe, Herrn Professor Dr. Oscar Cullmann zu seinem 60 Geburtstag überreicht* (Leiden: Brill, 1962), 261–271.

20. See I. Lønning, *Kanon im Kanon: Zum dogmatischen Grundlagenproblem des neutestamentlichen Kanons* (Oslo: Universitetsforlaget, 1972).
21. "Prefaces to the New Testament," *Luther's Works*, Vol. 35 (Philadelphia: Fortress, 1960), 396.
22. E. Käsemann, "The Canon of the New Testament and the Unity of the Church," in *Essays on New Testament Themes* (London: SCM, 1964), 95–107, 103.
23. C. H. Dodd, *According to the Scriptures: The Substructure of New Testament Theology* (London: Nisbet, 1952). Another, rather different book with the same title will be appealed to at the end of this essay.
24. In his commentary on II Timothy 3:17, Calvin writes: "In speaking of the Scripture Paul means what we call the Old Testament; how can he say that it makes a man perfect? If that is so, what was added later through the apostles would seem to be superfluous. My answer is that as far as the substance of the Scripture is concerned, nothing has been added. The writings of the apostles contain nothing but a simple and natural explanation of the Law and the prophets along with a clear description of the things expressed in them." [*The Second Epistle of Paul the Apostle to the Corinthians and the Epistles to Timothy, Titus and Philemon* (Grand Rapids: Eerdmans, 1964), 331.]
25. C. F. Evans, in P. R. Ackroyd and C. F. Evans, eds., *The Cambridge History of the Bible: Vol. 1, From the Beginnings to Jerome* (Cambridge: Cambridge University Press, 1970), 232.
26. P. Vielhauer, "Paulus und das Alte Testament," *Oikodome* (Munich: Kaiser, 1970), 196–228.
27. Paul M. van Buren, *According to the Scriptures: The Origins of the Gospel and of the Church's Old Testament* (Grand Rapids: Eerdmans, 1998), viii. The conclusion of the book makes a nice *inclusio*: "Are we to excise (anti-Jewish) passages from the New Testament, or ignore them, or just not use them? However that be decided, the prior question is, by what authority, according to what criterion, could any of these courses be chosen? This study has suggested an answer: by the authority of the Old Testament" (p. 134).

CHAPTER 11

Reading the Cross at Auschwitz

Holocaust Memories and Passion Narratives

TANIA OLDENHAGE

I am looking at a picture entitled *ausweglos* ("hopeless"). It is painted in shades of gray with the exception of the wooden color of a cross. The cross lies on Jesus' right shoulder. His left hand reaches over a barbed wire toward a group of veiled women. Behind the women runs a railroad track to the infamous entrance wall of Auschwitz-Birkenau. The picture belongs to a series of posters dedicated to this year's ecumenical Way of the Cross, a widespread church ritual during which young Christians meditatively trace Jesus' walk to Golgatha. The posters together with songs and prayers were published by Catholic and Protestant church organizations in Germany in order to guide and inspire local congregations in composing their Way of the Cross liturgy in the year 2001.[1] As a teenager I used to participate in these annual events and glancing through the materials I remember the feelings I had when I walked through the streets of my German hometown with Jesus' suffering on my mind. Looking at the poster of Jesus in front of the Nazi death camp, I also wonder how exactly this year's youth groups combined the memories of Golgatha with the memories of Auschwitz. How did young Germans manage to contemplate the suffering and death of Jesus while at the same time reflecting on the suffering and death of millions of Jews during the Holocaust?

Jesus' cross placed within the landscape of Auschwitz is no invention of the German ecumenical committee but a long-standing, well-known trope that has attracted much academic discussion. The trope has been developed in different ways by Christian theologians seeking to integrate the events of the Holocaust into their thinking, and it can be found in art, music, literature, liturgy, and poetry.[2] But the trope is also contested and has been criticized and repudiated by both Jewish and Christian thinkers.[3] During the 1990s its controversial potential exploded when the supporters of the Carmelite convent in Auschwitz planted a cross close to the barracks in the memorial camp. For the Carmelites, as for the German liturgists, Jesus' crucifixion may have seemed the most compelling symbol through which to remember the victims of the Holocaust. But for others, and especially for the Jewish survivors of Auschwitz, this same symbol evokes centuries of Christian anti-Jewish violence that makes its presence in the memorial camp intolerable.[4] The cross at Auschwitz, in its literal manifestation in Poland, but also in its countless representations in art and discourse, is charged with problems. Doesn't the cross at Auschwitz impose on us the idea that there is some meaning to be found in the suffering of the Jews because we (Christians) are so used to the redemptive meaning of the suffering of Christ? Isn't there a danger that through the cross we figure Jews as martyrs, tortured and murdered for some higher goal? And how can we bear the cross as a meaningful sign after Auschwitz when we know that it incited Christians to hate, persecute, and kill their Jewish neighbors for centuries, when we know that there are still people today who believe that the Jews will be punished because they crucified our Lord?

I

In his recent book *Constantine's Sword*, the Catholic writer James Carroll makes frequent references to the cross at Auschwitz in an effort to persuade his readers once and for all that this trope is unacceptable.[5] As he tells us, seeing the Carmelite cross at the memorial camp in Auschwitz was an experience so disturbing that in its aftermath Carroll was prompted to investigate and publicly narrate the long and jarring history of violence associated with the cross of Jesus.[6] In a monumental narrative that traces the causal links from the first to the twentieth century, Carroll shows how the cross turned under Constantine from a device of Roman state terror into a sign of Christian domination and was used throughout the centuries against those who did not conform to the Christian norm, especially Jews. From Constantine to the crusades to the antisemitic articles of the French paper *La Croix* in the nineteenth century, the history of the cross's disastrous effects on Jews, according to Carroll, led not inevitably, but logically to the Nazi genocide. Confronting his audience with this bleak narrative, Carroll argues that the symbol of the cross should be, if not abandoned, at least deemphasized.[7] What he calls the "Church's fixation on the death of Jesus"[8] should give way to a recovery of alternative ways to interpret not only the death but also the life of Jesus. The Carmelite cross, finally, should be removed from the camp in Auschwitz by the Church in a ritual of penance.[9]

I agree with Carroll's claim that the Carmelite cross is unacceptable because its prominence violates the right of Jewish visitors to remember the dead on their own terms. But I disagree with Carroll's sweeping claim that the symbol of the cross should be pushed to the background of contemporary Christian imagination. It seems to me that from a Christian perspective, it is quite impossible not to make the associative link between Auschwitz and Jesus' crucifixion, regardless of how problematic it is. And I would argue that rather than prohibiting or repressing this link, we should examine its various motivations, contexts, and implications. This argument is not only based on my observation that despite all the good reasons not to Christianize the Holocaust by interpreting it as a twentieth-century calvary, the cross at Auschwitz keeps reappearing at so many corners of contemporary Christian life. More importantly, I base my argument on the critical approach to Holocaust literature developed by the Jewish scholar James Young in his groundbreaking work *Writing and Rewriting the Holocaust.*[10] Young persuasively argues that post-Holocaust generations cannot know and understand the events of the Holocaust without the help of the figures and narratives of their own cultural and religious reservoirs. He writes: "How victims of the Holocaust grasped and responded to events as they unfolded around them depended on the available tropes and figures of their time no less than our own responses now depend on the figures available to us in a post-Holocaust era."[11] Holocaust remembrance is shaped by the particular sense-making strategies available through the language and traditions of those who seek to remember. If this is true, and if this insight applies also to people whose main figures are Christian, then the Christianization of the Holocaust—at least to a certain degree—is inevitable. When the liturgical committee in Germany configured Jesus' walk to Golgatha against the background of Auschwitz-Birkenau, it was caught up in this inevitable process. The interpretive link between Jesus' passion and Auschwitz was made and will continue to be made, appropriate or not, because Jesus' passion stands at the heart of the Christian tradition.

It is precisely this centrality of Jesus' passion that Carroll wants to relinquish. Yet his own autobiographical narrative unwittingly testifies to the reasons why such an endeavor would be futile. As Carroll tells his readers, the impulse for writing his history of the cross came to him during a visit at the memorial camp in Auschwitz. Walking through the exhibits, Carroll was suddenly struck by the sight of the tall Carmelite cross:

> In coming to the death camp, I had resolved to guard against conditioned responses, even as I felt them: the numbness, the choked-back grief, the supreme sentimentality of a self-justifying Catholic guilt. I had visited the barracks, the ovens, the naked railway platform, the stark field of chimneys, more or less in control of my reaction. But before the cross some-

> thing else took over. Even as I knew to guard against the impulse to "Christianize the Holocaust," I was doing it—by looking into this abyss through the lens of a faith that has the cross embedded in it like a sighting device.[12]

Carroll's experience exemplifies what Young would call the inevitable and often involuntary process of grasping the events of the Holocaust through one's own tropes and figures. In Carroll's terms, the cross is his "sighting device," even though he hates the fact and later in the paragraph calls it an "imprisonment" inside Christian categories.

What interests me especially about this narrative is Carroll's loss of control at the sight of the cross. After being able to walk through the exhibits with a strained sense of composure, he sees the cross and is suddenly overcome by something more powerful than the fear of dubious emotions: "something else took over." Carroll does not say what exactly took over, but I surmise that his self-control broke down because the cross forced him to make a connection between the horrific things he saw while walking through the camp exhibits and his own self. As long as he was not confronted with something that concerned himself, Carroll was able to keep the horror at a distance. But at the sight of the cross, Carroll could not not be moved, despite the sentimentality of it all, because the cross stands at the heart of his own identity as a Catholic.

Carroll's final interpretation of this moment sounds as though he regained his composure: "Yet I reacted as I imagine a Jew might have. The cross here was simply wrong."[13] Against this straightforward conclusion I want to retain the important ambivalence expressed in Carroll's narrative. Carroll did not react like a Jew but like a Christian. He does love the cross, as he tells his readers, and this is the reason why the cross was capable of breaking through his detached posture, releasing a considerable amount of energy that led him, after all, to write a 600-page genealogy of the cross at Auschwitz. The Carmelite cross in the memorial camp may be "simply wrong." But the cross at Auschwitz as configured in Carroll's mind was valuable. How else could he have worked through the legacy of the Holocaust if not by exploring the relationship between these events and his own beliefs? Carroll's critique of the cross, in my opinion, is the result of an important mourning process that would not have been possible without bringing the cross in relation to the Holocaust.

I would not want to ban the cross from Holocaust remembrance. Instead I would like to suggest a shift that again is inspired by the work of Young. For Young the task is not to "remove the Holocaust from the realm of imagination, . . . and place it off-limits" (p. 133) so that it cannot be appropriated by the wrong interpretive tradition.[14] Instead Young wants to examine the precise meanings created and reflected in such interpretations and to study how they affect people's understanding of the Holocaust and their actions.

This approach would take a close look at specific configurations that use the Christian cross as a "sighting device" for Holocaust remembrance, while keeping in mind that not all configurations are the same. It would ask about the social and political context of each "cross at Auschwitz" and include in its analysis the social location and perspective of the person or the group who holds on to it. This approach would thoroughly differentiate between Polish nuns wishing to pray for the dead within the borders of a former death camp and German ecumenical youth groups meditating on Jesus' passion on the streets of their hometown with pictures of Auschwitz in front of them.[15] It would differentiate between an attempt to integrate the crucifixion into the long history of Jewish suffering and another that interprets the cross at Auschwitz under the paradigm of liberation theology. None of these configurations of the cross is innocent, but all of them create powerful meanings in the minds of contemporary Christians, and the particularities of these meanings, as well as the differences between them, should be examined.

This approach would ask not only how the events of the Holocaust are interpreted through the Christian trope of the cross but also how the Christian trope, in its turn, is recast as it is brought into the shadow of Auschwitz. The Christian trope of the cross is no monolith but grew over many centuries based on narratives that refuse to deliver clear, single meanings. The New Testament traditions about the death of Jesus are complex, often contradictory, the result of the hermeneutic work of different early Christian writers and communities, consisting of diverging plots, themes, and character constructions. Each post-Holocaust reach for these traditions necessarily makes choices and is an interpretive activity in its own right. To be able to examine and assess this activity, a nuanced grasp of the biblical passion narratives is necessary. What is called for, in other words, are the skills of New Testament scholars! In fact, I would like to propose that the approach to Christian Holocaust remembrance described above should be introduced into biblical studies. It seems to me that the hermeneutic movement between New Testament traditions and the events of the Holocaust could be an important topic for post-Holocaust biblical scholarship.

II

An explicitly post-Holocaust reading of the passion narratives has been offered by biblical scholar John Dominic Crossan in his book *Who Killed Jesus?*[16] Like Carroll, Crossan is motivated by the recognition that the Christian passion stories,

> have been the seedbed for Christian anti-Judaism. And without that Christian anti-Judaism, lethal and genocidal European anti-Semitism would have been either impossible or at least not widely successful. What

> was at stake in those passion stories, in the long haul of history, was the Jewish Holocaust.[17]

Because he is a biblical scholar, Crossan's response to this critical insight does not take the form of a history of the church, but leads him to investigate the historical background of the passion narratives. Crossan wants to find out how much these narratives are grounded in historical reality. His answer is: not very much. Most of what we read in the gospels are not actual events faithfully remembered and diligently reported but the result of what Crossan calls "prophecy historicized."[18] To come to terms with the traumatic event of Jesus' shameful execution, Jewish Christians tried to imagine, to write and rewrite this event as though Jesus' suffering and dying fulfilled biblical prophecy. According to Crossan, Jesus' learned followers went to their sacred Scripture, the Hebrew Bible, and looked for cues that would allow them to interpret the crucifixion as a meaningful event.

> Their questions are these: Was Jesus' death a divine judgment against his program? Did God destroy Jesus? How does it now stand between God and Jesus? And the question above all was this: Do *we* have a future? Like any people asking if they have a future, they went back into their past to see what it might indicate. Searching the Scriptures was internally constitutive for their faith and their identity. . . . They knew, of course, what they were looking for in those texts. Could God's Holy One (by whatever title) be killed, and what sort of vindication would God obtain for him?[19]

These early Christian scribes laid the groundwork for the passion stories driven by the desire to have in Jesus not a cursed victim of Roman state terror but God's Holy One. Under this hypothesis Crossan demonstrates how the different scenes of the passion narratives were shaped in creative interaction with biblical texts.

Unlike Carroll, Crossan never draws clear conclusions from his analysis for our post-Holocaust time. Although he repeatedly emphasizes the ethical responsibility of biblical scholars to make a general public aware of the passion stories' lack of historicity,[20] Crossan never indicates how Christians should integrate his scholarly theses into their post-Holocaust consciousness, granted they agree with them. How, for example, should a Christian community willing to learn from Crossan respond to his historical judgment that the trials of Jesus so central to the passion stories are literary creations based on Psalm 2 and never actually took place?[21] Perhaps Crossan hopes that once uncovered as "unhistorical" the destructive tale of the Jews as "Christ-killers" will gradually lose its persuasive power among Christians. Perhaps he hopes that Christian communities will modify, or rather correct, their passion memories according to his findings by dropping, for example, from their Good Friday liturgy any reference to the alleged Jewish cries "Crucify him!" during the Roman trial.

I believe that these are legitimate hopes. But I also think that Crossan fails to deal with the ways in which the canonical passion stories informed and will continue to inform Christians after the Holocaust, whether or not these stories are historical. Crossan's historical-critical study needs to be opened up to a genuinely hermeneutic approach to the passion narratives, one that reckons with the contemporary effects of biblical texts. To do so, I would like to point to the striking parallel between the interpretive activity that Crossan ascribes to first-century Jewish Christian writers coming to terms with Jesus' violent death and the interpretive activity of both Jews and Christians writing to come to terms with the Holocaust. I would like to argue that regardless of how disparate the Nazi genocide and Jesus' crucifixion are, the two events in their aftermath triggered literary responses that are at least structurally comparable. Not all, but some twentieth-century writers, in responding to the events of the Holocaust, have taken recourse to biblical texts. And not unlike those first-century writers who interpreted Jesus' death in creative interaction with their sacred Scriptures, some writers and poets interpreted the events of the Holocaust by rereading and rewriting biblical tropes and narratives.[22] Searching the Scriptures, in other words, is a hermeneutic activity that distinguishes, however differently, both postcrucifixion and post-Holocaust literature.[23]

One of the better known *Jewish* examples of post-Holocaust literature is Elie Wiesel's midrash "The Sacrifice of Isaac: A Survivor's Story."[24] Of all the biblical narratives perhaps none resonates more powerfully and disturbingly with Wiesel's Holocaust experiences than the story of God commanding Abraham to kill his son Isaac as a burnt offering on Mount Moriah. "This very ancient story," Wiesel writes, "is still our own and we shall continue to be bound to it in the most intimate way. We may not know it, but every one of us, at one time or another, is called upon to play a part in it."[25] Wiesel writes that Jews have been bound to "this very ancient story" for centuries due to the never-ending experience of destruction. Through the experience of the Holocaust, the story gained new relevance: "We have known Jews who, like Abraham, witnessed the death of their children; who, like Isaac, lived the *Akeda* in their flesh."[26] The Holocaust is the reference point for Wiesel's thoughts on "The Sacrifice of Isaac" and invigorates his retelling and reimagining of the biblical story. This process crystallizes itself in Wiesel's almost explicit identification with the figure of Isaac:

> As the first survivor, he had to teach us, the future survivors of Jewish history, that it is possible to suffer and despair an entire lifetime and still not give up the art of laughter. Isaac, of course, never freed himself from the

> traumatizing scenes that violated his youth, the holocaust had marked him and continued to haunt him forever. Yet he remained capable of laughter.[27]

One finds here, as Young points out, not only an interpretation of Holocaust experiences through an ancient biblical text but also a reinterpretation of the biblical text through Wiesel's own experiences of surviving Auschwitz and Buchenwald. "Wiesel necessarily transmits his own story,"[28] Young writes, and thereby the biblical story "is recast and reunderstood in light of new experiences, taking on new, often startling, meanings and significance."[29] That Isaac "never freed himself from the traumatizing scenes" on Mount Moriah is an insight that we will not find in the biblical text. It is Wiesel's own experience of survival that brings this insight to the story. Because Wiesel knows what it means to survive traumatic events, he is able to raise a new question, and that is the question of how Isaac was able to continue to live (and laugh) after having almost been slaughtered by his own father.

Wiesel's post-Holocaust midrash contains an important aside that is relevant to my concerns. In an effort to guard his reading against Christian appropriations, Wiesel draws clear boundaries between the sacrifice of Isaac and the crucifixion of Jesus. Isaac, for him, is *not* a precursor of Christ, because

> In Jewish tradition man cannot use death as a means of glorifying God. . . . To invoke the *Akeda* is tantamount to calling for mercy—whereas from the beginning Golgatha has served as pretext for countless massacres of sons and fathers cut down together by sword and fire in the name of a word that considered itself synonymous with love.[30]

Jesus' crucifixion is not an adequate figure for Wiesel, not only because the idea of a redemptive death runs against Jewish beliefs, but also because of the Christian symbol's violent legacy.

Wiesel rejects Golgatha as an interpretive figure; but when a *Christian* writer turns to the Scriptures in an effort to come to terms with the Holocaust, he or she will inevitably find Golgatha in his or her fund of figures. The biblical reservoir of contemporary Christians, in contrast to the one of Wiesel and in contrast also to the one of first-century Jewish Christians, consists not only of the Hebrew Scriptures but also of the New Testament. "Searching the Scriptures" for Christians means searching both "Old" and "New" Testament. A Christian writer's list of biblical archetypes will include next to Adam, Abel, Isaac, Moses, and Job, the characters of the New Testament, not only Jesus, but also Peter, John, Mary, Herod, and Pilate. And of all the biblical narratives available to Christians, perhaps none resonates more powerfully and disturbingly with the events of the Holocaust than the passion narratives.

III

I take it to be essential, then, to differentiate between *Jewish* and *Christian* post-Holocaust readings of Scripture. Searching the Scriptures will produce different meanings depending on who is doing this work and what is meant by "Scriptures." Although Jewish writers often struggle with the failure of biblical archetypes to adequately capture the massive scale of suffering during the Holocaust,[31] Christian writers are confronted with problems of their own. Most importantly, and as Wiesel himself suggests, Christians who turn to the New Testament would have to reckon with the legacy of anti-Judaism that comes with so many of these Christian canonical texts. Christians trying to understand the Holocaust through the lens of the passion narratives would have to deal with the fact that these stories, in Crossan's words, "send people out to kill,"[32] and thus with the irony that the very "Scripture" informing one's post-Holocaust reflections fueled Christian hatred against Jews in the first place. A Christian post-Holocaust writer necessarily draws from a poisoned religious reservoir, from a tainted tradition.[33]

Most Christian writers, moreover, while approaching the Scriptures in an effort to remember the Holocaust, will bring to this work experiences, concerns, and memories that differ from the ones informing Wiesel's *midrashim.* This is especially true when these writers are not only *Christian* but also *German* and therefore are informed by experiences, concerns, and memories arising out of the perpetrator culture.[34]

One such Christian post-Holocaust writer is Marie Luise Kaschnitz. Born in 1901, Kaschnitz was in her 30s and 40s when the events of the Holocaust took place. In the grand scheme of things, and according to her own self-understanding after the war, she belonged to the side of the perpetrators. At the center of Kaschnitz's Holocaust poetry are not experiences of suffering and victimization, as is the case with Wiesel's writings, but a sense of having become guilty. Haunted by feelings of shame and failure, she, too, felt the impulse to write about her experiences during the Holocaust, and as a Christian she did so by accessing a Christian fund of figures. The following lines are from Kaschnitz's poetic cycle "Zoon Politikon," published in the mid-1960s.[35]

> Why did the disciples pretend to sleep on the Mount of Olives?
> Why did nothing really get better since Auschwitz?
> To be of evil.
> That's what we are.
> We are of evil.

In these lines Kaschnitz slowly approaches the notion of "being evil," trying it on, so to speak, testing it, and eventually embracing the attribute, assigning it to herself. The insight that "we are of evil" can be understood as the main theme of the entire poetic cycle whose sociopolitical context are the Auschwitz trials that took place in Frankfurt in the mid-1960s. These trials were West Germany's most prominent proceedings against former Nazis and brought the evidence of Nazi atrocities back into public discourses and into daily news coverage. The trials had a particularly powerful impact on Kaschnitz, because she attended the proceedings.[36] Her lines exemplify how Germans, faced with the horrific crimes committed in the name of their country, understood the horror from their own perspective and with recourse to their Christian tradition.

The figures that apparently most resonated with Kaschnitz's experience are Jesus' disciples in the garden of Gethsemane: "Why did the disciples pretend to sleep on the Mount of Olives?" This question alludes to the following episode, differently recounted in the synoptic gospel. Here is the episode, according to the gospel of Mark:

> They went to a place called Gethsemane; and [Jesus] said to his disciples: "Sit here while I pray." He took with him Peter and James and John, and began to be distressed and agitated. And said to them, "I am deeply grieved, even to death; remain here, and keep awake." And going a little farther, he threw himself on the ground and prayed that, if it were possible, the hour might pass from him. He said, "Abba, Father, for you all things are possible; remove this cup from me; yet not what I want, but what you want." He came and found them sleeping; and he said to Peter, "Simon, are you asleep? Could you not keep awake one hour? Keep awake and pray that you may not come into the time of trial; the spirit indeed is willing, but the flesh is weak." And again he went away and prayed, saying the same words. And once more he came and found them sleeping, for their eyes were very heavy; and they did not know what to say to him. He came a third time and said to them, "Are you still sleeping and taking your rest? Enough! The hour has come; the Son of Man is betrayed into the hands of sinners. Get up, let us be going. See, my betrayer is at hand." (Mark 14:32–42)

This episode recounts Jesus' anticipation of his coming arrest, suffering, and dying. Asking his disciples to stay awake during these hours, Jesus leaves them to pray and returns to them three times. Three times the disciples have fallen asleep.

According to John Dominic Crossan, early Jewish Christian exegetes created the Gethsemane story with the help of their sacred Scriptures.[37] Crossan demonstrates that Mark 14:32–42 was shaped against the background of a story found in II Samuel 15–17, whose protagonist is not Jesus but King David. The story tells how David, threatened by his son, betrayed by his adviser, and abandoned by many of the Israelites, went up to the Mount of Olives weeping.

Crossan argues that the early scribes used this story as a model for imagining the hours before Jesus' arrest: like the great king of Israel, Jesus went up to the Mount of Olives, betrayed, abandoned, and sorrowful. I would like to make a similar argument with regard to Kaschnitz's postwar poem: just as the first-century scribes took recourse to the King David story in their efforts to interpret Jesus' suffering, the twentieth-century poet Kaschnitz took recourse to the Jesus story in her efforts to interpret the events of the Holocaust:

> Why did the disciples pretend to sleep on the Mount of Olives?
> Why did nothing really get better since Auschwitz?

What triggers this linkage between Gethsemane and Kaschnitz's own time is the theme of failure. The disciples fail to meet Jesus' request to keep awake; Kaschnitz's post-Holocaust world fails to learn from the crimes of Auschwitz.

The theme of failure is also prominent in one of Kaschnitz's self-reflections, which I believe offer important clues for understanding her poem. In her autobiographical essay, "Wie man da stand," Kaschnitz describes her life in Nazi Germany in the 1940s.[38] She spent the war years in Frankfurt, withdrawn into an internalized, passive opposition to the Nazi regime. As her essay indicates, Kaschnitz listened to foreign radio stations, hoped that Hitler would lose the war, but never engaged in acts of resistance that would put her own life in danger.[39] Kaschnitz's failure to actively help her threatened fellow human beings, her unwillingness to take risks, produced a growing feeling of unease, a simmering guilty conscience, which, however, did not lead her to break out of her paralysis.[40] It was only after the war that she was able to account for these feelings.

Against the background of these self-critical reflections, the sleeping disciples on the Mount of Olives gain interpretive power. Kaschnitz, it seems to me, reads herself through the figure of the disciples not unlike the first-century Christian scribes read Jesus through the figure of King David. Deploying the sleeping disciples, Kaschnitz resorts to the one figure in her biblical reservoir that perhaps best captures her experience during the war. The sleeping disciples turn into a figure for herself, the non-Jewish German, minding her own business while people close by are arrested and deported. Sleep itself turns into a metaphor for the "evil" with which Kaschnitz identifies a few lines later. "To be of evil" for her means not to be cruel but to have "very heavy eyes"; not to enjoy other people's suffering but to be dumbfounded when asked for support. As we read in Mark 14:40: "[Jesus] came and found them sleeping, for their eyes were very heavy; and they did not know what to say to him." Once the linkage between Kaschnitz and the disciples is made, the Gethsemane story comes to life casting light on Kaschnitz's self-understanding.

But Kaschnitz not only lets the biblical story cast light on her experience. She also reinterprets the biblical story and thereby engages in the same process that Young describes with regard to Wiesel's midrash: the biblical story "is recast and reunderstood in light of new experiences, taking on new, often startling, meanings and significance." Kaschnitz does not faithfully copy the sleeping disciples as they appear in the gospels. Instead she modifies them in a striking way:

> Why did the disciples pretend to sleep on the Mount of Olives?

There is no indication in the biblical story that the disciples *pretend to* sleep. To the contrary, in light of Mark's overall portrayal of Jesus' disciples as weak and fallible, their threefold surrender to sleepiness, despite Jesus' request, makes perfect sense. But Kaschnitz turns the disciples' failure into a willful act thereby transforming the biblical characters for her own interpretive purposes. Kaschnitz's question suggests that the disciples, in fact, were not asleep but wide awake, since a person pretending to sleep is usually anything but sleepy. With this modification Kaschnitz brings new meaning both to the story of Gethsemane and her own biography. Sleep, her question suggests, can be a deliberate disguise allowing one not to interfere in a dangerous or uncomfortable situation. Kaschnitz's poem evokes the disturbing scenario that the disciples did not spend their last hours with Jesus in blissful ignorance but instead knew quite well of the danger threatening Jesus' life and peace of mind—just as Kaschnitz was aware of the terror going on around her: "of course it is not true that we did not know anything, one did hear this or that. . . . Small warnings, small admonitions and sleepless nights. I, a coward by nature and equipped with a tormenting power of the imagination, kept my mouth shut."[41] The sleeping/sleepless German writer in Frankfurt interprets and is interpreted by the sleeping/sleepless disciples on the Mount of Olives.

Kaschnitz's poetry is not unproblematic. If there is some validity to my reading, her lines imply a comparability between Jesus' abandonment by the disciples and the abandonment of German Jews during the war and thus bring with them all the troublesome issues that come with any attempt to interpret the Holocaust through the lens of Jesus' passion. But to speak in the words of James Young, we should "focus not on these writers' poetic license to others' suffering but rather on the meanings created and reflected in such figures" (p. 99). Just as Wiesel is intimately bound to the story of Isaac's sacrifice, Kaschnitz is bound to the story of Gethsemane and plays a part in it that would be worthwhile to explore more thoroughly than I was able to in this limited space.

IV

In this essay I have tried to make a case for introducing an approach into New Testament studies capable of exploring Kaschnitz's engagements with both the

Holocaust and Jesus' passion, and of investigating, more generally, what James Young calls the "reciprocal movement between [biblical] figure and events" (p. 106). Such a post-Holocaust hermeneutics will not try to delimit proper interpretations of New Testament texts after Auschwitz. Neither will it demonstrate how the events of the Holocaust are properly understood in light of the New Testament.[42] Instead it would focus on the ways in which the Holocaust has already informed Christian readers of the Bible. It would examine how these readers interpreted the Nazi crimes as well as their own position vis-à-vis these crimes, and how, finally, the events of the Holocaust have changed their understanding of biblical texts. "The actions we take in the current world in light of the Holocaust are necessarily predicated on our understanding of the Holocaust," Young writes.[43] Examining the ways in which New Testament texts have influenced Christian efforts to understand the Holocaust is therefore an important task.

NOTES

1. The *Ökumenischer Kreuzweg der Jugend* 2001 is a joint project of the *Bund der Deutschen Katholischen Jugend*, the *Arbeitsgemeinschaft der Evangelischen Jugend*, and the *Arbeitstelle für Jugendseelsorge der deutschen Bischofskonferenz.* The pictures are by German artist Günter Fischermann.
2. One of the sources of this trope is a Christian interpretation of an execution scene recounted in Elie Wiesel's memoir *Night*, trans. Stella Rodway (New York: Bantam Books, 1982). This Christian interpretation can be found in the book's foreword by Catholic writer François Mauriac. The interpretation was transported into theological discourses especially by Jürgen Moltmann and Dorothee Sölle. A well known example of how the trope appeared in art during the Holocaust is "White Crucifixion" by the Jewish artist Marc Chagall. A recent example in the realm of music is "Deus passus" by German composer Wolfgang Rihm.
3. For a powerful critique of the trope as it relates to Wiesel's memoir see Naomi Seidman, "Elie Wiesel and the Scandal of Jewish Rage," *Jewish Social Studies: History, Culture, and Society* 3 (Fall 1996): 12ff.
4. For a detailed discussion of the Jewish–Catholic clash of sensibilities, see James Young, *The Texture of Memory: Holocaust Memorials and Meaning* (New Haven: Yale University Press, 1993).
5. James Carroll, *Constantine's Sword: The Church and the Jews* (New York: Houghton Mifflin Company, 2001).
6. Ibid., 11.
7. Ibid., 587.
8. Ibid., 583.
9. Ibid., 604.
10. James Young, *Writing and Rewriting the Holocaust: Narrative and the Consequences of Interpretation* (Bloomington and Indianapolis: Indiana University Press, 1988).
11. Ibid., 84.
12. Carroll, *Constantine's Sword*, 11–12.
13. Ibid., 12.

14. Young, *Writing and Rewriting*, 133. I am especially inspired by Young's discussion of Sylvia Plath, a non-Jew with no personal connection to the Nazi genocide, who has used in her poetry the suffering of Jews during the Holocaust in order to figure her own personal pain. Plath has been accused of exploiting other people's suffering, which, in its enormity is utterly incomparable with a woman's domestic chagrin. However, instead of policing the use and abuse of her Holocaust metaphors, Young draws attention to the cultural processes that have enabled Plath's poetry.
15. I am examining the German Way of the Cross 2001 under the critical paradigm offered by James Young in another research project.
16. John Dominic Crossan, *Who Killed Jesus? Exposing the Roots of anti-Semitism in the Gospel Story of the Death of Jesus* (San Francisco: HarperSanFrancisco, 1995).
17. Ibid., 35.
18. Ibid., 4. Crossan's idea of the passion narratives as "prophecy historicized" has strongly influenced Carroll's work. See, especially, Carroll, *Constantine's Sword*, 129.
19. Crossan, *Who Killed Jesus?*, 12.
20. Ibid., 35–38.
21. Ibid., 117.
22. I realize that my argument may seem dangerous to some. If Crossan's work is centered around a denial of the historicity of the passion narratives, am I not close to suggesting something similar concerning the historical details of the Holocaust? Let me therefore emphasize that I contextualize my argument within contemporary Holocaust literary studies, a discourse based on the insight that the historical facts and events of the Holocaust are always necessarily shaped by their representation. Saul Friedlander's volume *Probing the Limits of Representation* (Cambridge, MA: Harvard University Press, 1992) offers several helpful discussions of this topic and its controversy. See also James Young's critique of those who insist that Holocaust writings be limited to the literal documentation of facts, *Writing and Rewriting*, 15–39.
23. As David Roskies has shown, in *Against the Apocalypse: Responses to Catastrophe in Modern Jewish Culture* (Syracuse: Syracuse University Press, 1999), when Jewish writers after the Holocaust take recourse to biblical archetypes they continue a long and complicated Jewish tradition of responding to catastrophe.
24. Elie Wiesel, *Messengers of God: Biblical Portraits and Legends* (New York: Random, 1976), 69–97.
25. Ibid., 70.
26. Ibid., 95.
27. Ibid., 97.
28. Young, *Writing and Rewriting*, 109.
29. Ibid., 106.
30. Wiesel, *Messengers of God*, 76.
31. Young, *Writing and Rewriting*, 95–98. In his book *Against the Apocalypse*, Roskies offers detailed discussions of how Jewish writers dealt with this challenge both before, during, and after the Holocaust.
32. Crossan, *Who Killed Jesus?*, 32.
33. I borrow the idea of a poisoned reservoir from Eric Santner, *Stranded Objects: Mourning, Memory, and Film in Postwar Germany* (Ithaca: Cornell University Press, 1990). The idea of a tainted tradition is taken from Nancy Harrowitz, ed., *Tainted Greatness: Antisemitism and Cultural Heroes* (Philadelphia: Temple University Press, 1994).
34. See Björn Krondorfer's important argument that we should pay attention to the social locations of post-Holocaust writers, especially when these writers are working from within the

perpetrator culture; Krondorfer, "Of Faith and Faces: Biblical Texts, Holocaust Testimony and German 'After Auschwitz' Theology," in *Strange Fire: Reading the Bible after the Holocaust*, ed. Tod Linafelt (New York: New York University Press; Sheffield: Sheffield Academic Press, 2000), 86–105.

35. Translations of Kaschnitz's poetry are my own, from Marie Luise Kaschnitz, *Zeiten des Lebens* (Freiburg: Herder, 1991), 68–73. I historicize and discuss the first segment of "Zoon Politikon" in *Parables for Our Time: Rereading New Testament Scholarship After the Holocaust* (New York: Oxford University Press, 2002).
36. Dagmar von Gersdorff, *Marie Luise Kaschnitz. Eine Biographie* (Frankfurt: Insel Verlag), 297.
37. Crossan, *Who Killed Jesus?*, 76–78.
38. Marie Luise Kaschnitz, "Wie man da stand," in *Exil, Widerstand, Innere Emigration: Badische Autoren zwischen 1933 und 1945*, ed. Hansgeorg Schmidt-Bergmann (Karlsruhe: Literarische Gesellschaft [Scheffelbund], 1993), 53–57.
39. Ibid., 55.
40. Ibid., 54.
41. Ibid., 57.
42. For a similar argument, see Tod Linafelt, in his introduction to *Strange Fire*, 18.
43. Young, *Writing and Rewriting*, 10–11.

CHAPTER 12

Did Christianity Die in Auschwitz?

ROLF RENDTORFF
(TRANSLATED BY ARMIN SIEDLECKI)

Elie Wiesel once said: "The sincere Christian knows that what died in Auschwitz was not the Jewish people but Christianity."[1] Let us consider this statement more closely. First: The Jewish people did not die in Auschwitz. We would not be gathered here today if the plans of those had worked who conceived of Auschwitz and who made it a reality. Their diabolical machinery of extermination has murdered millions of Jews, but at the same time it contributed to a new form of existence that the Jewish people as a people have assumed: as a Jewish state in the land that has been their home since the time of their biblical ancestors. The Jewish people did not die, and let us thank God that they did not die.

I

But what about Christianity? What does Christianity have to do with Auschwitz? I am convinced that the acknowledgment of a joint responsibility and guilt for Auschwitz is one of the most important realizations, perhaps *the* most important realization by many Christians of the past few decades. Some Christians have been talking about this responsibility for some time now, and more recently the Rhineland Synod of the Evangelical Lutheran Church in Germany has acknowledged it publicly—clear and unmistakably—for the first time in the history of Christianity. Since then the Catholic bishops of Germany as well as other Catholic and Protestant groups have made similar statements. Perhaps such official Church pronouncements are a sign that Christianity has not yet died.

On the other hand, it is precisely here that the truth of Elie Wiesel's statement becomes most obvious. It took the realization and acknowledgment of joint guilt by Christians with regard to the Holocaust to dissuade Christianity from a very dangerous path, which it had pursued for much too long. I think that the remark cited at the beginning of our discussion—as well as many other remarks by Elie Wiesel—contains first and foremost a critique of the way Christians understand themselves.

Christianity perceives itself as a message of love, the love of God for all human beings and the love of human beings for one another; a message of grace in which we share and on which we base our lives. How can a Christian religion that sees itself in this way give rise to enmity against another group of human beings? Is such a form of Christianity not a contradiction unto itself?

Above all, can a Christian religion in which antisemitism has largely become a constitutive element still appeal to him whose name this religion bears: to Jesus, whom we call Christ? In the writings of Elie Wiesel we frequently come across passages in which this question is posed, albeit in passing, as he never considered it to be his place to teach Christianity to Christians. He did, however, see it very much as his responsibility to confront Christians with a critical challenge: Is that which you call Christianity really the message of Jesus? He offers us two possible answers to this question. First, it is Christianity rather than Judaism that has deceived Jesus. In other words, it is not Jesus who is to blame, but his Christian "followers," who did not in fact follow his message, and who established a type of Christianity that led to Auschwitz, where the religion was to reduce itself to absurdity.

The other possible answer is significantly harsher. "Any messiah in whose name men are tortured can only be a false messiah."[2] But is Auschwitz then not only the fault of the Christian followers? Is Christianity itself based on false assumptions? Did Christians indeed follow a false Messiah? Upon closer consideration it becomes evident that these two questions are merely different aspects of a much larger problem. The problem is not the Messiah himself, but rather the way he is seen and understood by his followers and with the implications of such this perception. Could it be that the Christian messiah—the Messiah who became the cornerstone of the Church—is a Messiah in whose name people are tortured and murdered? Certainly not! Torture and killing in the name of the Church, and therefore in the name of her lord Jesus Christ, are completely outside the scope of the foundational scriptures of Christianity, the New Testament.

Unfortunately, this does not make things any easier for us. If we acknowledge the joint responsibility of Christians for the Holocaust, we must ask how it could have happened in the first place. It is not enough to say "Never again," because the roots of the problem are significantly deeper. We can identify certain developments in the history of the Church that have led to such a militant self-understanding of Christianity.

Undoubtedly the first crucial turning point is the alliance of Christianity with political power at the time of the emperor Constantine in the early fourth century, which was very soon followed by the first persecution of Jews through the political authority of a state, which also considered itself Christian. One could say that it is here that Christianity first embarked on a path that continued throughout the entire Middle Ages and that intensified into modernity until it reduced itself to absurdity in Auschwitz.

However, the fact that an alliance of Christianity and political power could yield such anti-Jewish results demonstrates very clearly that the basic elements of Christian antisemitism had already existed before, and that these elements had now merely attained a repeatedly dangerous position of authority. We must therefore go back to the roots of Christian antisemitism.

II

This leads us back to the topic of anti-Judaism in the New Testament. It is no longer disputed by anyone that there are anti-Jewish statements in the New Testament. I am not referring to the disputes between Jesus and the Pharisees. These are so to speak inner-Jewish controversies, in which Jesus is understood as a Jewish teacher and preacher, who argues with other Jewish authorities over the correct interpretation of the scriptures. However, it must also be pointed out that the way in which the Pharisees are portrayed in some New Testament texts already points to an early form of antisemitism. I am thinking, for example, about Matthew 23, where the Pharisees are called hypocrites in a lengthy accusation; it is from here that we derive the usage of the word Pharisee as an invective in our own language.

We have to deal primarily with those texts that speak stereotypically about "the Jews" and that clearly portray the Jewish people in a negative light, especially in antithetical comparison with the Christian community. Some of these texts have left a deep impact on Christian antisemitism. This applies above all to the infamous trial scene in Matthew's gospel:

> So when Pilate saw that he could do nothing, but rather that a riot was beginning, he took some water and washed his hands before the crowd, saying, "I am innocent of this man's blood; see to it yourselves." Then the people as a whole answered, "His blood be on us and on our children!" So he released Barabbas for them; and after flogging Jesus, he handed him over to be crucified. (Matthew 27:24–26; NRSV)

The situation is clear. Pilate is not convinced of Jesus' guilt. The gospel writer Matthew therefore lets a crowd of Jewish people assume responsibility for the execution of Jesus. Because the statement "his blood be on us and on our children" is found only in Matthew, I suggest that we read it in conjunction with another passage in the gospel of Matthew, namely the parable of the great banquet (Matthew 22:1–14). Here I must briefly address an exegetical detail. The parable of the great banquet is found in two of the gospels. In Luke, the invited guests decline their invitation with various excuses whereupon the host rounds up the poor, the blind, the lame, and finally the homeless to let them attend his feast (Luke 14:16–24). Matthew politicizes this parable. The host is a king, who arranges a wedding banquet for his son and who invites prominent guests from other cities. The invited guests, however, do not only decline the invitation, but they mistreat and kill the king's servant who is to remind them of the invitation.

> The king was enraged. He sent his troops, destroyed those murderers, and burned their city. (Matthew 22:7; NRSV)

There can be no doubt that this passage was written in retrospect of the destruction of Jerusalem in 70 C.E. Matthew interprets the destruction of Jerusalem as a punishment for the Jews, which serves at the same time as the fulfilment of what the crowd had called out during the trial of Jesus: The blood of Jesus was on them.

We know the horrifying consequences of this text. However, it is very remarkable that the statement "his blood be on us and on our children" was used as an argument against the Jews only after Christianity had formed its alliance with political power. This shows in a poignant way how Christianity has developed in the wrong direction. In conjunction with political power, theological arguments have become weapons. As André Schwarz-Bart writes in his novel *The Last of the Just*: "They have turned around the cross and have made it into a sword."

It would be an oversimplification to say that this problem no longer concerns us today, because Christianity no longer has any political power. It still remains our problem that antisemitic thought is deeply incorporated into our Christian tradition. Even if we no longer want to draw political consequences from it, the idea "the Jews have killed Jesus" still resonates with many Christians, a resonance that, I would like to believe, appears self-evident only because it is without reflection.

For Christian theology and for the church this antisemitic position has taken the form of a doctrine about the rejection of Israel. It is very strange that especially the apostle Paul is often cited as the author of such a doctrine of rejection, even though he himself vehemently opposed such a position. In the letter to the Romans he writes:

> I ask, then, has God rejected his people? By no means! I myself am an Is-

> raelite, a descendant of Abraham, a member of the tribe of Benjamin. God has not rejected his people whom he foreknew. (Romans 11:1–2a; NRSV)

Here we come across a crucial point: How shall we understand the election of Israel and does this election relate to the self-understanding of the early Christian community.

III

How could the idea arise that God has rejected the Jewish people? After all, Jesus and his disciples, as well as the authors of most New Testament texts, were themselves Jews. Here we encounter a fundamental problem in Christian self-understanding. The first Christians were Jews, and although they themselves never had any doubt about their Jewish identity, the recognition of Jesus as God's Messiah was a crucial conviction for them. This led to a certain line of thought: Jesus was sent by God as the Messiah to God's people Israel; if one part of the people recognize and acknowledge this while the other part does not, then those who recognize and believe it constitute the "true" Israel and the other part does not, or at least not anymore. This way of thinking is characteristic of minorities who do not possess a high degree of confidence. One could call such minorities sects, without attaching any negative connotations to this term. The first Christian community was a sect within Judaism. Its members believed that God's Messiah had appeared in the person of Jesus and that the last days were therefore at hand. Almost by necessity this perception gave rise to the question about the status of the "rest" of Israel, which was in fact the majority.

Soon another problem arose: An increasing number of non-Jews or "Gentiles" joined the Christian community. Because they themselves were not Jews, the question that posed itself for them was of a different kind altogether. They had joined a community that perceived itself as called and chosen by God. This calling, however, was tied to Jesus as God's Messiah. Therefore some or even many of them would probably not have considered the status of Jews who did not believe in Jesus as their concern. Or they might have said: God has rejected Israel and we have now come to assume its place. Such a position, which seems to have existed among Christians in Rome, is addressed by Paul: "God has not rejected his people." Paul thereby acknowledges very explicitly his own Jewishness: "I myself am an Israelite, a member of the tribe of Benjamin."

One can see that in the conflict between the first generation of Jewish Christians and those who came from outside Judaism, the history of Christianity could have taken a different turn. There was an infamous attempt in the second century by Marcion to liberate the church completely from its Jewish origins and especially to dispense of the Old Testament. This would have given rise to a form of Christianity that would not have seen itself as standing in continuity with Judaism. The Church has rejected this attempt and has held on to the Old Testament as an indispensable part of its holy scriptures. At the same time the Church also acknowledged that it cannot understand itself in any other way than in continuity with Judaism. Paul formulates his own self-proclaimed allegiance to the people of Israel by referring to himself explicitly as a descendant of Abraham. He therefore situates himself along this line of continuity.

Again there is the twofold question: What is the status of Christians who are not Jews, and what is the status of Jews who do not recognize Jesus? The Church has frequently answered this question by putting itself in the place of Israel. It turned the Jewish Bible—for Jesus and the first generation of Christians simply "the scriptures"—into the "Old Testament" as part of its new, two-part "Holy Scriptures." The Church understood this first part as a component of the Christian Bible and applied all divine promises and covenants with Israel that can be found in it to itself. It had "disinherited" Israel, or more precisely it believed it was able to disinherit Israel.

Now this theological question is taking on an increasingly more political significance. If the Jewish Bible belongs only to Christians, a decisive element of identity has been taken from the Jewish people. They are declared so to speak as nonexistent. This point has been described very appropriately by the Rhineland Synod:

> Throughout centuries the word "new" has been used against the Jewish people in the interpretation of the Bible. The new covenant was understood in contrast to the old covenant, the new people of God were seen as the replacement of the old people of God. This disregard of the chosenness of Israel and its condemnation to non-existence have persistently characterized theology, teachings and actions of the church until today. We have therefore also become guilty of the physical destruction of the Jewish people.[3]

We have condemned Israel to nonexistence by appropriating for ourselves everything that used to be Israel's and, as we now begin to recognize, still belongs to Israel. Because Christianity and the Church have declared the Jewish people throughout many centuries as nonexistent, there was no resistance by Christians or by the Church when Jews were dispossessed and murdered. On the contrary, there are many examples in the history of the Church in which the persecution, dispossession, and murder of Jewish people took place precisely by Christian sanction and authority.

This is where we must begin our investigation into the question of what it means to be Christian after Auschwitz.

To be sure, there is a plethora of ethical, political, and other aspects that

Christians must also address and discuss, but this is a specifically Christian discourse, which attempts to respond to Elie Wiesel's question.

Why did Christianity declare the Jews nonexistent? I believe the answer is very obvious: because Christians believed (and often still believe) that they occupied the place that the Jewish people should occupy if they existed. Christians believed to be the "new Israel," the "true Israel," which implied that the "old Israel" must have perished in the destruction of Jerusalem by the Romans. Christians believed that God had made a "new covenant" with them that replaced and invalidated the "old covenant." In other words, Christians developed a self-understanding in which there was no room for the existence of the Jewish people.

One of the results of this development was that the existing Jewish religion was hardly talked about at all. When I was a university student, most theological schools did not offer an opportunity to learn anything about contemporary Judaism.

One came across Jews in the Bible, also in the New Testament, but with the destruction of Jerusalem by the Romans they disappeared from the theologian's scope. Occasionally they resurfaced in the history of the Church, usually as victims of persecution by the Church, as, for example, at the beginning of the Crusades, when the crusader horde coming from France turned North and committed many massacres in the Jewish communities in the Rhineland, from Speyer and Worms, Mainz and Cologne, all the way to Xanten and Moers. Another example would be the history of the inquisition, with its climax in the expulsion of Jews from Spain in 1492. However, the Jewish people practically never appeared as a theological problem, let alone a challenge to Christian identity.

I would like to use a concrete example to illustrate another manifestation of this repression of real Judaism from Christian consciousness. Karl Barth was undoubtedly one of the most significant theologians of this century, possibly the most significant and certainly the most influential Protestant theologian in general. In a letter to his student Friedrich-Wilhelm Marquardt, Barth wrote in 1967:

> In personal encounters with actual Jews (even Jewish Christians), as long as I can remember, I always had to suppress a fully irrational aversion, an aversion which I was naturally able to suppress and completely conceal on the basis of all my presuppositions, but which I nonetheless had to suppress and conceal. "Shame," is all I can say to this allergic reaction as it were, but this is how it was and is.[4]

This is how it was and is, an irrational aversion. How many of us, including Christians and theologians, still have difficulty today saying the word "Jew" without embarrassment. Circumscriptions such as "Jewish people" or "Jewish citizens" are common examples of this embarrassment. Many examples could be cited to show that the existence of Jews is still not a matter of fact for many of us, undoubtedly because it confronts our very self-understanding.

IV

We are therefore forced to conclude that if we want to revise our relationship to the Jews and to Judaism, we must also revise our own self-understanding. It does not suffice simply to establish new relationships with the Jewish people. Of course, this is also important, but it does not address the core of the problem. We must begin by returning to the Jewish people what they legitimately possess and what we have illegitimately appropriated for ourselves. To be sure, this task is anything but easy, and it confronts us with questions that Christianity has not yet had to face throughout its history.

A deciding factor is the point of departure we choose for our considerations. We are used to proceeding on Christian assumptions and to formulating certain questions on that basis. Such a question would be: "What is the significance of Judaism from a Christian perspective?" In other words, we would attempt to assign a certain position to Judaism within the intellectual structure of Christianity. But this is precisely what is no longer possible, once we begin to pose such fundamental and radical questions as have now become unavoidable. We must first call into question a number of keystones in this intellectual structure. More than that, we have to invert the question itself. The point is no longer to define Israel from a Christian perspective, but rather to redefine Christianity in light of the continued existence of the Jewish people.

I do not wish to be misunderstood as calling into question the existence of Christianity and of the Church, let alone their right to exist. On the contrary, the perseverance of the Christian Church is a precondition for our new considerations. What must be reconsidered and reformulated is the definition of Christian identity, which must be carried out in view of Israel.

What does this mean? We must attempt to combine two different tasks. On the one hand, we must return to the beginnings of Christian history, to its place of origin, and we must try to understand what had happened at that time. In doing so, we must examine with openness, even critical openness with regard to the New Testament as the foundational document of Christianity, whether decisions that were made in the past can still stand in light of our new and different position, and whether the Church in subsequent centuries has remained true to the decisions of the New Testament. The second task then must be to put any new insights that result from this examination into appropriate, theological formulations.

Let me begin the first task with a quotation. My first teacher with regard to Christian–Jewish relations was Krister Stendahl, the great Swedish-American theologian, who had shaped the Divinity School at Harvard for decades. In 1967 he made the following observations about a colloquium at Harvard.

> Something went wrong in the beginning. I say "went wrong," for I am not convinced that what happened in the severing of the relations between Judaism and Christianity was the good and positive will of God. Is it not possible for us to recognize that we parted ways not according to, but against the will of God?
>
> I know that this is a strange way to speak. I know that it may be branded as historical romanticism, an attempt "to turn the clock back." But why call it "to turn the clock back"? Why not say instead that the time has come for us to find the alternatives which are the theological expressions of our repentance and of our understanding as they force themselves upon us today?[5]

At the time I was very impressed by these statements, which have made a lasting impression on me. Something went wrong in the beginning. What could have gone wrong? Stendahl is asking if the separation between Judaism and Christianity was necessary and if it corresponds to the will of God. In response I would suggest the following answer: Early Christianity should have maintained its cognizance that was part of Judaism.

This is, in my estimation, the decisive point of departure for a search of lost alternatives. To illustrate the extent to which this alternative had been excluded, I quote from another great theologian of the twentieth century. In his famous series of lectures *The Essence of Christianity* delivered during the winter semester of 1899/1900 at the University of Berlin, Adolf von Harnack described the appearance of Jesus:

> He immediately confronted the official leaders of the people, and with them the common nature of humanity in general. They imagined God as a despot, who watches over the ceremony of his house-order, while he lived in the presence of God. They perceived him only in his laws, which they had turned into a labyrinth of ravines, false paths and secret side-exits, while he saw and felt him everywhere. They possessed thousands of his commandments in which they believed to be able to recognize him, while he had only his one commandment, by which he knew him. They had turned religion into an earthly business—nothing is more reprehensible—, while he proclaimed the living God and the nobility of the soul.[6]

Jesus himself becomes an anti-Jew, and the Jews are but the reprehensible counterpart to Jesus!

In subsequent decades, these lectures by Harnack appeared in no less than 14 printings and were translated in as many languages. His remarks are therefore quite representative of a general Christian position at the turn of the century. They exemplify in a very explicit way the fundamental oppositions between Judaism and Christianity according to Harnack and many of his contemporaries. They also illustrate the effects of the negative image of the Pharisees in the New Testament mentioned earlier. I will decline to comment on the style of the description of Jesus as reflecting the pathos of the turn of the century, but I would add a few more remarks by Harnack about the subsequent development of Christianity.

> It was Paul who led the Christian religion out of Judaism.... It was he who considered the gospel as something new, which supersedes legalistic religion. . . . Paul contrasted [this new religion] with the Israelite religion: Christ is the fulfilment of the law. Not only did this new religion survive uprooting and transition, it even proved to be inherently oriented towards transition, as it went on to offer strength and support to the Roman empire and all of Western culture.

Another passage again concerns the disciples of Jesus, who followed the new teachings of Paul:

> History distinguished here quickly and with unmistakable clarity the core from the shell. The shell was the Jewish context of Jesus' message. We must also regard as shell certain verses like "I was sent only to the lost sheep of the house of Israel." [Matthew 15:24] Through the power of Christ's spirit, the disciples were able to break through such limitations.[7]

I have deliberately chosen to cite this representative voice of Christianity from the turn of the century more fully, because it shows quite clearly how Christianity, or at least the liberal, Protestant majority in Germany and in the Western world, understood itself at the time. I could have quoted theologians of later generations, from Rudolf Bultmann to the present, who give expression to the same basic understanding about the relationship between Jews and Christians. Harnack's comments about the impact of Christianity on the Roman empire also demonstrate that he viewed the alliance between Christianity and political power as something quite positive.

It is not my place to chide earlier generations. On the contrary, I would like to point out again it was only after the Holocaust, after the terrible misuse of this power in conjunction with the growing tradition of Christian antisemitism, that we—Christians of our generation—were able to recognize these misguided developments. *That* is the Christian religion that died in Auschwitz.

For this reason Stendahl's call for a search for lost alternatives is so important. Stendahl himself has made a first, still somewhat hesitant attempt to point out the direction that a new beginning could take.

> Even if we were granted that our intentions were serious when we describe our plea as one borne out of repentance and humility—for we are the ones to ask that we be recognized as a peculiar kind of Jews, and it is up to "Judaism" to see if that is possible—it must be recognized that such a question is a new one, and utterly unexpected from our divided and common history.[8]

At the time, this was indeed a strange way to speak, but it shows very clearly where Stendahl saw the critical turn in the wrong direction. It was precisely what for Harnack—and for many before and after him—constituted the "essence of Christianity": the separation from Judaism, the surpassing of Judaism, the fundamental contrast to Judaism. To this "essence" Stendahl responds with the antithesis: We must return to our Jewish origins.

It is not sufficient to acknowledge that Christianity has its origins in Judaism, because the critical question concerns the relations between the two after the establishment of an independent Christian religion. It also not enough to say that Jesus was born a Jew, because it leaves all possibilities about his later development open. Pilate knew it, and he inscribed it on the cross for all posterity: Jesus was crucified as the "king of the Jews." Jesus was and remains a Jew.

Several years ago, David Flusser, an important Jewish Jesus scholar in Jerusalem, published a book with the title *Christianity—A Jewish Religion.* It is a provocative title, surely unpopular with many, which Flusser justifies as follows:

> Historically speaking, Christianity could only develop into a world-religion, because it had been . . . a Jewish faith and a Jewish religion. . . . It is quite understandable that Christianity spread among non-Jews, as many Gentiles were attracted to Jewish monotheism with its belief in an ethical deity, the loving concern for one's neighbor, the care for the poor and disabled, as well as its reverence for life. These Gentiles were able to accept Christianity because Judaism had already established itself as a religion, and because many who converted to Christianity were already familiar with Judaism and were knowledgeable about the Jewish scriptures, as Paul informs us.[9]

Flusser's suggestions that Christians are peculiar kinds of Jews and that their faith is a Jewish faith sounds almost like a direct answer to Stendahl. The common ground between the two is above all the conviction that the first, fundamental step toward a redefinition of Christianity must be the close and insoluble fellowship with Judaism. A Christian religion that attempts to define itself without this fellowship exists only in a vacuum.

Implicit in this position is the impossibility of any Christian form antisemitism, because this would compromise the very foundations of Christianity. Thus the first quality that should characterize a new Christian identity should be the cognizance of its Jewish roots. It is here that we must begin our discourse about the Christian affiliation with Judaism and the implications of this affiliation.

The treatment of these questions is still very much in the beginning phase, and there are only a few who have tackled them, because they touch in fact the very foundations of the definition of Christian self-understanding. Let me begin with the critical point: If we proceed from the assumption that the Jewish people stand in direct continuity with God's chosen people Israel in the Hebrew Bible, then they can also claim the biblical designation "people of God." This raises the question whether we as Christians can also lay claim to this designation, as the Church has done for centuries with much matter-of-factness. This shows again that we could do certain things only as long as we did not acknowledge that the people of Israel continue to exist with unbroken continuity. Can we still do it now that we have once again become aware of the real embodied existence of the Jewish people?

This question seems to lead us into a dilemma. If we continue to refer to ourselves, or to Christian religion, or to the Church, as the people of God, we are taking away from the Jewish people what is rightfully theirs. If we decline to apply this designation to ourselves, it could seem as if we were pulling the rug out from under our own feet. The designation "people of God" is indeed very significant, and the idea of chosenness is closely connected to it, to use only one example. But could we perhaps view ourselves as members of the people of God alongside the Jews and together with the Jews? Can the idea and the concept of the "people of God" support such an extension?

The Rhineland Synod has tried to make a distinction in its declaration of 1980.

> We believe in the continued election of the Jewish people as people of God and recognize that the church through Jesus Christ has entered into the God's covenant with his people.[10]

The concept of covenant is used very deliberately here and is explicitly distinguished from the concept "people of God." The latter is reserved for the Jewish people, who alone are called "people of God." Christians have entered the covenant together with the people of God. This declaration is governed by the intention not to take away from the Jewish people what is rightfully theirs, but at the same time to situate the Church as close as possible to the biblical tradition and to emphasize its bond with the Jewish people. In recent years this question has prompted lively discussions, in which biblical–theological studies intersect with considerations about the fundamental relationship between Christians and Jews and between the Church and Israel.[11]

Another consideration is found in Friedrich-Wilhelm Marquardt's "Prolegomena zur Dogmatik," which bears the poetic title "Theology's Distress and Visitation."[12] He uses the image of Abraham's children to describe the ongoing relationship between Israel and the Church. We have already seen that Paul explicitly emphasizes his descent from Abraham, and in the letter to the Galatians he explains in detail that all who believe are children of Abraham (Galatians 3). This could also be an approach to the question of how we could think about and give expression to the affiliation of Christians and the Church with the divine history of election without interfering with the rights of the Jewish people.

As I said before, we are only now beginning to deal with this question, and there are few who have addressed it. However, the first step is always the most important, and in conclusion I would like to direct our attention once more to it. Christian anti-Judaism, which gave rise to antisemitism, has its roots in the belief that Christians can assume the position of Israel. This was possible only by theologically disowning Israel, a step that soon proved to be not only a theological development, but that also involved a "condemnation to non-existence," as the Rhineland Synod has put it. Because Israel no longer existed theologically and in the faith of the Church, there was no reason to be concerned about the fate of Jews who were living among us.

This is the dark side of the history of the Church. At the same time, Christianity has also invalidated a very crucial element of its own identity, by forgetting its own Jewish roots, or to be more precise, the fundamental Jewish element in its own identity. We must try to restore both. In this way, the new insights that we have won through the acknowledgment and confession of Christian guilt for the Holocaust could help Christians to develop a new self-understanding, which is anchored in new ways in its origin and its roots.

NOTES

1. R. McAfee Brown, *Elie Wiesel: Messenger for all Humanity* (Notre Dame: University of Notre Dame Press, 1983), 171.
2. Elie Wiesel, *The Oath*, trans. Marion Wiesel (New York: Random House, 1973), 138.
3. Rolf Rendtorff and H. H. Henrix, eds., *Die Kirchen und das Judentum: Dokumente von 1945–1985* (München: Christian Kaiser Verlag, 1988), 595.
4. Karl Barth, *Briefe 1961–1968: Gesamtausgabe V/6*, eds. H. Stoevesandt and J. Fangmeier (Zürich: Theologischer Verlag, 1975), 420–421.
5. Krister Stendahl, "Judaism and Christianity II—After a Colloquium and a War," *Harvard Divinity Bulletin* (New Series) 1 (Autumn 1967): 2–9.

6. Adolph von Harnack, *Das Wesen des Christentums* (München: Siebenstern Taschenbuch, 1964 [1900]), 42.
7. Ibid., 110–112.
8. Stendahl, "Judaism and Christianity II," 6.
9. David Flusser, *Das Christentum—eine jüdische Religion* (München: Kösel Verlag, 1990), 165.
10. Rendtorff and Henrix, eds., *Die Kirchen und das Judentum*, 594.
11. Cf. articles by Rendtorff, Crüsemann, and Zenger in *Kirche und Israel* 9 (1994), vols. 1–2.
12. Friedrich-Wilhelm Marquardt, *Von Elend und Heimsuchung der Theologie: Prolegomena zur Dogmatik* (München: Kaiser Verlag, 1988), esp. §6.

PART IV

Jews and Gentiles, in the New Testament and Today

CHAPTER 13

The Passion after the Holocaust

JOHN DOMINIC CROSSAN

> It is vital that the Passion Play be continued at Oberammergau; for never has the menace of Jewry been so convincingly portrayed as in this presentation of what happened in the times of the Romans. There one sees in Pontius Pilate a Roman racially and intellectually so superior, that he stands out like a firm, clean rock in the middle of the whole muck and mire of Jewry.
>
> —*Adolf Hitler* (July 5, 1942)[1]

How should we Christians read the passion of Jesus after the Holocaust? How do we face that story now when we see within it roots that enabled if not caused such terrible evil? Anything said by one Jewish group against any or all other ones in that first century was a fight within the family of Judaism, a strife of options within an ancient people, land, and tradition under the pressure of Greek cultural internationalism and Roman military imperialism. As the name-calling and story-mongering of one group inside become the inheritance of another group outside, the ground was prepared by rhetorical invective, dismissive rejection, and demonized disdain so that, in the awful fullness of time, genocidal action becomes not just possible but almost inevitable. How—now, after that—do we Christians read the passion and consider it good news?

Text and Stage

The villagers of Oberammergau have dramatically portrayed the passion of Jesus every decade since their ancestors vowed to do so in gratitude for deliverance from plague in 1633. After the initial production in 1634, it was repeated on the decade since 1680 but with some significant omissions, such as 1770 and 1940, and some special additions, such as 1934 and 1984. Today, the gently sloping and aircraft-hanger-like auditorium of 1900 holds almost 5000 spectators, hosts around 500,000 visitors over its summer-long run, has magnificent acoustics, costumes, scenery, and music, as well as a theater-wide, open-air stage that can accommodate between 200 and 300 men, women, and children for the crowd scenes.

After the omission in 1940, the play was revived in 1950 (with Adenauer and Eisenhower attending), but that production and the next in 1960 were still unchanged since the 1930 play. What I saw in the early fall of 1960 was what Hitler had seen twice, in August of 1930 and of 1934, once before and once after he became Chancellor of Germany. I knew none of that at the time but afterward, and continually across the years, one feature, and actually only this one feature, has always stuck in my mind. It was the crowd scene and the trial before Pilate.

The play takes about six hours but it is divided on either side of a long lunch-break. At the start, in early morning, I watched a huge crowd, with children conspicuously present, reenact the triumphal entry (actually, an antitriumphal one) on Palm Sunday. By late afternoon, I watched that exact same crowd reenact the scene before Pilate. It was the same shouting crowd in each case but first they cried out for Jesus and then against him, first it was acceptance and then it was rejection. I knew that, of course, from the gospels' passion narratives, but it was only when I saw it staged as drama rather than read as story that it seemed so problematic. How and why had exactly the same people changed so radically? It seemed inept *as drama* whatever one might think of it as history or gospel. I do not hint for a second that my life-long study of the historical Jesus was consciously generated by that experience, although such logic is always beguiling as one looks backward after the facts. I do know that my first scholarly journal article, published in 1965 in *Theological Studies*, was on "Anti-Semitism and the Gospels," and that the crowd scene before Pilate was one of its focal points.

In the decades of the 1970s through 1990s, local, national, and international discussions as well as criticisms from both Roman Catholic authorities and American Jewish groups led to a revised play for the fortieth production in 2000. The play had never been a straightforward dramatization of a single, chosen gospel or even of a harmonized fourfold gospel. It had always been a creative reproduction based on those texts and dramatic imagination and expansion. Many of those additions contained unfortunate stereotypes redolent of theological anti-Judaism if not racial antisemitism. Much of that was removed in the 2000 version and the changes made were certainly for the better. But all those changes, even or especially those clearly for the better, only emphasized this question. Will it ever be possible to get it right? And, more importantly, is the difficulty with the villagers of Oberammergau or the gospels of the New Testament? After the Holocaust and within the dark shadow of its remembrance, is it the dramatic staging of the passion play or the liturgical reading of the passion narrative that is the heart of the problem?

I returned in 2000 to see the play once more. Through the courtesy and generosity of Professor Ingrid H. Shafer of the University of Science and Arts of Oklahoma, I was able to study her English translation of the text before going there in late August. Although I received an English and German text with my ticket, it would hardly have been possible to watch and read simultaneously, so what I record next is due to preliminary preparation.

On the one hand, that infamous verse in Matthew 27:25 in which "the people as a whole answered, 'His blood be on us and on our children!'" is now completely absent. In itself, that phrase meant that the speakers accepted responsibility for the death sentence. It was most probably Matthew's own creation interpreting the destruction of Jerusalem in 70 C.E. as the inevitable result and divine punishment for that responsibility. But, thereafter, it was often the basis for Christian charges of deicide against Judaism itself. "The people" meant the Jewish people of all times and all places, past, present, and future. But, of course, even if that statement were taken as factual and historical, it no more implicated all Jews of then or thereafter than Pilate's judgment implicated all Italians anywhere forever.

On the other hand, although certain changes are definite improvements, their detailed statistics are certainly not. The key question is whether there was then and should be now two views about Jesus, one completely for him and one completely against him. Should the play show such a divergence and debate within Jerusalem concerning Jesus? And if so, how evenly or clearly should it be represented. Here are the changes and their statistics.

1. In Act III of the play, because of the crowd's acclaim at Jesus' entry into Jerusalem, there is a debate about him among the high-priestly authorities. There are nine individuals who speak against him a total of sixty-five times: Caiaphas (21), Nathaniel (15), Archelaus (11), Annas (6), Ezekiel (4), Dathan (4), Solomon (2), Amiel (1), and Zadok (1). There are three individuals who speak for him a total of eighteen times: Nicodemus (12), Gamaliel, (3), and Joseph of Arimathea (3). That is much more of a debate than one finds in the gospels and the last three voices one hears are those of the pro-Jesus speakers. Still, the imbalance is quite heavy.
2. In Act VII, in the "interrogation" Caiaphas speaks fourteen times and Annas five times against Jesus but Gamaliel speaks for him six times. Debate once again and imbalanced once again.
3. In Act IX, we come climactically to the trial before Pilate and that crucial interaction between high-priestly authorities, shouting crowd(s), and a reluctant governor. The crowd is now divided into four segments: Crowd A, B, C, and D. The former triad shout against Jesus forty-one times either as single or combined units: A (10), B (7), AC (6), B C (5), ABC (5), AB (4), and C (4). The D crowd shout for him three times. Also, each has a Leader but while the pro-speaker is called "the leader of the D people" (D *Volksführer)* and speaks twice, his opponent is simply "the leader of the people" *(Volksführer)* and speaks eight times. Once again there is some debate but imbal-

ance operates most powerfully here. Besides, all those numbers come from a preparatory close reading of the text. None of that is very evident to an audience that, whether it knows German or not, sees and hears only a very large crowd all shouting for Barabbas and against Jesus, all demanding "Crucify him. Crucify him."

4. Finally, that last point emphasizes the difference between a text read and a drama performed. In terms of stage presence Caiaphas totally overshadows Pilate. The Jewish high-priest and not the Roman governor dominates the scene. He does not out-talk Pilate, he simply outdresses him. Earlier, Caiaphas had entered the Jewish trial on a *sedes gestatoria* with six or eight bearers but Pilate gets no such dramatic entrance and is hardly distinguishable from the others around him. He is bare headed and wears an elegant red-ribbed tunic while Caiaphas has an even more elegant white one as well as a white cloak and a very high headdress.

After having seen the unchanged 1960 version and the changed 2000 version, I am convinced of one point. No matter how that play must continue to change, the core of its problem is not the Bavarian interpreters but the gospel writers. It is necessary, after the Holocaust, to ask this basic question. Granted that even if everything in the passion narratives were history, they would not justify for an instant any theological anti-Judaism or racial antisemitism, what exactly in there is history? Specifically, for here and now, how do we read that central scenario of the open amnesty and shouting crowd(s), of Barabbas and Jesus, of demanding Caiaphas and reluctant Pilate, of Roman innocence and Jewish responsibility? Is that fact or fiction, history or parable?

Barabbas and Jesus

In this study I presume certain historical conclusions as present presuppositions. In the first place, Matthew and Luke take their passion narratives from Mark; and second, John takes its passion narrative from those synoptic gospels. We are not dealing, in other words, with four independent accounts but with one single interdependent tradition. Against that background, the lines of change and development become particularly significant.

The Open Amnesty

The term "open" is very important. It is not at all unusual for rulers to grant amnesty to individuals or even groups and to do so at certain occasions that might make them predictable. But Mark 15:6 ("for whom they asked") followed by Matthew 27:15 ("whom they wanted") note that the Passover amnesty allowed the crowd to choose the prisoner to be released. Pilate, in other words, ceded choice to them. That is certainly possible but also bureaucratically unlikely. There is, of course, no other evidence of this privilege outside that Markan source. Note, for example, that John 18:39 has Pilate say only that "you have a custom that I release someone for you at the Passover." And Luke, who probably knows the way of Roman government best of all New Testament authors, omits completely any mention of amnesty or Barabbas. Finally, writing against the Roman governor of Egypt in his *Flaccus*, Philo of Alexandria mentions what good governors might do for condemned prisoners on the occasion of highest festival. It is not even selective let alone open amnesty but only postponement. "With all rulers, who govern any state on constitutional principles, and who do not seek to acquire a character for audacity, but who do really honour their benefactors, it is the custom to punish no one, even of those who have been lawfully condemned, until the famous festival and assembly, in honour of the birth-day of the illustrious emperor, has passed" so that "the very time itself gave, if not entire forgiveness, still, at all events, a brief and temporary respite from punishment" (81, 83). Philo can imagine at best a temporary delay rather than an open amnesty. None of that disproves Pilate's open Passover amnesty, it just makes it very unlikely.

The Reluctant Pilate

Several first-century Roman governors of Judea are known to us only by their names, but Pilate, apart completely from the gospels, is well known from both the first-century Jewish philosopher Philo and also from the first-century Jewish historian Josephus. And precisely what they describe negatively, namely his handling of trials and crowds, is precisely what the gospels describe positively.

1. Pilate and Trials. In his *Embassy to Gaius* Philo describes Pilate as "a man of a very inflexible disposition, and very merciless as well as very obstinate." He speaks of "his corruption, and his acts of insolence, and his rapine, and his habit of insulting people, and his cruelty, and his continual murders of people untried and uncondemned, and his never ending, and gratuitous, and most grievous inhumanity." He mentions him as "being exceedingly angry, and being at all times a man of most ferocious passions" (301–303). That may well be rhetorical overkill but it is precisely Pilate that Philo chooses as a specific example of a very bad governor.

2. Pilate and Crowds. First he brought iconic military standards into Jerusalem and an unarmed crowd's unexpected readiness for mass martyrdom forced him to remove those religious offenses (*Jewish Antiquities* 18.55–59). But when they tried such nonviolent resistance a second time over his use of Temple money for a Jerusalem aqueduct, Pilate infiltrated civilian-dressed soldiers among them, and "many of them were actually slain on the spot" (*Jewish Antiquities* 18.60–62). In the end, Pilate was removed from office by his immediate superior, the Syrian legate Vitellius, and sent to explain his actions before Tiberius in Rome. Those actions, not unexpectedly, involved "the slaughter" of a Samaritan crowd *(Jewish Antiquities* 18.85–89).

3. Pilate and Caiaphas. That Pilate and Caiaphas cooperated well together is indicated in several ways. Pilate was prefect from 26 to 36 and Caiaphas was high-priest from 18 to 36. Such longevity points to successful collaboration since prefects could appoint and depose high-priests at will. Further, whether John 11:47–50 is fact or fiction, it is a quite responsible reaction to Jesus. Neither Jewish nor Roman authorities thought him a military (bandit) threat, any more then Antipas thought John the Baptist was one before him *(Jewish Antiquities* 18.55–89). The leaders in violent military threats did not die alone but nonviolent politico-religious threats did so as example and warning. There is, then, no surprise in Josephus's statement that "Pilate, upon hearing him [Jesus] accused by men of the highest standing amongst us, had condemned him to be crucified" *(Jewish Antiquities* 18:64). But the Syrian legate eventually removed both Pilate and Caiaphas from office, remitted certain taxes, returned the high-priestly vestments to Jewish control, and was "received in magnificent fashion" in Jerusalem at Passover *(Jewish Antiquities* 18.90). That collaboration was, apparently, not so successful even from Rome's own point of view. The passion story, however, does not speak of collaboration but rather of a high-priest who stirs up the crowd(s) and forces the hand of a very reluctant Pilate. This just and righteous governor knows that Jesus is accused because of high-priestly "envy" (Mark 15: 10), insists that he is "innocent" (Luke 23:22), and gives in only when he "saw that he could do nothing, but rather that a riot was beginning" (Matthew 27:24) or lest he seem no longer "Caesar's friend" (John 19:12).

Despite all of that, the gospels record Pilate's patient debate and reluctant submission before a high-priestly-led crowd demanding what he does not want to do. None of that disproves Pilate's reluctance, it just makes it very unlikely. No doubt that discrepancy can be explained by proposing biographical and psychological profiles of Pilate, by imagining a tortured conscience caught between personal self-interest and professional legal justice, or by presuming a husband who listened to his wife for a change. But, as with amnesty and Barabbas, what here is fact and what fiction, what history and what parable?

The Markan Parable

A parable is a fictitious story with a pedagogical point and, just as the historical Jesus used parables about God so early Christianity used parables about Jesus. My proposal is that Mark created both the open Passover amnesty, the shouting crowd, and its choice of Barabbas over Jesus to make a very specific point. He is writing in the immediate aftermath of Jerusalem's destruction in 70 during the great war with Rome of 66–74. He is creating a parable, a fictional story claiming that Jerusalem brought destruction upon itself because long before it had chosen the wrong leader, the wrong savior, the wrong son of the wrong father (Barabbas). Instead of choosing the nonviolent way of Jesus, they had chosen the way of violent rebellion. Hence his emphasis in 15:7 that "Barabbas was in prison with the rebels who had committed murder during the insurrection."

That explanation explains, first, the (historical) implausibility of the open Passover amnesty, the reluctant but crowd-forced Pilate, and the Caiaphas–Pilate disagreement. It was invented parabolically. Second, it explains Mark's redactional purpose against the background of his gospel narrative in general and its passion story in particular. Finally, it fits with the character of gospel as actualization of the good news for then-as-now and now-as-then, as a creative integration of the Jesus of the 30s into the time and place of an evangelist.

But that solution only relocates the problem. Mark could have established his parabolic point without depicting a reluctant Pilate seeking to free a Jesus he knew was innocent. The crowd could simply have chosen Barabbas over Jesus before a Pilate unconcerned one way or another. Why, especially in the aftermath of Roman slaughter in 70 C.E., does a Roman governor in the year 30 receive such benign treatment?

Roman and Jew

The question of Pilate's portrayal intensifies as one watches how the Markan story is adapted in subsequent and dependent gospel retelling. The general tendency is to increase Jewish responsibility and to decrease Roman culpability. What started as the crowd for Barabbas will end as the Jews against Jesus.

The Shouting Crowd(s)

The "crowd" scene changes rather dramatically as it moves from Mark through Matthew and Luke into John. Watch, especially, how the purpose and volume of the "crowd" changes across that development.

1. Purpose of the Crowd. There is, across the four texts, a subtle shift from a demand for Barabbas's release (and therefore against Jesus') to one against Jesus' release (and therefore for Barabbas'). In Mark 15:6–8 (and Matthew 27:15–17a) there is the custom of an open Passover amnesty, a rebel named Barabbas in prison, and a crowd who come before Pilate to obtain the customary privilege.

Now at the festival he used to release a prisoner for them, anyone for whom they asked. Now a man called Barabbas was in prison with the rebels who had committed murder during the insurrection. So the crowd came and began to ask Pilate to do for them according to his custom.

How should that be read? Do they come for just anybody? Are they aware or unaware of Barabbas? Is his release what they demand in that last verse? Because the first verse mentions "anyone for whom they asked," and the second verse mentions Barabbas, I interpret that last verse as meaning that they came and asked for Barabbas. In that reading, therefore, they do not arrive *against* Jesus but for Barabbas. Next, in Mark 15:9–14, Pilate offers them Jesus, and "the chief priests stirred up the crowd to have him release Barabbas for them instead." In other words, they must refuse Pilate's alternative of Jesus in order to get Barabbas freed.

But the much shorter versions in both Luke 23:18–19 and John 18:39–40 (respectively below) mention Jesus before Barabbas and shift the emphasis so that the action now seems more against Jesus than for Barabbas:

> Then they all shouted out together, "Away with this fellow! Release Barabbas for us!" (This was a man who had been put in prison for an insurrection that had taken place in the city, and for murder.)

> "But you have a custom that I release someone for you at the Passover. Do you want me to release for you the King of the Jews?" They shouted in reply, "Not this man, but Barabbas!" Now Barabbas was a bandit.

The change is delicate but definite: the crowd, encouraged by its religious authorities, begins by wanting Barabbas freed (and therefore Jesus rejected) and ends by wanting Jesus crucified (and therefore Barabbas accepted).

2. Volume of the Crowd. If that development is somewhat oblique, this next one is very obvious. It concerns the identity, volume, and responsibility of the crowd. Here is how it changes across those four texts:

Mark	*Matthew*	*Luke*	*John*
15:8, 11, 15	*27:15, 22, 25*	*23:4, 13, 18*	*18:31, 36, 38;19:7*
"the crowd"	"the crowd"	"the chief priests and the crowds"	"the Jews"
"the crowd"	"the crowds"	"the chief priests, the leaders, and the people"	"the Jews"
"(they)"	"(they) all"	"(they) all together"	"the Jews"
"the crowd"	"all the people"		"the Jews"

That hardly needs any commentary. From a simple reference to "the crowd" in the initial Markan text, it escalates steadily through Matthew's and Luke's "the people" into John's "the Jews."

Notice, however, the special Lukan additions in 23:27 where "a great number of the people followed him, and among them were women who were beating their breasts and wailing for him," as well as in 23:48 "when all the crowds who had gathered there for this spectacle saw what had taken place, they returned home, beating their breasts." On the one hand, we have "the crowds . . . the people . . . all together" *against* Jesus, but, on the other we have "a great number of people . . . all the crowds" for Jesus.

A Pre-Markan Parable?

The standard explanation for why the gospels steadily increase Jewish and decrease Roman responsibility is that their authors consider the latter a far greater threat. Although Josephus's statement of accusation by Jewish authority but crucifixion by Roman power was quite accurate, the evangelists, it is said, wanted to relieve Pilate of responsibility even though Jesus had certainly died by Roman judgment, under Roman control, and on a Roman cross. The gospels' solution was their creation of a reluctant governor asserting Jesus' innocence but bowing to open amnesty, the crowd's choice, and high-priestly demand. That, of course, would make those writers deliberate liars, asserting what they knew was not true for reasons of safety and security. Is that our best explanation?

The Passover amnesty and the choice of Barabbas over Jesus can be plausibly explained as a Markan post-70s creation, a contemporary parable explaining Jerusalem's destruction for having chosen the wrong Bar-Abbas ("son of the father"), having trusted in the violence of the Zealot over the nonviolence of Jesus. But precisely *that* background militates against Roman exculpation. How could Mark create a parable about Roman innocence in the year 30 after the knowledge or experience of Roman violence in the year 70? My proposal is that not Mark but a pre-Markan source created that particular parable and that its content was dictated by its time and place of origin and not by an effort to lie about Roman responsibility. I outline the argument for this pre-Markan parable over four steps.

*1. **Step One.*** From 1967 to 1980 George Nickelsburg made these four proposals. First, there is a story of the persecution, vindication, and exaltation of the Righteous One that extends from extrabiblical Ahikar to intrabiblical Joseph, Esther, Daniel, and Susanna. In this narrative genre of innocence unjustly accused "the protagonist is a wise man in a royal court. Maliciously accused of violating the law of the land, he is condemned to death. But he is rescued at the brink of death, vindicated of the charges against him, and exalted to a high position (sometimes vizier, sometimes judge or executioner of his enemies), while his enemies are punished." This genre's hero or heroine is always saved from death, before death, but at the very last moment, as it were. Second, there is also a tradition visible in Wisdom 2:12–20 and 4:18–5:14 in which innocence is not vindicated before but only after death. Because "the protagonist is, in fact, put to death . . . [h]e is exalted to the heavenly court, where he serves as a vice-regent of the heavenly king," a development "inherent in the servant theology of Second

Isaiah [52–53]." No doubt that former tradition indicated a situation of political discrimination while the latter indicated one of lethal persecution. Third, the "story of the righteous man in Wisdom is a variation on the model of the wisdom tale, with the framework of the Isaianic exaltation scene shaping Wisdom 5."[2] In other words, the postmortem tradition "stands in the tradition" of the premortem one. Finally, "the Markan passion narrative" has as its "generic model" those stories about "the rescue and vindication of a persecuted person or persons."[3] Of course, despite that generic basis, Jesus is not vindicated *premortem,* not rescued by present divine intervention (as with Joseph or Esther, Daniel or Susanna), but will be vindicated *postmortem* by future divine consummation (as with the Wisdom 1 or the Suffering Servant). How, one might ask, could it be otherwise for Jesus?

2. Step Two. From 1985 to 1991 I made the following four proposals, very much based on Nickelsburg's seminal suggestions, but also arguing that it could be and was otherwise for the passion tradition of Jesus. First, the fragmentary *Gospel of Peter is* a second-century text that deliberately harmonized *both* the canonical passion–resurrection stories *and* another noncanonical passion–resurrection narrative that I termed the *Cross Gospel* for easy reference. Second, I also argued that the *Cross Gospel* was earlier than and the major source for the entire canonical tradition. Third, the passion narrative, from *Cross Gospel* to John, was not derived from history remembered but from prophecy historicized. Fourth, my best location for that alleged *Cross Gospel's* origins was a pro-Roman Jewish site like Sepphoris.[4]

In Nickelburg's very persuasive reconstruction the *premortem* tradition led to the *postmortem* tradition of the Righteous One's public vindication by God. But my alleged *Cross Gospel's* passion–resurrection is even closer to those *premortem* vindication stories than is Mark. Jesus, of course, cannot be saved from the cross like Daniel from the lions or Susanna from the judges. So, here, no pure premortem salvation is possible. But the *Cross Gospel* is as close as one can get to that generic model. For here Jesus appears in risen triumph before the very Jewish authorities themselves and they must thereafter concede what has happened to Pilate who then proclaims himself "clean from the blood of the Son of God, upon such a thing have you decided" (*Gospel of Peter* 11:46). As in those stories, the neutral ruler comes down eventually on the side of the unjustly accused. In this story Jesus' vindication is already present in sight and not just future in faith.

3. Step Three. In 1989 Gerd Theissen made these four proposals. First, there existed a consecutive pre-Markan passion story. Second, its time and place could be recovered "taking for granted that narratives are marked by the conditions under which their narrating community lives." Third, "the choice, shaping, and stylizing of traditions into a connected Passion account was specially feasible in the 40s." Fourth, "probably we can limit the phase in which this Passion tradition underwent its critical shaping still more: it could well have been composed in light of the persecutions that occurred during Agrippa I's reign (41–44 C.E.).[5]

4. Step Four. I had the same reaction to Theissen's thesis as I earlier did to Nickelsburg's, namely that it works much better for the alleged *Cross Gospel* than for Mark. I immediately abandoned my suggestion of locating it at Sepphoris in the mid-50s and thought instead of Jerusalem in the early 40s.[6]

My alleged *Cross Gospel's* version of the passion–resurrection is strikingly different from any of those in the New Testament. Pilate and his soldiers are completely innocent and withdraw from the single unified trial at which all the authorities are initially present. Jesus is not crucified by Pilate and soldiers but by Herod (not identified as Antipas) and the Jewish people. One's immediate reaction is to consider this the most anti-Jewish of all the passion accounts and that is the position of many contemporary scholars: the *Gospel of Peter* is simply a crude pastiche of the canonical gospels rewritten to render anti-Judaism as virulent as possible.[7] But actually the story continues in a even more surprising manner. The miraculous events at the crucifixion, which go almost unnoticed by the people in the canonical gospels, now generate fear and doubt among those who have crucified Jesus. A split starts between Jewish authorities and Jewish people. The former ask Pilate for soldiers to help them guard the tomb lest a stolen body create a resurrection legend among people now ready to believe it. Roman and Jewish authorities are there at the tomb and actually see the resurrection itself but the Jewish authorities beg Pilate for a cover-up lest "the people of the Jews" stone those leaders for having led them astray in executing Jesus. That story is, in other words, as anti-Jewish authorities as one could imagine but also as pro-Jewish people as one could imagine.

I do not think for a moment, of course, that this story is historical. But my question is this: What is the most plausible chronological location for a story in which (1) the Romans are absolutely innocent (Pilate's hand-washing is more valid in *Peter* than in Matthew where his soldiers still execute Jesus), (2) the Jewish authorities are supremely guilty, much more so than in any canonical gospel, but (3) the "people of the Jews" are so repentant that their own leaders dare not tell them the truth of the resurrection that they themselves have witnessed? Unless we are dealing with complete fools, when and where would such a story have been credible, not true, not historical, but just fictionally believable? The more my colleagues insist that the story is quite fantastic, the more I agree, but press the question: who, where, when, why would such a story have been usable?

The best answer I have is that offered by Theissen for his proposed pre-Markan passion story. And I apologize (without repentance) for using his idea in a way he may not appreciate. That *Cross Gospel* version would have been credible to Christian Jews between 41 and 44 C.E. when Herod Agrippa I was King of the Jews as his grandfather Herod the Great had been a half century earlier. First, the Romans were a little farther in the background hidden behind a Jewish king (distance as innocence) and the Syrian legate Petronius had just stalled on Caligula's command to erect his statue in Jerusalem's Temple. Second, Josephus says that Herod Agrippa I "enjoyed residing in Jerusalem and did so constantly; and he scrupulously observed the traditions of his people. He neglected no rite of purification, and no day passed for him without the prescribed sacrifice" *(Jewish Antiquities* 19.33 1*)*. Next, he restored the high-priestly dynasty of Annas to power (19.3 13–3 16). Then, not surprisingly, Acts 12:1–11 tells how Agrippa attacked the Twelve, executing James, son of Zebedee, and imprisoning Peter. Roman authorities rather than Jewish regal or sacerdotal authorities must have looked very good to Jerusalem's Christian Jewish community in the early 40s. It was also early enough in the night for those latter to dream that all their fellow Jews, if only they were not lead astray by their leaders, would join the Christian Jewish program.

There is one very important footnote to this interpretation. We have always known that the gospels are not straightforward history or biography, but that they take, adapt, and create events from the 30s and update them to the lives and times of Christian communities in the 70s, 80s, and 90s. *But not only do they update the words and deeds of Jesus, they also update the friends and enemies of Jesus.* In other words, whenever a gospel writer describes the passion of Jesus, the tendency is to overlay the heroes and villains back then with those of immediate present experience. That happens spontaneously, automatically, and more or less unconsciously. Pre-Mark did it by inventing a superinnocent Roman authority and superguilty Jewish authority. Mark did it by inventing an open Passover amnesty and a Jerusalem crowd that chose a violent Barabbas over a nonviolent Jesus. Post-Mark did it, as Christian Judaism became more and more marginalized within its own people, by expanding the enemies of Jesus in the year 30 from "the crowd" in Mark, through "all the people" in Matthew, and into "the Jews" in John. General Roman innocence and general Jewish guilt were never true but they came not from deliberate lying propaganda but from inevitable gospel process.

Conclusion

I repeat that even if everything in the passion stories of the gospels were historically accurate, it would no more justify theological anti-Judaism let alone racial antisemitism than it would theological anti-Romanism or racial anti-Italianism. Also, if modem interpreters take it all as factually inerrant, that does not necessarily make them anti-Jewish. But precisely after the Holocaust, that question of historicity must be pressed as relentlessly as possible. No doubt it should have been done in any case and the lines drawn between what were historical reconstructions and what were theological interpretations made openly explicit. But reading "after the Holocaust" involves two changes: not doing what we should never have done in the first place, and doing what we should have done in any case. First, what, in our very best reconstruction, is the historicity of Jesus' passion? Second, how does that best reconstruction avoid either brutalizing non-Christian Jews as killers or else brutalizing Christian Jews as liars?

NOTES

1. Quoted in James Shapiro, *Oberammergau: The Troubling Story of the World's Most Famous Passion Play* (New York: Pantheon, 2000), 169.
2. George W. E. Nickelsburg, *Resurrection, Immortality, and Eternal life in Intertestamental Judaism* (Harvard Theological Studies 26; Cambridge, MA: Harvard University Press, 1972). My citations are from pp. 170 and 66. This is the published version of his Ph.D. dissertation, written at Harvard Divinity School in 1967, under Krister Stendahl.
3. George W. E. Nickelsburg, "The Genre and Function of the Markan Passion Narrative," *Harvard Theological Review* 73 (1980): 153–184. My citation is from pp. 155–156.
4. For the *Cross Gospel* proposal see *Four Other Gospels: Shadows on the Contours of Canon* (Minneapolis, MN: Winston/Seabury, 1985), 123–181 [Sonoma, CA: Polebridge Press, 1992, pp. 85–127] and especially *The Cross that Spoke: The Origins of the Passion Narrative* (San Francisco, CA: HarperSanFrancisco, 1988). For that as well as its Sepphoris location see *The Historical Jesus: The Life of a Mediterranean Jewish Peasant* (San Francisco, CA: HarperSanFrancisco, 1991), 354–394 (especially p. 387), and also *Who Killed Jesus? Exposing the Roots of Anti-Semitism in the Gospel Story of the Death of Jesus* (San Francisco, CA: HarperSanFrancisco, 1995), 223.

   Those second and third proposals were strongly opposed by the late Raymond E. Brown in "The Gospel of Peter and Canonical Gospel Priority," *New Testament Studies* 33 (1987): 321–343, and also in *The Death of the Messiah: From Gethsemane to the Grave. A Commentary on the Passion Narratives in the Four Gospels*, 2 vols. (The Anchor Bible Reference Library; New York: Doubleday, 1994), 1317–1349. But his position on that first proposal is much more ambiguous. I had proposed a consecutive and independent three-act drama of juridical execution, guarded burial, and visible resurrection in that *Cross Gospel*. Brown actually agrees that there is such a consecutive and independent source within the *Gospel of Peter* but it is only a two-act drama of guarded burial and visible resurrection: "GPet . . . had a source besides Matt, namely, a more developed account of the guard at the tomb. (That point is also supported by the consecutiveness of the story in *GPet.)* The supplying of the centurion's name, the seven seals, the stone rolling off by itself, the account of the resurrection with the gigantic figures, the talking cross, the confession of Jesus as God's Son by the Jewish authorities, and their fear of their own people—all those elements could plausibly have been in the more developed form of the story known to the author of *GPet* and absent from the form known to Matt" *(Death,* 1307). My response was and is that such a two-act drama could never have existed without some initial act that (1) detailed a juridical execution and that also (2) explained why the tomb needed to be guarded. I find it most economical to locate that required first act exactly where it is, before those other two in the *Gospel of Peter* itself.
5. Gerd Theissen, *Lokalkolorit und Zeitgeschichte in den Evangelien* (Novum Testamentum et Orbis Antiquus 8; Göttingen: Vandenhoeck & Ruprecht, 1989); translated into English as *The Gospels in Context: Social and Political History in the Synoptic Tradition*, trans. Linda M. Mal-

oney (Minneapolis, MN: Fortress Press, 1991). The difficulties in establishing pre-Markan passion texts are clear from the 35 examples studied comparatively by Marion L. Soards as "Appendix IX: The Question of a Premarcan Passion Narrative," pp. 1492–1524 in Brown's *The Death of the Messiah* (see note 4 above).

6. John Dominic Crossan, *The Birth of Christianity* (San Francisco: HarperSanFrancisco, 1998), 481–573.
7. Examples are Susan E. Schaeffer, "The Gospel of Peter, the Canonical Gospels, and Oral Tradition," Ph.D. dissertation, Union Theololgical Seminary in NY (under Raymond E. Brown), and Alan Kirk, "Examining Priorities: Another Look at the Gospel of Peter's Relationship to the New Testament Gospels," *New Testament Studies* 40 (1994): 572–595.

CHAPTER 14

Restoring the Kingdom to Israel

Luke–Acts and Christian Supersessionism

CRAIG C. HILL

A driving force in recent biblical scholarship is the desire to interpret the New Testament from a point of view that is fair to Judaism.[1] This attitude has made possible new insights, especially into the contingent nature of many of the New Testament's harshest statements concerning Judaism, statements that become especially disturbing in light of the Holocaust. Most scholars now recognize that, for example, when Matthew speaks of the Pharisees and John of the Jews, their statements are less eternal, dominical truth than situational, even personal polemic. Thus, contemporary scholarship has made great strides in exposing our common failure to assess the New Testament's sometimes vitriolic treatment of the Jews in a way that is honest both to Jewish and to Christian history.

A second, less prominent consequence of this attitude is the reinterpretation of many New Testament passages whose exegesis had been prejudiced by anti-Jewish assumptions.[2] It might come as a surprise to discover that, at times, the New Testament is not so anti-Jewish as some commentators have assumed it to be.

A third result of scholarship's changing outlook is the reclamation of New Testament material, albeit not a substantial corpus, that is in some respect favorable toward Judaism. Here it should be noted that overcorrection is the shadow of good intentions. In looking for the sympathetic one must not fall prey to the temptation to turn New Testament authors into religious universalists or cultural pluralists. You won't find "diversity" in Metzger's list of frequently used words. Still, texts such as Luke 1:6, the complimentary depiction of the righteous Jews Elizabeth and Zechariah, were not wished into existence. A reappraisal of the New Testament's treatment of Judaism must be open to discovering the occasional good as well as the all-too-frequent bad.

Supersessionism

Scholars who work in the area of Christian supersessionism encounter a daunting set of theological problems. For example, if one allows, as increasing numbers of Christians do, that Judaism is a religion of grace, then in what sense if any is Christ necessary? Most pointedly, must Jews believe in Jesus to be in covenant with God? A growing number of scholars attempt to answer such questions in a manner that honors Jewish faith and that recognizes the ongoing validity and vitality of Judaism. Such thinkers are almost universally agreed in their opposition to "Christian supersessionism," although a good deal of latitude is exercised in the identification of their common adversary. For our purposes, let me describe two broad and yet distinct types. The first, which I shall call *thoroughgoing supersessionism,* holds that the Church has fully superseded, that is, has taken over the place of Israel. For all intents and purposes, the Church *is* Israel, and the religion of Judaism no longer has a purpose or a place. This is the ideological background to the statement made in 1980 in a speech by Rev. Bailey Smith, then president of the Southern Baptist Convention, that "God does not hear the prayer of a Jew."

Is "thoroughgoing supersessionism" to be found in the New Testament? The Gospel of Matthew certainly seems to push us in that direction. For example, it is only in Matthew that Jesus is reported as telling the Jews, "The kingdom will be taken from you and given to a people that produces the fruits of the kingdom" (Matthew 21:43), and "the heirs of the kingdom will be thrown into the outer darkness, where there will be weeping and gnashing of teeth" (Matthew 11:12; cf. 22:7–9). The Gospel of John is another strong candidate. The lines are cleanly drawn: those who believe in Jesus are in, those who do not, including most Jews, are out, as in John 1:11–12:

> He came to what was his own, and his own people did not accept him. But to all who received him, who believed in his name, he gave power to become children of God. . .

If the Jews are not children of God, then what is their status? In one of the Bible's most notorious passages, Jesus tells his Jewish opponents,

> You are of your father the devil, and you choose to do your father's desires. . . . Whoever is from God hears the words of God. The reason you do not hear them is that you are not from God. (John 8:44–47)

A second, more moderate viewpoint is also represented in the New Testament. Like the proverbial half-empty/half-full glass, it is difficult to name, being only partly supersessionist. It accepts that Israel has an ongoing existence and significance in the plan of God and so is distinct from the Church; in that sense, it is not supersessionist. Nevertheless, it believes that Jews must be saved through faith in Christ, even if such faith comes only at the eschaton; in that sense, it could be called supersessionist. For lack of a better label, I shall refer to this perspective as *semisupersessionism.* This viewpoint is most famously represented in Paul's deliberation on the fate of Israel in Romans 9–11. Verses 25–36 of Chapter 11 in particular have become a *locus classicus* of contemporary Christian theological reflection about Judaism. These verses do challenge the characteristically knee-jerk Christian dismissal of Judaism (although such a dismissal might not be absent from Paul's earlier letters; see I Thessalonians 2:14–16, if genuine, Galatians 4:24–25, and the especially problematic Galatians 6:16, "the Israel of God").

It appears that by the time of Romans, the Pauline calculus no longer contained, if it ever did, the equation "Israel = Church." Contrary to Matthew 21:43, the kingdom cannot simply be wrenched from the Jews and given to others. At stake is the faithfulness of God. It is God who elected Israel, a fact that Jewish unbelief cannot annul. "The gifts and calling of God are irrevocable" (Romans 11:29). Therefore, Israel, historical Israel, has a future. Paul solves the problem posed by the apparent failure of the mission to the Jews by moving the solution outside of present-day history and thus outside of normal historical agency, namely, human evangelism. Thus finally shall all Israel be saved, and thus finally shall God be shown righteous.[3] Understandably, Romans 11 is *the* text to which modern Christian interpreters turn when searching for a way out of thoroughgoing supersessionism. As we shall see, the applicability of Romans 11 to Luke–Acts is one of the key issues in recent Lukan study.

A third option would be straightforward *nonsupersessionism.* According to this perspective, two separate and enduring covenants exist: the Abrahamic/Mosaic covenant and the covenant inaugurated by Christ. It is only Gentiles who need enter the people of God through Jesus. Jews and Gentiles were, are, and forever will be saved in different ways. Is such a view to be found in the New Testament? Some, most notably Krister Stendahl,[4] have thought so, but their arguments have not persuaded most scholars. The necessity of Christian faith for Jews as well as Gentiles appears basic to the New Testament authors, including Paul in Romans 11. Many contemporary Christians reject all forms of supersessionism; one only wishes that they had better support from the New Testament in doing so.

Luke–Acts

The issue of anti-Judaism is at the white-hot center of current discussion of Luke–Acts.[5] A sizable group of scholars has invested considerable labor in reevaluating these texts in light of present-day theological sensibilities. Similarities in motivation have not, however, produced uniformity in results. Many interpreters, such as Jack Sanders, have concluded that the traditional Protestant reading of Luke–Acts is essentially accurate.[6] Luke concluded that God had "written off the Jews" (Haenchen's famous phrase[7]); the prerogatives of Israel had become the possession of the Church. Our job is not to explain or make excuses for Lukan anti-Judaism but rather to expose and repudiate it. Other interpreters, such as Robert Brawley,[8] have stressed the many positive characterizations of Jews and Jewish practice in Luke–Acts and the many favorable references to Jewish history and expectation.

The extent and persistence of these disagreements are surely due to the ambiguity of the evidence. In fact, Luke has both positive and negative things to say about Jews, and it is not difficult to show the narrative in either light. A truly satisfying reading of Luke–Acts must take both favorable and unfavorable elements fully into account. But what of Israel specifically? Where do the Gospel of Luke and the book of Acts fit on the supersessionism spectrum? As one might imagine, opinion is as divided. A plurality of scholars continue to see Luke as a thoroughgoing supersessionist. The church alone is the locus of God's activity and the fulfillment of God's promises to previous generations. The mission to the Jews might or might not have been abandoned (depending on one's interpretation of Acts 28:26–28), but historical Israel in effect has. The future belongs solely to the Church. Among the many fine scholars who take this line is Luke Johnson, who, in his popular textbook *The Writings of the New Testament: An Interpretation*, titles his discussion of Acts chapters 1–8 "The Restored Israel in Jerusalem." He then writes, "What is most striking about Luke's perception is that believing Jews and Gentiles together make up the authentic Israel, the people of God."[9]

On the other side of the issue are those scholars (a "mighty minority," to borrow Jervell's phrase) who have argued that Luke continued to expect, along the lines of Romans 11, that Israel—that is, historical Israel—would be restored at the return of Christ. As Arthur Wainwright puts it:

> It cannot be denied that Luke recognizes a movement away from Jews to Gentiles, and that as far as he is concerned they have forfeited their status with God as the chosen people. But it does not follow that they have been irrevocably rejected by God.[10]

And David Tiede has pointed helpfully to the tension that exists between the first chapters of Luke and the final chapter of Acts.[11] Where a particular scholar comes down on the question of Luke and Israel is in no small part determined by the manner in which he or she chooses to adjudicate this tension.

Luke Chapters 1–2 repeat and appear to validate Jewish expectations of national restoration:

1. In Luke 1:32–33, Gabriel tells Mary:

   He [your son] will be great, and will be called the Son of the Most High, and the Lord God will give to him the throne of his ancestor David. He will reign over the house of Jacob forever, and of his kingdom there will be no end.

2. The Magnificat (Luke 1:46–55) includes, among others, the following statements:

   He has brought down the powerful from their thrones, and lifted up the lowly. . . . He has helped his servant Israel, in remembrance of his mercy, according to the promise he made to our ancestors, to Abraham and to his descendants forever. (Luke 1:52, 54)

3. Zechariah, "filled with the Holy Spirit" (Luke 1:67), prophesied concerning Jesus:

   Blessed be the Lord God of Israel, for he has . . . raised up a horn of salvation for us in the house of his servant David . . . *that we should be saved from our enemies, and from the hand of all who hate us;* to perform the mercy promised to our fathers, and to remember his holy covenant, the oath which he swore to our father Abraham, *to grant us that we, being delivered from the hand of our enemies,* might serve him without fear. . . (Luke 1:68, 69, 71–73)

4. Simeon, who had been "looking forward to the consolation of Israel" (Luke 2:25), states,

   Master, now you are dismissing your servant in peace, according to your word; for my eyes have seen your salvation, which you have prepared in the presence of all peoples, a light for revelation to the Gentiles and for glory to your people Israel. (Luke 2:29–32)

   And, in a verse that previews the narrative of Luke–Acts, adds,

   This child is destined for the falling and the rising of many in Israel . . . (Luke 2:34).

5. Likewise, we hear of the prophet Anna, who spoke "about the child to all who were looking for the redemption of Jerusalem" (Luke 2:38).

So, Luke begins his story by raising readers' expectations concerning the fulfilment of Jewish hopes. How does Luke–Acts end? With Paul's denunciation of Jewish unbelief in Acts 28:23–31.[12] For a great many scholars, Acts 28, the end of the story, trumps Luke 1–2, its beginning. For example, Joseph Tyson, an especially thoughtful interpreter of Luke–Acts, writes:

> Thus, in my judgment, it is better to read the end of Acts as proclaiming the end of the mission to the Jews than it is to read it as maintaining a continued openness to the Jewish people. If this is right, the end of Acts pro-

> vides a resolution to the apparent ambivalence of the narrative . . . a resolution without ambivalence or ambiguity: an image of Jewish people as rejecting the gospel and thus as a people without hope.[13]

Hard words, but representative of what is probably the majority opinion. What then of Luke 1–2? Scholars who see the author of Luke–Acts as fully supersessionist (usually the same ones who see Acts 28 as a declaration of the end of the Jewish mission) have a variety of ways of dealing with the promises of Luke 1–2. To some, it appears that the promises will remain forever unfulfilled, due, from Luke's point of view, to Jewish obduracy. This is a tale of what might have been, not what will be. It is on this basis that Robert Tannehill has written of Luke–Acts as a "tragic" narrative.[14]

The traditional and most popular strategy is to spiritualize and universalize the prophecies contained in Luke 1–2. For example, F. F. Bruce wrote that although Jesus, the "son of David had not overthrown the Gentile oppressors or established national independence for Israel" as had been prophesied earlier in Luke's Gospel,

> Yet the promises on which those hopes were based were not forgotten in the early church: their fulfillment was recognized. . . . But it was a fulfillment on a plane other than what formerly had been envisaged. The promises made to the house of David were fulfilled in the resurrection and exaltation of Jesus, the Son of David.[15]

David Moessner's approach is similar in his article "The Ironic Fulfillment of Israel's Glory."[16] He challenges the notion that Luke intended his readers to take the promises of Chapters 1–2 "at face value." The truthfulness of these "reliable witnesses" is relativized; they speak only for "pious Israel" and do not comprehend the plan of God. "The tension, I would submit, is ironic. That is to say, what certain characters believe and express as a hope or promise on one level is meant to be perceived by readers on a different level." A significant problem with Moessner's argument is the fact that it ignores parallel sayings (e.g., Luke 21:24 and Acts 1:6; see below) credited to the disciples and Jesus, whose reliable witness cannot be so easily undermined. Nevertheless, Moessner's work stands as one of the most interesting defenses of the traditional interpretive strategy.

A third and far less common approach is that advocated by Michael Wolter in his provocative article "Israel's Future and the Delay of the Parousia, according to Luke."[17] Wolter holds out for the future, literal fulfilment of the promises of Luke 1–2, but he believes that, according to Luke, the recipients would be Christians, not non-Christian Jews:

> The hopes expressed by Zechariah (1:68–75), Simeon (2:29–32), and Hannah (2:38) can thus be understood as representing the author's own implicit position because as unfulfilled hopes they point beyond the Lukan present and not to some point before Luke's writing. . . . The difference now is that Israel will include completely different people, and the apportionment of salvation and condemnation will be decided by completely different criteria than implied by the "near expectation" in Luke 19:11 and Acts 1:6.[18]

Other scholars challenge the conclusion that Acts 28 announces the formal cessation of the Jewish mission and the end of Jewish opportunity. They point to the fact that Acts 28:28 is paralleled by Paul's statements at both Pisidian Antioch (Acts 13:46) and Corinth (Acts 18:6); in both cases, Paul resumed preaching to Jews upon arrival at the next city. Rather than see the three pronouncements as being cumulative, so that Acts 28:28 is the last word, a number of interpreters regard the three instances as establishing a pattern of expectation that extends into the future. In any case, the declarations applied only to Paul and in each instance served to justify his preaching to Gentiles. They also note that Jews almost certainly are among those converted by Paul at Rome (Acts 28:24), and that the most natural reading of the "all" in v. 30 would include such Jews as are mentioned in v. 24. Writes James D. G. Dunn:

> The mistake of those who see here the account of an irretrievable breakdown between Christianity and Judaism has been to assume that the third report of such a denunciation by Paul of this fellow Jews was intended to be the final. On the contrary, Luke was well aware that the real history continued beyond the limits of his narrative (cf. 1.11!). . . . [W]hat Luke records is not so much a final scene as a *definitively typical scene*—the ongoing debate between believers in Messiah Jesus and traditional Jews as definitive for Christianity; the debate continues, some Jews being persuaded, others disbelieving.[19]

Similarly, David Tiede concluded that

> Simeon's dire oracle concerning the falling of many in Israel and a sign spoken against has already been amply fulfilled within the narrative and at its end (Acts 28) and probably in Luke's world. But the restoration, the consolation, the redemption, the repentance, the forgiveness, the reign of God which Simeon and all those other worthies in Israel expected has only begun to be inaugurated in the present time of Luke's story.[20]

I would also make the observation that Luke was hardly in a position to announce or enforce the universal cessation of "the Jewish mission." Also, it is important to remember that Luke did not discover the failure of the church's preaching to the Jews; it was already obvious to Paul, who nevertheless refused to "write off" Israel. It is worth noting that there is nothing in Paul's other writings, not even in Romans itself, that would lead us to anticipate the startling declaration of Romans 11:26, "And so all Israel will be saved." In other words, Paul himself is the best evidence that it was possible to portray Judaism most unfavorably and to make exclusivist Christian claims while still holding to a future restoration of Israel. That does not prove that Luke held such a view, but it does mean that we cannot preclude the possibility based on his negative characterizations of the Jews.

A number of scholars refer to Romans 11 when commenting on Luke–Acts, but, unsurprisingly, they do so in opposing ways. One side contrasts the two authors. Michael Wolter is typical of this group:

> Like Paul, Luke picks up the motif of obduracy on the part of the people of God to explain Israel's "utterly incomprehensible" historical refusal to believe, and in this respect he and Paul do indeed have something in common. This does not by a long shot mean, however, that the two rhetorical questions in Rom. 11:1, 11, concerning Israel's present status before God and its future can be imputed to Luke as well; for a qualitative distinction obtains between Luke and Paul, making such a transference utterly anachronistic—namely, the distance of more than thirty years between Paul's Letter to the Romans and Luke's two-volume work in the light of the absent parousia. Hence it was nothing other than the delay of the parousia itself that made it impossible for Luke to speak about "Israel" in the same way that Paul did.[21]

In other words, Paul could believe in future restoration because he believed in an immediately approaching eschaton. Luke took the long view, according to which Israel was replaced by an enduring Church. One might well ask if this polarization of Paul and Lukan eschatologies is justified. The influence of Hans Conzelmann upon Wolter's work is evident especially at this point.

The other side sees a great deal more affinity than contrast between the two authors. Wrote Arthur Wainwright:

> Like Paul in Romans 11, Luke appears to look forward to a time when they [the Jews] will be reinstated. His references to the restoration and redemption of Israel provide a clue to his theological presuppositions. . . . [T]here is no good reason to suppose that when he speaks of the restoration of Israel he is alluding to the Church. He is referring to the Jewish nation.[22]

Can Romans 11 help us to understand Luke–Acts on this point? The future salvation of Israel and the reversal of the eschatological timetable are striking and important ideas that might have lived on in some form in Pauline Christianity.[23] What follows is an attempt to set forth some further arguments in favor of this position.

As it is commonly interpreted, Romans 11:25–36 makes, among others, the following three points:

1. Jewish unbelief has occasioned a period of Gentile opportunity: "you [Gentiles] were once disobedient to God but now have received mercy because of their [the Jews'] disobedience" (v. 30; see also vv. 11 and 15).
2. The period of Gentile evangelization is impermanent: "a hardening has come upon part of Israel, until the full number of the Gentiles has come in" (v. 25).[24]
3. After the mission to the Gentiles is complete, history as we know it will come to an end, and God will act to bring faith to Israel: "so all Israel will be saved; as it is written, 'The Deliverer will come from Zion, he will banish ungodliness from Jacob'; 'and this will be my covenant with them when I take away their sins'" (vv. 26–27).

It is important to note that each of the three points has a counterpart in Luke–Acts. The first is the assertion that Jewish unbelief has occasioned a period of Gentile opportunity. The pattern in Acts of Jewish refusal leading to Gentile evangelization is obvious enough on both macro and micro levels. I have already mentioned the prophecy of Simeon, who said both that Jesus would be "a light for revelation to the Gentiles" and that he would be "destined for the fall and rise of many in Israel" (Luke 2:32, 34). The twinned themes of God's favor toward Gentiles and Jewish rejection of Jesus are put front and center in Luke's version of Jesus' Nazareth sermon (Luke 4:16–30), which serves as Jesus' first public proclamation in Luke's Gospel. Acts 1–7 records an increasing Jewish opposition to Christian preaching in Jerusalem that leads ultimately to the death of Stephen, whose speech centers on the theme of Jewish rejection, and the scattering of the Church, a consequence of which is the Gentile mission (Acts 8:4; 11:19) and the fulfilment of Christ's command in Acts 1:8.[25] Similarly, on a micro level, it is Paul's practice in Acts always to speak first to Jews; only when they reject him does he venture to preach to Gentiles (e.g., Acts 13:44–47 and 17:1–5). Why has Christian proclamation eventuated in an increasingly Gentile church? The answer is clear: it is the Jews' own fault.

Of particular importance is the statement made by Peter to the Jews in Acts 3:19–21:

> Repent therefore, and turn again, that your sins may be blotted out, in order that times of refreshing may come from the presence of the Lord, and that

> he may send the Christ appointed for you, Jesus, whom heaven must receive until [the] times of [the] restoration of all things [*apokatastaseōs pantōn*], which God spoke by the mouth of his holy prophets from of old.

It may be that Luke believed that the *parousia* would already have occurred had the Jews responded to the early preaching of the disciples. As we noted above, in Acts the Gentile mission begins only after Jewish unbelief had crystallized. Perhaps, as Terrance Donaldson has suggested in a different context,[26] just such a view stands behind Paul's statements in Romans 11 concerning the hardening of Israel as the *cause* of the Gentile mission: "*through their trespass* salvation has come to the Gentiles . . . *their failure means* riches for the Gentiles . . . you have now received mercy *because of their disobedience*" (v. 30).[27] Also, Acts 3 and Romans 11 are both reminiscent of the well-known rabbinic tradition that "If Israel repented a single day, immediately would the son of David come."[28]

Note too that Acts 3:19–21 links the eschaton, Jewish national repentance ["your sins blotted out" (Acts) = "banishing ungodliness from Jacob" (Romans)], and Jewish acceptance of Jesus. For both Paul and Luke, these ideas belong together. Moreover, the "restoration of all things" is to take place at the *parousia.* Restoration is emphatically a *future* category for Luke. This is evidenced by Luke's treatment of Mark 9:12, which reads: And Jesus said to them, "Indeed, Elijah having come first does *restore all things* [*apokathistanei panta*]. . ." (v. 13: "But I tell you that Elijah has come. . .").

Luke moves the Malachi 3:24 [ET 4:5] quotation to Chapter 1:17, but, unlike Mark, does not use the Septuagint, which translates the Hebrew term *shuv* ("turn") with the Greek verb *apokathistēmi* ("restore"; in Mark's "restore all things"); instead, Luke deliberately returns to the original sense of the Hebrew text, choosing the verb *epistrephō* ("turn"). Also, Luke does not follow Mark in paraphrasing "the hearts of the fathers to the children (etc.)" as either restoring or turning "all things." The result? Luke 1:16–17 has plainly to do with John's preaching of repentance and not with an already-commenced restoration of Israel. The point is underscored by Luke's own addition to Malachi: the phrase "and he will turn [*epistrephō* again] many of the sons of Israel to the Lord their God" (v. 16).

Two further observations on this point: First, Mark's broad paraphrase of the Septuagint, associating Malachi 3:24 [4:5] with the restoration "of all things," is consistent with Ben Sira's use of the same verse in Ecclesiasticus 48:10, in which we are told that Elijah will come "to turn the hearts of parents to their children, and to restore[29] *the tribes of Jacob.*" Luke strips the verse of its apparently common restoration associations; restoration is yet to come. Yet Luke does make further use of Mark 9:12. The Markan phrase "restore all things" resurfaces in Acts 3:21, in which it is addressed to a Jewish audience and refers unambiguously to the situation following the return of Christ. Such displacement of Markan material in Acts is not unique and such relocations on the part of Luke are both intentional and meaningful.

The only other use of restoration language by Luke also concerns a future restoration of historical Israel. The reference is of course Acts 1:6, in which the question is posed to Jesus, "Will you at this time restore [yet again, *apokathistēmi*] the kingdom to Israel?" Most scholars have treated this question as though it came straight from the lips of the New Testament equivalent of the Keystone Cops, the Markan disciples. C. S. C. Williams, for one, makes this judgment explicit:

> The hardness of the disciples' hearts is apparent here *as in Mark's Gospel;* they awaited a material kingdom, for the spirit was not yet poured out on them to give them *a more enlightened conception of it.*[30]

But these are not the Markan disciples. Luke's design is clear: through the time of Jesus' death, the disciples are uncomprehending [as is stated at the time of the third passion prediction, "They understood nothing about all these things; in fact, what he said *was hidden from them*. . ." (Luke 18:34)]. But after the resurrection, Jesus, "beginning with Moses and all the prophets . . . interpreted to them the things about himself in all the scriptures" (Luke 24:27). Again, in Luke 24:45, he "*opened their minds* to understand the scriptures." Prior to their question about the kingdom in Acts 1:6, we are told that Jesus taught the disciples over a period of forty days "about the kingdom of God" (v. 3).

It is certainly not in the Lukan scheme of things that the final utterance of the disciples to their Lord should manifest base ignorance of his teaching. Jesus does *not* correct their perception, just their priorities. "*It is not for you to know* the times or seasons that *the Father has set* by his own authority." This statement functions much like that of the angel that immediately follows: "Why do you stand looking into heaven?" It does not undermine the expectation of Christ's return but shifts the focus to the task at hand. "What will be, will be"; in the meantime, there's work to be done. "You will be my witnesses. . . ."

It is worth noting how the beginning of Acts aligns with the beginning of Luke. Of particular note is Gabriel's promise to Mary in Luke 1, which includes the first mention of a *basileia* ("kingdom") in Luke–Acts: "He will reign over the house of Jacob forever, and of his kingdom there will be no end" (v. 33). Luke 1:33 and Acts 1:6 are then echoed in the concluding verse of the entire narrative, in which we are told that Paul continued "preaching the kingdom of God" (Acts 28:31). It is not the case that the expectations created by Luke 1–2 are either subverted or fulfilled in the later narrative.

The second point made above with reference to Romans 11 was that the present period of Gentile opportunity is impermanent ("a hardening has come upon part of Israel, until the full number of the Gentiles has come in"; v. 25).

Consider the Lukan version of the "Desolating Sacrilege" pericope:[31] "Jerusalem," Luke alone writes, "will be trampled on by the Gentiles, *until the times of the Gentiles are fulfilled*." Granted, Luke 21:24 says nothing about Gentile evangelization (which is obvious enough elsewhere, in any case), but it, like Romans 11, periodizes the present as the Gentile age, a time fated to last until the eschaton (v. 27). Note too Luke's implication that there will come a day after "the times of the Gentiles" when Jerusalem will once again be the providence of Israel. This harks back to the figure of Anna in Luke 2:38, who anticipated "the redemption of Jerusalem." So, "Jerusalem will be trampled on by the Gentiles, until [*achriou*] the times of the Gentiles are fulfilled" (Luke); "A hardening has come upon part of Israel, until [*achriou*] the full number of the Gentiles has come in" (Romans).

I have already shown that the linkage between the eschaton and Jewish belief in Jesus (Paul's "Point Three") is found in Luke's statement in Acts 3:19–21. I should also mention in this context Luke 13:35, part of Jesus' lament over Jerusalem: "I tell you, you will not see me again until you say 'Blessed is the one coming in the name of the Lord.'" The last part of this verse is a quotation from Psalms 118 [ET 117]:26, which "appears to have had a [tradition of] messianic interpretation."[32] It is possible that this saying, paralleled in Matthew 23:37–39, reflects an early Christian belief, as in Acts 3, that Jesus' return would be occasioned by Jewish belief. This is not identical to Paul's claim in Romans 11:26–27, that is, that Israel would be redeemed at the time of the parousia itself, but the ideas are very similar. Logically, Paul's view might have been a modification or extension of that reported in Luke and Matthew. Indeed, Romans 11:11–15 may well presuppose such a belief: "I magnify my ministry in order to make my own people jealous . . . *for what will their acceptance be but life from the dead!*"

Paul in Romans does not inform us about the time following the return of Christ. To some extent, Luke does, but what he says has more in common with traditional Jewish restoration eschatology than most Christian exegetes either have recognized or have been willing to admit.

It is instructive to compare Luke's Parable of the Pounds with Matthew's Parable of the Talents. Luke greatly expands the eschatological dimensions of the parable. This is clear enough in the Lukan introduction: "he . . . told them a parable . . . because they supposed that the *kingdom of God* was to appear immediately" (Luke 19:11–27; cf. Matthew 25:14–30). Matthew tells of a man going on a journey, but Luke of "a nobleman [who goes] . . . to a distant country *to get royal power for himself* and then return." The theme of the accession of the resurrected Jesus to the Davidic throne is common in Luke; see Luke 1:32; 19:12; Acts 2:30; etc. It is this in all likelihood and not the restoration of Israel that stands behind Acts 15:16 ("After these things I will return and I will rebuild the tent of David, which has fallen"),[33] a passage that is frequently cited in defense of supersessionism. As many interpreters now realize, the rebuilding of David's "hut" (*skenē*) is a reference to the reestablishment of the Davidic dynasty, in line with the promise of II Samuel 7:16: "Your house and your kingdom shall be made sure forever before me; your throne shall be established forever."[34] Because Jesus has taken the Davidic throne, James argues, the Gentile mission foreseen in Amos 9:11–12 (by virtue of the LXX) may now commence.

When the nobleman "having received royal power" (v. 15; that is, Jesus, having been enthroned) returns, how does he reward those who have exercised good stewardship? In Luke, unlike Matthew, they are given charge over *cities* (vv. 17 and 19). Cities in the kingdom of God? This is of course reminiscent of the (possibly Q) saying in Matthew 19:28 and Luke 22:30: "You will sit on thrones judging the twelve tribes of Israel." Such talk of course appears to assume the restoration of the twelve tribes. In addition, we should pay attention to what Luke inserts before the saying. Luke 22:28–29:

> You are those who have continued with me in my trials; and I confer on you, just as my Father has conferred on me, a kingdom, so that you may eat and drink at my table in my kingdom, and you will sit on thrones judging the twelve tribes of Israel.

The disciples together with Jesus will rule over kingdoms, the sort of kingdoms in which one eats and drinks.

So, what of Acts 28:28: "Let it be known to you then that this salvation of God has been sent to the Gentiles; they will listen"? One possible answer is that it was not Luke's objective to defend the restoration of Israel, which both he and his "opponents" assume (albeit under very different terms), but to defend his understanding of what happens before the restoration, what is the present work of God. His strategy is twofold. First, demonstrate that Christianity, in particular, Gentile Christianity, is God's idea, God's initiative, God's plan. The attitude of the Christians is expressed by Peter in Acts 11: "Who was I that I could withstand God?" The attitude of right-thinking Jews is articulated by Gamaliel in Acts 5:

> Keep away from these persons and let them alone; for if this plan or this undertaking is of human origin, it will fail; but if it is of God, you will not be able to overthrow them. You might even be found [to be] opposing God!

Second, Luke demonstrates, above all to Jewish detractors, that this is not a Gentile religion or movement. It is, first and foremost, a work of God amongst and for the sake of the Jews. But few Jews respond; therefore, the grace of God has been and is continually extended to the Gentiles. Thus, the increasing Gentile dominance of the Church is, ironically, the result of Jewish choice. Note how often Luke refers to the Jews of Jesus' day, to "this generation" (*genea*) (e.g., 7:31; 9:41; 11:29–32; 50–51; 17:25; Acts 2:40), who would witness the destruction of Jerusalem. That is the focus of judgment. It is, in a sense, self-defense. Acts 28:28 justifies a Gentile, not a supercessionist, Church.

Conclusion

Docetists read the Gospel of John and find in it support for their denial of the humanity of Jesus. Did the author of John doubt Jesus' humanity? No, but it *is* overshadowed in the book by Jesus' divinity. Why? For the simple reason that John's opponents required no convincing of Jesus' humanity. But one-front arguments lend themselves to one-sided interpretations. It is possible to read Luke–Acts in such a way as to believe that the Church is restored Israel. Why? Because shared convictions are not defended. Hence the Church overshadows Israel in Luke–Acts.

As a final argument, I invoke the plausibility of the ordinary. Would not the early Christians have remained, so far as possible, within the realm of Jewish expectation? Surely they would have done so for practical, theological, and evangelical reasons. What should be of surprise are those places in which the Church threw off Jewish understanding. But these do not surprise us, because we stand in a tradition that sees the Jewish–Christian relationship as those who lived after its divorce came to see it. Those who participated in and tried to make sense of the Jewish–Christian union were sensitive to issues that have become almost insensible to us.

Similarly, we should not be astonished if it turns out that Luke owes a thing or two to Paul after all. At the very least, Luke was probably associated with a Pauline church; apart from some such connection, his considerable interest in Paul is without explanation. One is right to be cautious about making claims concerning Luke's knowledge of Pauline theology, and indeed the above argument is not entirely dependent upon them,[35] but we should not rule them out in advance. Sometimes the truth is the darnedest, most unorthodox, most unexpected thing of all. So learned Paul's apparently self-certain, self-congratulatory Gentile readership in Rome. For Paul, who knows God as "unsearchable . . . and inscrutable" (Romans 11:33), not all truth is calculable; there is mystery. Surprisingly, mysteriously, even against the logic of Paul's own earlier assertions, Israel has a future. It cannot be otherwise.

Ironically, it may be that operating from within their own Gentile–Christian perspective, most modern interpreters of Luke–Acts have themselves overcalculated, have been unobservant of the unanticipated, and so have failed to recognize this same mystery at the heart of Lukan eschatology: Israel has a future.

Romans 11:13: "Now I am speaking to you Gentiles. . . ." It may be that we have been a little too quick to assume identity with Paul and not with those whom Paul, and perhaps Luke as well, would correct.

NOTES

1. This essay revisits and expands a paper titled "A Future for the Historical Israel: A Link Between Pauline and Lukan Eschatology," which I delivered to the Pauline Epistles Section of the AAR/SBL annual meeting in Washington, D.C. on 20 November 1993.
2. Jacob Jervell's work on Luke–Acts is perhaps the best known example.
3. The interpretation of Romans 11 is treated in more detail in my essay on Romans in the *Oxford Bible Commentary* (Oxford: Oxford University Press, 2001).
4. *Paul among Jews and Gentiles* (London: SCM, 1977), 4.
5. Note in particular the impressive collection of fifteen essays by an international panel of scholars in *Jesus and the Heritage of Israel*, ed. David P. Moessner (Harrisburg: Trinity, 1999). Further examples beyond those mentioned elsewhere in this article include Walther Eltester, "Israel im lukanischen Werk und die Nazarethperikope," in *Jesus in Nazareth*, eds. E. Grässer et al. (Berlin: Walter de Gruyter, 1972), 76–147; Bradley J. Chance, *Jerusalem, the Temple, and the New Age in Luke–Acts* (Macon, GA: Mercer, 1988); Stephen G. Wilson, *Related Strangers: Jews and Christians 70–170 C.E.* (Minneapolis: Fortress, 1995); and David Ravens, *Luke and the Restoration of Israel*, (Sheffield: Sheffield Academic Press, 1995). Also notable is Henry W. L. Rietz's unpublished paper "The Restoration of Israel: the Birth Narrative of Luke–Acts."
6. See Jack T. Sanders, *The Jews in Luke–Acts* (London: SCM, 1987).
7. Ernst Haenchen, *The Acts of the Apostles: A Commentary*, trans. Bernard Noble and Gerald Shinn, rev. R. M. Wilson (Oxford: Basil Blackwell, 1971), 128.
8. Robert L. Brawley, *Luke–Acts and the Jews: Conflict, Apology, and Conciliation* (Atlanta: Scholars, 1987).
9. Luke T. Johnson, *The Writings of the New Testament: An Interpretation* (Philadelphia: Fortress, 1986), 228.
10. "Luke and the Restoration of Israel," *Expository Times* 89 (1977–78): 76. Cf. Helmut Merkel, "Israel im Lukanischen Werk," *New Testament Studies* 40 (1994): 371–398.
11. David L. Tiede, *Prophecy and History in Luke–Acts* (Philadelphia: Fortress, 1980), 16.
12. Two textual variants are of particular interest in this passage. Verse 29, "And when he had said these words, the Jews departed, holding much dispute among themselves," is part of the Western expansion of Acts. It provides a smoother transition to verse 30 and makes clear the conclusion that some Jews did believe Paul's preaching. This last point is also made by the variant of verse 30, which clarifies that amongst the "all" who came to Paul were "both Jews and Greeks." These additions do not prove that Luke had "written off" the Jews, but they do demonstrate that some early Christians wanted to make clear that the text should not be read in that way.
13. Joseph Tyson, *Luke, Judaism, and the Scholars* (Columbia, SC: University of South Carolina Press, 1999), 144–145.
14. For example, in Robert C. Tannehill, "The Story of Israel within the Lukan Narrative," in David Moessner, ed., *Jesus and the Heritage of Israel: Luke's Narrative Claim upon Israel's Legacy* (Harrisburg: Trinity, 1999), 327.
15. F. F. Bruce, "Eschatology in Acts," in *Eschatology and the New Testament: Essays in Honor of George Beasley-Murray*, ed. W. Hulitt Gloer (Peabody, MA: Hendrickson, 1988), 53.

16. In Tyson, *Luke–Acts and the Jewish People: Eight Critical Perspectives* (Minneapolis: Augsburg, 1988), 35–50.
17. In Moessner, *Jesus and the Heritage of Israel*, 307–324.
18. Ibid., 323.
19. James D. G. Dunn, *The Acts of the Apostles* (Narrative Commentaries; Valley Forge, PA: Trinity Press International, 1996), 353 (italics mine).
20. David L. Tiede, "Glory to Thy People Israel," in Tyson, *Luke–Acts and the Jewish People*, 34.
21. Michael Wolter, "Israel's Future and the Delay of the Parousia, according to Luke," 317.
22. "Luke and the Restoration of the Kingdom to Israel," 76.
23. Cf. Merkel, "Israel im Lukanischen Werk," 397.
24. Cf. Romans 15:19 ("I have fully preached the gospel of Christ") and Mark 13:10 (Matthew 24:14). Interestingly, the "Gentile condition" is absent from Luke–Acts.
25. That is not to say that Christian preaching to Jews ceases at this point in the narrative. What is clear is that the Jews *as a nation* do not repent, in stark contrast to the hope expressed in Acts 3:19–21. Paul himself knew of the conversion of individual Jews when he composed his lament Romans 9:1–5. It is the absence of national repentance that is key for Paul and quite possibly also for Luke.
26. Terrance Donaldson, "'Riches for the Gentiles' (Rom 11:12): Israel's Rejection and Paul's Gentile Mission," *JBL* 112 (1993): 94.
27. The Gentile mission is a counterpart to the distruction of Jerusalem, also thought to have been the result of Jewish unbelief (Luke 13:35).
28. P. Ta'anith ["feast"] 64*a*. This subject is addressed in A. Cohen, *Everyman's Talmud* (New York: Schocken Books, 1975), 351–352. Compare Canticles Rabba: "If the Israelites would but repent for one day, they would be redeemed, and the son of David would come straight away, as it says, 'Today, if you would hear his voice' (Ps. xcv, 7)" [as noted in C. G. Montefiore and H. Loewe, *A Rabbinic Anthology* (Cleveland and New York: Meridian Books, 1963), 318].
29. *Katastēsai* (aorist infinitive of *kathistēmi*).
30. C. S. C. Williams, *A Commentary on the Acts of the Apostles* (New York: Harper & Brothers, 1957), 56 (italics mine).
31. Found also in Mark 13:14–20 and Matthew 24:15–22.
32. I. Howard Marshall, *Commentary on Luke: A Commentary on the Greek Text* (Grand Rapids: Eerdmans, 1978), 577.
33. Contra Jacob Jervell, *Luke and The People of God. A New Look at Luke–Acts* (Minneapolis: Augusburg, 1972), 51–52.
34. For example, Mark L. Strauss, *The Davidic Messiah in Luke–Acts: The Promise and its Fulfillment in Lukan Christology* (Sheffield: Sheffield Academic Press, 1995), 190; Joseph A. Fitzmyer, S.J., *The Acts of the Apostles* (Anchor Bible; New York: Doubleday, 1998), 555; and Robert C. Tannehill, *The Narrative Unity of Luke–Acts: A Literary Interpretation, volume 2* (Minneapolis: Fortress, 1990), 188.

    It is possible to read *anastrepsō* ("I will return") as referring to a still-future restoration of the Davidic throne. Obviously, this interpretation would lend weight to a nonsupersessionist construal of Luke–Acts. Against such a reading is the fact that the quotation from Amos is meant to validate a present-day mission to Gentiles. It is difficult (although not impossible) to see how a future renewal of the Davidic line might be thought to provide such justification. At the same time, it is important to note (in concert with the above-mentioned scholars) that the restoration of *Israel* is not in view in Acts 15:16–17.
35. It is conceivable that Luke came to conclusions similar to those of Paul on his own or under some other influence.

CHAPTER 15

The Jew Paul and His Meaning for Israel

JAMES D. G. DUNN

I

To speak of "the Jew Paul" has an unnerving ring about it. The tradition in Protestant New Testament scholarship has been rather to distance Paul as far as possible from his Jewish heritage. The classic Reformation "law/gospel" antithesis usually carried with it as its fateful shadow the more virulent antithesis "Judaism/Christianity," with the assumption that it was Paul's formulation of the gospel in conflict with his Jewish opponents that is crystallized in that antithesis. At the beginning of the modern period of Pauline scholarship, F. C. Baur formulated Paul's theological significance in terms of Christianity's breaking through and free from the bounds of national Judaism.[1] And a hundred years ago Adolf Harnack could characterize Paul's greatness as lying in the fact that he broke tyranny of the law and transplanted the gospel into the Gentile world.[2] There is no need to dwell on the horrors of sixty years ago. But the fact remains that it was still easier in the Bultmann and post-Bultmann generation—the post-Holocaust decades—to speak denigratingly of the Jew as Paul's opponent, as the type of "sinful; self-reliance" and "unceasing self-assurance,"[3] rather than of Paul himself as "the Jew."

On the Jewish side Paul remained more of an enigma than a co-religionist. S. Schechter, for example, found the Apostle to the Gentiles "quite unintelligible" when set alongside the theology of the Rabbis as he knew it.[4] And although some did try to dialogue with Paul and even to speak for him, the crude dismissal of Paul by Hyam Maccoby as a fake Pharisee (in reality a Gentile adventurer)[5] probably resonated more fully with older incomprehension. Even the highly sympathetic treatment of Alan Segal, *Paul the Convert*, is subtitled, *The Apostolate and Apostasy of Saul the Pharisee.*[6] This negative attitude to Paul from the Jewish side is, of course, deeply rooted in the history of Christianity's beginnings. We need only recall the reports that apparently circulated within Jerusalem even during Paul's life—"They (the zealous Jewish converts) have been told about you that you teach all the Jews living among Gentiles to forsake Moses . . . and not to circumcise their children or to observe the customs" (Acts 21:20–21)—or the denigration of Paul as the enemy of Peter that is a feature of the pseudo-Clementines.[7]

Against the background of this fairly uniform history, what can be said, what should be said about "Paul the Jew"? Given that Paul throughout the last two millennia has been so consistently seen and heard as an archetypal spokesman for Christianity, can it be that he still has something to say to his own people the Jews? And given that what he has been heard to say has been so consistently negative toward the Jews, has he anything else to say? After Auschwitz is Paul too much of an embarrassment to contemporary Jewish–Christian dialogue for his letters to have any claim on the attention of those engaged in and anxious to forward that dialogue?

II

It is important to realize at once how much the issue of Paul the Jew has become confused by terminology. The point is now widely recognized with regard to the term that was still common in theological circles forty years ago—*Spätjudentum* as the description of the Judaism of Paul's time. The obvious rationale for describing (late) Second Temple Judaism as "*late Judaism*" is that Judaism ceased to have any significance for theology after the establishment of Christianity; what preceded Christianity was therefore "late." In other words, Judaism's only function was to prepare the way for and to serve as the defining antithesis to Christianity. But, of course, "Judaism" continued, and continues to this day; if first-century Judaism was "late Judaism," how should we characterize nineteenth- or twentieth-century Judaism? And if we now acknowledge more willingly that (Rabbinic) Judaism emerged from the same matrix of Christianity,[8] then the question of Paul the Jew reemerges, since it becomes conceivable that he as a Jew still has something to say about that on-going Judaism, and perhaps even to that on-going Judaism.

Another word illustrative of the blinkered viewpoint that has characterized so much Christian scholarship on the subject of Jews and Judaism in the past 200 years is the term "Judaizers." Since Baur, "Judaizers" has been the common term used to refer to Paul's opponents, particularly in Galatians. But the reason why it has become so common a title is presumably that is characterizes these opponents, as Jews, or more accurately as Christian Jews, and as Jews who were determined to impose on others the rules and constraints of Judaism. Thus it has come to denote not just a certain body of Jews, but certain Jews as representative of Judaism. And even when the point is made that these "troublemakers" were actually Christian (Jewish) missionaries, the overtone still hangs heavy round the term—"Judaizers" as characterizing "Judaism" as a whole by their/its restrictiveness. And yet, most/many who use the term in this way know quite well that the verb "to judaize" in its use at the time denoted the adoption of Jewish ways by *non*-Jews,[9] so that the more appropriate use of the derived noun "Judaizers" would be to refer to "judaizing" *Gentiles.* The difference does not amount to much in itself. What I refer to here, however, is the change of tone in the word that the transition in usage has occasioned from a term denoting a positive approbation for Judaism and Jewish ways (Gentiles who wanted to live like Jews) to one that marks out Judaism as exclusive, dismissive, and uncompromisingly demanding in its encounters with sympathetic Gentiles.

Nor should it be forgotten that the term "Judaism" itself has created its own problems within this discussion. It is so easy to slip into the assumption that there was a constant that can be designated "Judaism" and that remained constant from Maccabean times,[10] through the first century C.E., and beyond. It was this assumption, too little examined for too long, that allowed such an eminent scholar as J. Jeremias in effect to reconstruct the Judaism of Paul's time from a wide spread of particularly rabbinic evidence spanning several centuries. The more recent reaction that speaks of several or many "Judaisms" during late Second Temple Judaism goes only part of the way to redraw the picture. For such a characterization ("many Judaisms") is one that only a modern, sociologically conscious perspective could acknowledge. It was certainly not a perspective operative at the time of Paul. Had they used the term at all, the "sects" of the time would more likely have recognized either one Judaism that embraced a number of differing halakhoth, or their own halakhah as defining the one true Judaism.[11]

This last problem becomes serious for us, since two of the very few attested uses of the term "Judaism" prior to the destruction of Jerusalem appear in Paul's letter to the Galatians (1:13–14).[12] Read in the light of the traditional attitudes to Jews and Judaism, it seemed most natural to take these two verses as indicating Paul's abandonment of "Judaism," that is, the normative Judaism assumed to remain constant more or less from the Maccabean settlement through to the rabbis and beyond. But in light of the considerations just alluded to, it makes better sense to see Paul's conversion as a break from "Judaism" as defined by zealous Pharisees, but not necessarily as a break from the diverse reality of Second Temple Judaism as a whole. The issue, of course, deserves much fuller discussion than can be provided here. But the very fact that there is an issue to be raised at this point should give pause to any who are interested in the topic, "Paul the Jew."

The issue becomes that much more significant, and sensitive, when we include consideration of what has been called "the new perspective" on Paul.[13] In brief, the argument of "the new perspective" is that Second Temple Judaism has been misrepresented in New Testament scholarship. In the traditional perspective, "Judaism" could be characterized as legalistic, teaching righteousness gained by good works, and requiring sinless perfection as both necessary and attainable. As noted already, Jewish scholars who tried to take some account of the New Testament could not understand this portrayal of Judaism: it was not Judaism as they knew it. A few from the Christian side had tried to protest against the misrepresentation, but to no avail.[14] It was Sanders who demonstrated most clearly that in contrast to the Judaism of Protestant antithesis, the Judaism of Second Temple Judaism was fundamentally a religion of grace. Its starting point was the free and gracious election of a slave people. Its keynotes were repentance and forgiveness (terms hardly found in Paul!), with a basic premise of the sacrificial system being that God had freely provided atonement for sin. Obedience was seen not as an attempt to gain favor with God, but as the response required of the people chosen, marking out their responsibility on how to live as the people of God (Exodus 20:1ff).[15] They looked for a righteousness defined as living in accordance with the covenant made with them by God, but did not teach or expect perfection.

The point here again is that when "Judaism" is freed from such misunderstandings, it becomes necessary to realign Paul in relation to Judaism. No longer can he himself simply be characterized as setting his face against "Judaism," no longer his teaching simply summed up as (Christian) gospel against (Jewish) law. A much more nuanced portrayal becomes both necessary and possible. Such a portrayal would have to include, for example, the fact that Paul drew his understanding of divine righteousness directly from his ancestral scriptures,[16] the fact that, as a passage like 1QS 11:11–15 from the Dead Sea Scrolls reminds us,[17] the teaching of grace toward sinners is first Jewish before it is Pauline, and the fact that Paul protested so consistently the importance of the law for his converts not least.[18] To develop such aspects would take us too far from our present concerns. The important point for us is the fact that these questions are being put to such basic terms and traditional perspectives should be sufficient signal to us that a fresh look is called for at Paul the Jew.

III

As the first step, it should be reaffirmed that Paul was indeed a Jew. The point is usually simply taken for granted. But Hyam Maccoby for one has questioned it.[19] Maccoby finds the portrayal of Paul, in Acts and in the Pauline letters, incredible, and finds a more plausible explanation for Paul's origin in a piece of hostile black propaganda attested only in the fourth century.[20] The attempt, however, is self-condemned by the arbitrariness of its evaluation of the data, and no reputable scholar to my knowledge has followed Maccoby, whose argument at this point is a testimony more to the residual suspicion, not to say extreme dislike for Paul on the part of some Jews, than to credible historical scholarship.

The tradition of Paul's Jewish ancestry is most clearly asserted in Acts. "I am a Jew, from Tarsus in Cilicia," testifies the Paul of Acts 21:39, "brought up in this city, at the feet of Gamaliel, trained in accordance with the strictness of our ancestral law, being a zealot for God," he adds some verses later (22:3). Given the degree of "re-Judaization" of Paul usually attributed to Luke, the author of Acts,[21] such evidence might be discounted, if not entirely dismissed. And the suggestion that Saul received his "higher education" in Jerusalem has often been disregarded for similar reasons, Paul's assertion to the effect that he was unknown by sight to the churches of Judea (Galatians 1:22) being regarded as sufficient countertestimony.[22]

It is true that in his own letters Paul never calls himself a "Jew" in so many words. But the language of Galatians 2:15 should be sufficient self-attestation—"we are by nature Jews and not sinners from the Gentiles"—where Peter is the particular "other" embraced by the Jewish "we." The language is all the more noteworthy since it is untypical of Paul's language in regard to Gentiles elsewhere in his writings, but echoes and attitude not untypical of many Jews of the time.[23] Paul was evidently appealing to a characteristically Jewish attitude toward Gentiles ("Gentile sinners"), which he himself presumably had previously shared, but from which now he wished to wean his fellow Jewish believers.

More weighty are Paul's description of his preconversion state and status in two important passage—Galatians 1.13–14 and Philippians 3:4–6.

> Galatians 1:13–14—You have heard of my way of life previously in Judaism, that in excessive measure I persecuted the church of God and tried to destroy it; and that I progressed in Judaism beyond many of my contemporaries among my people, being exceedingly zealous for my ancestral traditions.

> Philippians 3:5–6—circumcised on the eighth day, of the people of Israel, of the tribe of Benjamin, a Hebrew of the Hebrews, in terms of the law a Pharisee, in terms of zeal a persecutor of the church, in terms of righteousness which is in the law blameless.

The testimony of these passages is enhanced by the fact that elsewhere also Paul was able to describe himself as (still) a "Hebrew" and an "Israelite" (II Corinthians 11:22; Romans 11:1). Several things may be noted here. First, the fullness of the genealogical claim: both ethnic (Israel) and tribal (Benjamin) identity; the genealogical "birthmarks" had evidently been of considerable importance to him. Second, the clear indication that circumcision was the prime religious identifier of Jewishness: it is placed at the head of the list in Philippians 3:5.[24] Third, the internal consistency in the testimony regarding the character of his previous way of life "within Judaism" as a "Hebrew" (Philippians 3:5; II Corinthians 11:22); the emphasis on his "zeal" (Galatians 1:14; Philippians 3:5), confirming the testimony of Acts 22:3. Fourth, the degree of Paul's previous commitment to his ancestral faith has similar multiple testimony: the deliberate doubling in "Hebrew of the Hebrews," in Philippians 3:5, of what was already a conscious archaism ("Hebrew"),[25] the claim to a zeal that deliberately aligned him with the earlier heroes of zeal within Israel's history.[26]

In view of the doubts expressed about the value of Acts' testimony it is worth making particular note of the fact that Paul calls himself a "Pharisee," and that the claim made in Galatians 1:14 (cited above) both confirms what we know of Pharisees from other sources,[27] and again confirms the testimony of Acts (22:3; 26:5). Because it is more or less inconceivable to imagine a self-proclaimed Pharisee who had sought to complete his education or training anywhere other than Jerusalem,[28] the circumstantial evidence in favor of Acts 22:3 in regard to Gamaliel as Paul's teacher must surely outweigh the speculative interpretations of Galatians 1:22 referred to above. In short, Paul's Jewish origins, both ethnic and religious, are indisputable.

IV

Given this clarification of background in the past two sections, it becomes possible to reevaluate the significance of Paul the Jew, become believer in Messiah Jesus, for Israel.

In the first place, we should not underestimate the importance of having the (some) letters written by a Jew in the period prior to the destruction of the Temple. Paul has too readily been assigned to the "Christian" section of ancient literature. But he wrote at a period when "Christianity" as a term had not yet been coined, and when the Jesus movement (how can we best speak of it with historical authenticity?) was still a Jewish movement, a messianic movement, a renewal movement within the wider reality of Second Temple Judaism. The "parting of the ways" between Judaism and Christianity was only beginning and was still far from complete.[29] Paul wrote Galatians 1.13–14 with a backward glance to his life "within Judaism," but his was a conversion not from one religion (Judaism) to another (Christianity), but rather from one "sect" within the diversity of Second Temple Judaism to another.[30]

His letters should therefore be designated as "Jewish" before they are designated "Christian." Paul, in other words, provides an invaluable testimony to the rich diversity of first-century Judaism.[31] That is important in the renewed appreciation of the diverse character of Second Temple Judaism occasioned by the discovery of the Dead Sea Scrolls in particular. For so much of the source material for that period leaves issues of date and provenance ambiguous.[32] And the initial confidence regarding the character and testimony of the Scrolls themselves has given way to much more uncertainty on just the same questions. Likewise the older confidence in reading the rabbinic traditions as testimony to Second Temple Judaism's halakhah and practices has been replaced by an ongoing dispute as to how much can be just so read. And the evidence from diaspora Judaism remains tantalizingly limited and too dependent on the interpretation of scattered epigraphic data. To have such an amount of first-hand testimony from the period itself (Paul's letters), whose date and provenance can be so precisely pinpointed, is therefore invaluable. Of course, the testimony is very individualistic, and Paul's particular stance on the interface of Judaism and the wider Gentile world will be regarded by many Jews as too unrepresentative and too uncomfortable. But so too in their different ways are the other two Jews who positioned themselves also on the same interface, and who left us an even greater literary deposit—Philo and Josephus. Judaism in reassessing the diversity of its character in that period and of its heritage from that period must pay due heed to Philo and Josephus. In which case, it can hardly shut its ears to or exclude Paul.

To be noted in particular is the simple fact that Paul is the only Pharisee writing in the pre-70 period from whom we have first-hand testimony.[33] Even though he converted from his Pharisaism (Philippians 3:7–11), he still provides invaluable evidence regarding the character of pre-70 Pharisaism. Here the self-testimony of Galatians 1:14 again needs to be recalled, attesting Saul the Pharisee's "far greater zeal for the ancestral traditions" and his almost competitive progress within Judaism ("beyond many of my contemporaries"). This testimony not only fits well with the evidence of Acts, the Gospels, and Josephus,[34] but it also provides crucial confirmation of the character and concerns of Pharisaic halakhah in the pre-70 period. As rabbinic Judaism tries to clarify the depth of its roots in and the extent of its heritage from Second Temple Judaism, Paul's is a voice that needs to be heard.

Furthermore, it is very arguable that the Christian Paul still evinces many of the benefits of his Pharisaic training (as in other passages, we should recognize the rhetoric of Paul's language in Philippians 3:7–8). Here we can indicate only the more obvious examples.

1. Paul's concern for righteousness straddles his conversion—the one "in terms of the law," the other "through faith," but the key term and common term ("righteousness") reflects and attests Jewish/Pharisaic priorities. Often

neglected is the fact that Paul's debt at this point includes his typically Jewish emphasis on final judgment. It is not simply the fact that he cites traditional Jewish theologoumena on the subject (Romans 2:6, 11; cf. particularly Psalms 62:12; Proverbs 24:12; Deuteronomy 1:17; 10:16–17). More sensitive, at times embarrassing on *both* sides of the Jewish–Christian dialogue, is the fact that in Romans 2:7–11 Paul himself speaks with such a characteristically Jewish voice. The degree of this overlap between traditional Jewish and Pauline teaching, despite the fountains of ink spilled on it, has still to be adequately illuminated, and Romans 2 generally remains one of the most challenging passages in any assessment of Paul the Jew and of his testimony regarding Israel and Israel's heritage for Christian theology.[35]

2. Moreover, *pace* Maccoby,[36] Paul's exegetical or expository technique was almost certainly carried over from his Pharisaic training. Consequently a passage such as Romans 4 (Paul's exposition of Genesis 15:6) can be regarded as a good example of authentically Jewish–Pharisaic midrash. And Paul no doubt could confidently expect any Jewish readers to resonate with the arguments of I Corinthians 9:8–10 or Galatians 3:16.
3. Among other points we should certainly at least mention Paul's repeated affirmation of the *Shema* (Romans 1:24–27; I Corinthians 8:4, 6; Galatians 3:20). Also his continuingly passionate denunciation of idolatry (Romans 1:23; I Corinthians 10:14–22; I Thessalonians 1:9) and *porneia* (Romans 1:24–27; I Corinthians 6:9–10). In each case the voice of Paul the Jew speaks loud and clear; the latter two points are hardly if at all affected by his conversion. Here Paul provides one of so very few Jewish voices that can attest to what living and working in the diaspora, in some of the great cities of the Roman Empire, was actually like for a pious Jew (or Christian who, like Paul, valued this Jewish heritage as constitutive also for his faith in Christ).

On this whole question, we are still at a very early stage in the reappraisal of Paul as a voice from within Second Temple Judaism, as a witness to Second Temple Judaism. The older generation of Jewish scholars, however sympathetic to Paul, were still too much distracted and misled by the Protestant Paul to recognize in him a genuinely Jewish interlocutor. Today, however, the opportunity to extend the fresh round of dialogue recently begun by Segal and D. Boyarin[37] needs to be seized.

V

A second point at which Paul calls for attention from his fellow Jews is with regard to their "own" identity.[38] As already noted, his own ethnic and religious origin as a Jew is beyond question. At the same time, however, it would not be inappropriate to question whether Paul the believer in Christ continued to identify himself as a Jew. The evidence here is ambivalent. Unlike the Paul of Acts, the Paul of the letters never says "I am a Jew." In Romans 2:17ff. he seems to set himself to criticize the "Jew." And in I Corinthians 9:20 he seems to sit loose with his identity as a Jew—"I become as a Jew." Yet at the same time, Paul insists that there is much "advantage" in being a Jew, something about the "Jew" that really does distinguish him from others in a positive way (Romans 3:1–2). The resolution to the quandary, however, is given in Romans 2:28–29: Paul seeks to rescue the characterization (and reality) of "Jew" from too much dependence on outward and visible appearance. Although he has himself used the term as an identifier in ethnic terms (Jew = not Gentile, a particular nation over all other nations), he prefers to define the character of "Jew" in terms of divine rather than human recognition ("whose praise comes not from men but from God"). This is not a denunciation of the "Jew," but an attempt in effect to recall his fellow Jews to the defining feature of "Jew-ness," their choice and approbation by God. This is the voice more of Paul the prophet than of Paul the apostate. In a day when Jewish identity is still a matter of debate within Israel, the voice of Paul the Jew still deserves a hearing.

The same point can be made with regard to the other principal marker of Jewishness, then as now—circumcision. Paul never called for the abandonment of circumcision; his own usage attests his continuing identification between "circumcision" and "Jew." He certainly disputed, and fiercely, the necessity for Gentile believers to be circumcised. But he never called for Jews to remove the marks of their circumcision, and there is no suggestion that he ever attempted epispasm for himself; Paul should never be lumped with the Hellenizers of the Maccabean period. On the contrary, Paul strongly advised against any such procedure. "Was anyone at the time of his call already circumcised? Let him not seek to remove the marks of circumcision" (I Corinthians 7:18). In contrast, his concern was the same as with the term "Jew": he saw it as something valuable, something advantageous (Romans 2:25–26; 3:1–2); but he was more concerned to see the realization of what the circumcision rite symbolized, the circumcision of the heart (Romans 2:28–29, the Spirit enabling true worship of God (Philippians 3:3); in terms of priorities, the ritual act and its enduring mark were of less importance than "keeping the commandments of God" (I Corinthians 1:19). Would those who walked in the steps of Deuteronomy and Jeremiah have disagreed?[39]

The same point is reinforced when Paul switches his talk from "Jew" and "circumcision" to his more favored "Israel." Here it is important to note that whereas Paul the believer could have said in a meaningful way, "I *was* a Jew," "I *was* circumcised" (cf. Philippians 3:5–8), he does say "I *am* an Israelite" (Romans 11:1; II Corinthians 11:22). At the same time it is equally to be noted that he says of his "kinsfolk in terms of the flesh," "they (too) *are* Israelites" (Romans 9:3–4).

In both cases "Israel" denotes the continuing identity of both Paul and his countrymen. But as with "Jew" and "circumcision," Paul's primary concern in Romans 9–11 is evidently to remind his readers of what constitutes Israel as Israel. Not ethnic identity or physical descent, not religious practice, but divine election and call (Romans 9:7–13, 23–24), divine mercy (9:15–18, 23; 11:30–32), and grace (11:5–6). Here again is nothing other than a recall of Israel, not to its ethnic roots and covenant obligations, but to its still deeper root in God's prevenient choice and overarching purpose.

Given the tradition of exegesis in regard to Paul and the law any attempt to extend the point to Paul's teaching on the law would far outrun the limits of this essay. We will have to be content simply to indicate how the argument would run at this point. It would call for a discussion that fully reflected all that Paul has to say on the law, recognizing, for example, the polemical context and character of so much of the fiercer language in Galatians, II Corinthians 3, and Philippians 3. It would require more attention to be given to the points of continuity between traditional Jewish teaching on the Torah and Paul's teaching on future justification/judgment such as we have already noted in Romans 2. And it would have to recall the continuingly positive attitude that Paul maintained with regard to the law in the well-known passages in Romans (3:31; 7:7–13; 8:4; 13:8–10). What would emerge in the event would be the same claim: that a Paul who emphasizes the importance of keeping the commandments (I Corinthians 7:19), and of the love command in particular, while at the same time relativizing the importance of circumcision and the food laws, was not so much ignoring or abandoning the law as prioritizing its diverse and sometimes incompatible imperatives.[40] In which case, one could hardly avoid asking here too whether such teaching is so remote from prophetic exhortations such as "I desire steadfast love and not sacrifice" (Hosea 6:6), or so distant in spirit from Hillel's negative version of the golden rule from the Talmud (Sabb. 31a), as to exclude itself from authentic Jewish discourse or to disqualify itself as the word of a Jewish preacher who still challenges his own people to examine their own priorities afresh.

VI

The third point at which Paul the Jew may be said to have continuing significance for Israel is in his conception of his own missionary work. For here too it has to be emphasized that Paul did not see his conversion as any kind of abandonment of Israel, but rather as a commission on behalf of Israel; or, as we may state it summarily, he saw himself as an apostle of Israel, rather than an apostate from Israel.[41] I have argued the point at length elsewhere, so will confine myself to bringing out its main features.

Paul evidently took some care to indicate to those with ears to hear how he understood the character of his apostolic commissioning from the first. In describing how it pleased God "who set me apart from my mother's womb, and called me through his grace, to reveal his Son in me, in order that I might preach him among the Gentiles," Paul was clearly and deliberately echoing the prophetic call of Jeremiah and of the Servant of Isaiah.

> Jeremiah 1:5—Before I formed you in the womb I knew you, and before you were born I consecrated you; I appointed you a prophet to the nations.

> Isaiah 49:1–6—The Lord called me before I was born, while I was still in my mother's womb he named me . . . . I will give you as a light to the nations, that my salvation may reach to the end of the earth.

In other words, Paul saw his commissioning in direct parallel to and continuity with these earlier prophetic callings. Which is also to say that he was deliberately reminding any of his Jewish brothers, who may have listened to his letter with some suspicion, that the most controversial feature of his ministry (his preaching to the Gentiles) was wholly in line with these precedents. The God who sent Jeremiah and the Servant "to the nations" was also the God who sent Paul to preach Jesus "among the nations." Which was also to remind them that God took responsibility for the nations as well as for Israel, and therefore to challenge also Israel as to its own continuing responsibility for the Gentiles. Such Jewish auditors would not quickly forget that the Servant of Isaiah (49:1–6) was explicitly identified as Israel (49:3). That is to say, Paul was in effect claiming that his missionary work among the Gentiles was in fulfilment of Israel's own responsibility to be "a light to the nations, that my (God's) salvation may reach to the end of the earth" (49:6). That challenge still stands.

A similar emphasis emerges later in the same letter, no doubt again deliberately. In Galatians 3:8 Paul makes a point of identifying the gospel with the promise made to Abraham: "In you shall all the nations be blessed."[42] What Paul does is to single out one strand of the threefold promise made repeatedly to Abraham in Genesis.[43] He refers shortly to the promise of seed (Galatians 3:16); he more or less ignores the promise of land (possibly alluding to it in Galatians 4:25–26), but it is the promise of blessing to the nations on which he here seizes. It could be fairly said that historic Israel, then as now, focused its own attention primarily on the first two strands of the Abrahamic promise.[44] That is to say, historic Israel has traditionally played down or even marginalized any obligation that the promise of blessing to the nations may have entailed.[45] In which case, it is hardly straining the exegesis to recognize in Paul's formulation an attempt both to justify his missionary calling in terms of Israel's own obligations, and in so doing also to remind them of their own responsibilities.

An Israel that takes its biblical roots seriously should not ignore Paul's argument and implied exhortation.

This aspect of Paul's self-apology sheds light on another much contested feature of his missionary practice. That is, the extent to which he channeled his missionary efforts directly to Gentiles and the extent to which he bypassed his fellow Jews in so doing. Here it becomes all too easy, and simplistic, to set Paul the self-proclaimed "apostle to the Gentiles" (Romans 11:13) in antithesis with the testimony of Acts that Paul's regular practice throughout his missionary work was to go first to the local synagogue (Acts 13:5; 14; 14:1; 16:13; 17:1; 10; 17; etc.)—as though he could fulfil his obligation "to the Gentiles" only by avoiding fellow Jews! The argument is naive. The fact that Paul remained in such close touch with other diaspora Jews,[46] and that he strongly affirmed the Jewish socializing restrictions against *porneia* and *eidolothuta*,[47] most naturally implies that he kept at least in quite close touch with the Jewish communities in many diaspora cities.[48] More to the point, the argument ignores the clear enough evidence that many diaspora synagogues attracted enquiring or sympathetic Gentiles to their practices and festivals.[49] The point is that a Jewish missionary looking for Gentiles who were likely to give a fair hearing to his message would turn most naturally to the synagogue as his first port of call, since that is where he would most easily find them. Add to this that Paul remained within the ambit of synagogue authority for some quite considerable period (submitted himself to severe synagogue discipline no less that five times—II Corinthians 11:24), and that his theological paradigm as filled out in Romans was "Jew first, but also Greek" (Romans 1:16),[50] and there is surely not much more to argue about.

This discussion feeds into the last main point: that Paul saw his apostleship to the Gentiles as itself playing a part in evangelizing Israel. In Romans 11:13–14 Paul makes the link explicit: "Inasmuch as I am apostle to the Gentiles, I magnify my ministry, in hope that I might provoke my kindred to jealousy and might save some of them." From the following verse it is not too hard to deduce that Paul saw his own ministry as (part of) the climactic events of the age, the last act on the human stage (I Corinthians 4:9), ushering in the final events of resurrection of the dead (Romans 11:15).[51] In other words, we should take Paul's protest of his deep concern for his people (Romans 9:1–3; 10:1; 11:1) seriously, as also his hope for a mercy extended to "all" that still attests to God's original calling of Israel (Romans 11:28–32). We rise on the visionary's wings at this point, high above the ambiguous and compromising realities of every day life and history reckoned in centuries and millennia. Nevertheless, visions are to be cherished for their inspirational power. And this particular vision remains a challenge to the hope not simply of Christians but also of Jews, a hope rising above ethnic and religious differences to the ultimate purpose of God. Is not this also of significance for Israel?

In short, Paul saw his mission and its outcome as wholly consistent with Israel's destiny. This not least constitutes his continuing importance for Israel: to challenge as a Jew what the meaning of Israel should be within and for the world. Where Paul would stand in the continuing spectrum of debate within present-day Israel and the Jewish diaspora is an imponderable question. But it is important that his challenge should be heard as coming from within Israel rather than as the voice of an apostate to the whole tradition of Israel.

VII

To sum up, once we have become alert to the prejudice and confusion that have been present in so much Christian talk of perspective on Jews and Judaism, we actually liberate Paul from the Babylonian captivity of that prejudice and confusion. We liberate Paul the Jew, who is of course never less than Saul the Pharisee become Christian, but is still Paul the Jew, to reemerge into and as a partner in a Jewish–Christian dialogue to which he had previously appeared a hindrance and a stumbling block. For this Paul still speaks in Jewish language and sentiment, and in so doing he bears testimony to a first-century Jewish diaspora presence and reality of which we have all too little other extended evidence. As a Jew, believing in the eschatological purpose of the one God of Israel, he attempts to plumb the depth of Israel's identity, and to recall his own people to their God-given identity. As a missionary prophet, convinced of his call to proclaim Israel's Messiah to the nations, he seeks to remind Israel of its own missionary calling and to bring it closer to fulfilment. Such a one will always be uncomfortable within a community more settled to conserving its traditions; Christianity has known its own Pauls in turn. Nevertheless, for Israel to turn its back on Paul is to diminish or even to cut itself off from that portion of its own identity and heritage that Paul still represents. To refuse Paul a voice in the contemporary Jewish–Christian dialogue is to revert to pre-Holocaust confrontationalism and supersessionism (in reverse!). In a post-Holocaust Jewish–Christian dialogue Paul could become a voice recognizable by both sides and a positive force for further rapprochement.

NOTES

1. F. C. Baur, *Paul: The Apostle of Jesus Christ*, 2 volumes (London: Williams and Norgate, 1873, 1875 [1845]).
2. A. Harnack, *What is Christianity?* (London: Williams and Norgate, 1900), lecture 10.
3. R. Bultmann, *Theology of the New Testament*, Vol. 1 (New York: Scribner, 1952), 242; E. Kasemann, *Commentary on Romans* (Grand Rapids: Eerdmans, 1980 [1973], 102); both with reference to the "boastful" motif in Romans 3:27.
4. S. Schechter, *Aspects of Rabbinic Theology* (New York: Schocken, 1961 [1909]), 18.
5. H. Maccoby, *The Mythmaker: Paul and the Invention of Christianity* (New York: Harper & Row,

1986). Contrast among earlier contributors particularly S. Ben-Chorin, *Paulus: Der Volkerapostel in judischer Sicht* (Munchen: List,1970).

6. A. Segal, *Paul the Convert: The Apostolate and Apostasy of Saul the Pharisee* (New Haven: Yale University Press, 1990).
7. *Epistula Petri* 2:3; *Clem. Hom.*17:18–19.
8. See, for example, A. Segal, *Rebecca's Children: Judaism and Christianity in the Roman World* (Cambridge, MA: Harvard University Press, 1986).
9. Esther 8:17 [LXX]; Theodotus in Eusebius, *Praep. Evang.* 9:22.5; Plutarch, *Life of Cicero* 7:6; Josephus, *War* 2:454.
10. When the term first appears—II Maccabees 2:21; 8:1; 14:38.
11. See further J. D. G. Dunn, "Judaism in the Land of Israel in the First Century," in *Judaism in Late Antiquity, Part 2: Historical Syntheses*, ed. J. Neusner (Leiden: E. J. Brill,1995), 229–261.
12. Cited below, in the next section.
13. As stimulated and provoked by E. P. Sanders, *Paul and Palestinian Judaism* (Philadelphia: Fortress, 1977); see J. D. G. Dunn, "The New Perspective on Paul," in *Jesus, Paul and the Law: Studies in Mark and Galatians* (Louisville: Westminster/John Knox Press,1990), 183–206.
14. Noteworthy were the contributions of G. F. Moore, James Parkes, and R. Travers Herford; see further the references in Sanders, *Paul and Palestinian Judaism*, 6, 33–59.
15. E. P. Sanders's much cited term for this is "covenantal nomism" (*Paul and Palestinian Judaism*, 75, 420, 544).
16. See the data in J. D. G. Dunn, *Romans*, Word Biblical Commentary (Dallas: Word Books, 1988), 40–42.
17. 1QS 11.11–15—"As for me, if I stumble, the mercies of God shall be my eternal salvation. If I stagger because of the sin of the flesh, my justification *(mshpti)* shall be by the righteousness of God which endures for ever . . . . He will draw me near by his grace, and by his mercy will he bring my justification (*mshpti*). He will judge me in the righteousness of his truth and in the greatness of his goodness he will pardon *(ykipper)* all my sins. Through his righteousness he will cleanse me of all the uncleanness of man and of the sins of the children of men" (Vermes).
18. See section V.
19. See note 5.
20. Epiphanius, *Panarion* 30.16:6–9, cited in Maccoby, *Mythmaker*, 182.
21. Summarized, e.g., by P. Vielhauer, "On the 'Paulinism' of Acts," in *Studies in Luke-Acts*, eds. L. E. Keck and J. L. Martyn (Nashville: Abingdon Press, 1966), 33–50.
22. Cf. G. Bornkamm, *Paul* (New York: Harper & Row, 1971), 15.
23. Psalms 9:17; Tobit 13:6; Jubilees 23:23–24; Psalms of Solomon 2:1–2; Matthew 5:47; Luke 6:33.
24. It is Paul who identifies Jews by the fact of circumcision, and, even more strikingly, Gentiles by the absence of circumcision (Romans 2:25–27; 3:30; 4:9–12; Galatians 2:7–8; Colossians 3:11), a peculiarly Jewish perspective on humanity.
25. So K. G. Juhn, *TDNT* 3.367–9; J. Wanke, *EDNT* 1.369.
26. Judith 9:2–4; Sirach 45:23–24; 48:2–3; I Maccabees 2:23–27, 54, 58.
27. Pharisees noted for their "*akribeia*" (Josephus, *War* 1:108–109; 2:162; *Life* 191; *Antiquities* 20:200–201).
28. M. Hengel, *The Pre-Christian Paul* (London: SCM, 1991), chap. 2.
29. J. D. G. Dunn, *The Partings of the Ways Between Christianity and Judaism and their Significance for the Character of Christianity* (London: SCM, 1991).
30. Segal, *Paul the Convert.*
31. Ibid., xi–xvi.

32. J. H. Charlesworth, ed., *The Old Testament Pseudepigrapha*, 2 vols. (Garden City, NY: Doubleday, 1983, 1985).
33. Josephus, of course, is a self-confessed practitioner of Pharisaic halakhah (*Life* 12); but even so he writes after the year 70.
34. Mark 2:23–3:5; Acts 22:3; 26:5; Josephus, *War* 1:110; 2:162; *Antiquities* 17:41; *Life* 191.
35. See further Dunn, *Romans* ad loc.
36. H. Maccoby, *Mythmaker*, chap. 7.
37. Segal, *Paul the Convert*; D. Boyarin, *A Radical Jew: Paul and the Politics of Identity* (Berkeley: University of California Press, 1994).
38. In what follows I draw on J. D. G. Dunn, "Who Did Paul Think He Was? A Study of Jewish Christian Identity," *New Testament Studies* 45 (1999): 174–193. See also particularly K-W. Niebuhr, *Heidenapostel aus Israel: Die jüdische Identität des Paulus nach ihrer Darstellung in seinen Briefen*, WUNT 62 (Tübingen: J. C. B. Mohr, 1992).
39. Deuteronomy 10:16; Jeremiah 4:4; 9:25–26; Ezekiel 44:9; 1QpHab 11:13; 1QS 5:5; 1QH 2:18; 18:20; Philo, *Spec. Leg.* 1:305.
40. See further J. D. G. Dunn, *The Theology of Paul the Apostle* (Grand Rapids: Eerdmans, 1998), Sections 6, 14, 23; here I engage most closely with H. Hübner, *Law in Paul's Thought* (Edinburgh: T & T Clark, 1984).
41. J. D. G. Dunn, "Paul: Apostate or Apostle of Israel?", *ZNW* 89 (1998): 256–271.
42. Generally regarded as a mixed quotation from Genesis 12:3 and 18:18.
43. (i) See (Genesis 12:2; 15:5; 17:4–5; 22:17); (ii) land (Genesis 12:7; 13:15; 15:18; 17:8); (iii) blessing to nations (Genesis 12:3; 18:18; 22:18; 26.4; 28.14).
44. Regularly echoed in the Old Testament (e.g., Deuteronomy 1:8, 11; 4:37–38; Joshua 1:2–6; Psalms 105:8–11; Jeremiah 3:18).
45. The emphases of Jonah and Isaiah 66:19 are relatively rare within the Old Testament.
46. For example, probably eight of those listed in Romans 16 were Jews (J. D. G. Dunn, *Romans*, 900).
47. See Section IV (3).
48. Compare the still stronger thesis of M. D. Nanos, *The Mystery of Romans: The Jewish Context of Paul's Letter* (Minneapolis: Fortress, 1996).
49. Bibliography in J. D. G. Dunn, "Who Did Paul Think He Was?," 185 n. 48.
50. See further J. D. G. Dunn, *Romans*, 40.
51. See J. D. G. Dunn, *Romans*, 658.

CHAPTER 16

Reading after the Holocaust

A New Testament Scholar Responds to Emil Fackenheim

LUKE TIMOTHY JOHNSON

I

Emil Fackenheim was born in Germany in 1916. He was seventeen years old when Nazi terror against Jews became overt in 1933, when it was confirmed that Jews were being sent to concentration camps. He was twenty-two years old in 1938 when he was interned at the Sachsenhausen concentration camp and twenty-three years old when, with the rest of his family except one brother, he emigrated to Canada in 1939. He became a Rabbi, and received his Ph.D. from the University of Toronto in 1945. Acclaimed as an interpreter of the German philosopher Hegel, he is best known for his theological works, *The Presence of God in History* (1970) and *To Mend the World* (1982). In 1987, he delivered the Sherman Lectures at Manchester University, and in 1990, published them, together with an essay he had originally composed in 1980, as the four chapters of a small book, *The Jewish Bible after the Holocaust: A Re-Reading.*[1] The book is powerful and provocative. Its simplicity of style and directness of speech give it power. Its fierce engagement with an entire intellectual (and political) history makes it provocative. From beginning to end, it is clear that this is no academic exercise but rather a passionate attempt to find a place on which to stand by a witness to the unthinkable whose vocation is to keep thinking, a highly personal effort by a leader of the people to make sense of a book that has, in the face of experience, seemed to lose its sense for the people.

Fackenheim's basic thesis is simple: the Holocaust makes (or ought to make) a fundamental difference in the reading of the Jewish Bible, certainly by Jews, but by Gentiles as well. He stands with Hegel and with Rosenzweig and Buber in his conviction that the hermeneutical task is always to bridge the gap between the past and the present (pp. 31, 40). With Buber's 1926 essay, "The Man of Today and the Jewish Bible," he agrees that "Each generation must struggle with the Bible in its turn and come to terms with it." But Fackenheim insists that there is not only a gap between the world of the Bible and the contemporary generation, there is also an experiential gap between the world of Buber (and the entire history of interpretation preceding Buber) and the interpreters on this side of the Holocaust. The "seamlessness" of interpretation has been utterly ripped by the *novum* (new/unprecedented thing) that is the Holocaust. Jews of today must therefore confront the "naked text" of the Bible without the assistance given by the centuries of interpretation that were based on the premise that God would always intervene to save the people, and entirely from the standpoint of the two salient experiences of this Jewish generation—the "children of Job"—the death that was Auschwitz and the resurrection that is the state of Israel.

The four chapters unfold his argument in straightforward fashion. In "The Hermeneutical Situation," Fackenheim indicates the gap between the situation of pre-1945 interpreters (including Jews like Rosenzweig and Buber) and post-1945 interpreters. Despite the *novum* of the Holocaust, however, no Christian theologian of major stature who began work before 1945, even those whose witness against Nazism was unequivocal, such as Barth, Bultmann, and Tillich, fundamentally altered his theological position because of that experience. The closest to doing so was Bonhoeffer. More surprising, not even Buber (who lived until 1965) managed to answer the plaintive question in *The Dialogue between Heaven and Earth* (in 1952), "Dare we recommend to the survivors of Auschwitz, to the Job of the gas chambers, 'Thank ye the Lord for he is good, for His mercy endureth forever'?" Fackenheim suggests that perhaps the time was not yet right for a truly post-Holocaust hermeneutic for the theologians of the generation of Job. It must be the task of the generation of Job's children.

The most difficult section of Fackenheim's argument—both textually and emotionally—is his second chapter, "Two Types of Murmurers: Rereading the Jewish Bible after Auschwitz." Here Fackenheim reveals himself as Rabbi as well as philosopher. He takes as his starting point the texts of Exodus 15:22–24 (the complaint of the people at Marah, immediately after the Song at the Sea), and Exodus 17:1–3 (the complaint of the people at Meribah and Massah for themselves and their children). He notes that the narrator and Moses and the entire history of interpretation blame the murmurers for their lack of gratitude and confidence. But Fackenheim takes his stand with the murmurers at Meribah and Massah, because they cried out not simply in behalf of themselves but also in behalf of their children. This Holocaust generation is separated from all previous interpreters on the same basis: the survival of the children. All previous interpretation worked retrospectively from the confident premise that "God sleeps not nor slumbers" in God's care for Israel. The Holocaust, however, has put precisely that confidence in question. Fackenheim makes powerful use of the diaries of Chaim Kaplan and Adam Czerniakow, and his own brother's suicide as witnesses against the premise that God unfailingly savers the people. He concludes, "This Jewish 'generation,' and those to follow, are of Job's children. As such they can no longer read the Ta'nach—read their whole history—in the age-old, time-honoured, venerable, pious, retrospect" (p. 47).

On what basis, then, can the Bible be read? In his third chapter, Fackenheim presents his bold alternative to the pious glosses of the tradition, "Sacred Scripture or Epic of a Nation: Re-Reading the Jewish Bible in Jerusalem." This generation must begin not only with the experience of the Holocaust, but equally with the resurrection of the people (and of hope) in the state of Israel. The text of Ezekiel 36:24, "I will take you from among the nations, and gather you out of all the countries, and will bring you into your own land," has been fulfilled, in an act as profound and unprecedented as the Holocaust itself. The Bible should therefore now be read not as *Heilsgeschichte* ("Sacred History"), but as *Geschichte* ("History plain and simple"), by which Fackenheim means the secular history of the Jewish people as recorded in these texts. The real demythologization of the Bible has not been accomplished by philosophers, but by the Jewish people themselves, "with their collective decision to stop relying on others, human or divine, with the collective Jewish decision to take the collective Jewish secular courage in its collective hands: with the act of ending Jewish exile by 'going up' to the Land" (p. 65). Reading from this standpoint affects *how* texts are read: Ezekiel's vision is not eschatological but actual; the real point of Jeremiah 31 is not the renewal of the heart but saving Rachel's children. It also affects *what* texts are central. Fackenheim prefers the secular account in II Kings 24:19–20 to the sacralized version in II Chronicles 36:11–17, 21. Most provocatively, he proposes the Book of Esther as a "canon within the canon," the secular tale that shows the people of Israel being saved from extermination by their own efforts: "What if this once-strange book in the Jewish Bible had to be moved from the periphery to the centre, so as to provide the new principle uniting the whole? What if what once had been the repository of divine Revelation had now to become the classic repository of Jewish mythology, that is, for the Jews what the Homeric epics have all along been for the Greeks?" (p. 62).

Fackenheim's fourth chapter, "The Children of Rachel, of Haman, of Job: Post-Holocaust Possibilities of a Fraternal Jewish–Christian reading of the Book Belonging to Both" (the original essay that propelled him in this direction), pulls together the themes established in the first chapters and elaborates them further. Two points in particular deserve notice. The first is that he recognizes the claim of modernity to an "objective" and "neutral" reading of the Bible to be false. Commentaries reveal how "objective" scholars betray their faith positions in their interpretations. Fackenheim's "fraternal reading" would seem to be largely a willingness to recognize and accept the different starting points and conclusions of Jewish and Christian readers, rather than an effort to find a common meaning. "Post-Holocaust" here becomes something very much like postmodern. The second is that despite his call for a secular reading of the Bible, Fackenheim by no means eliminates the possibility of an on-going relationship between Israel and Israel's God: "Even so I make bold to assert that a Jewish 'life with God' is still possible, for it is real." But the reader notices this important condition: "Where? In Israel, a new Mordecai for a new age in the history of Judaism, guarding the Jewish remnant, and obligated to guard it—but strong enough for the task only through the hope for help 'from another place' (Esther 4.14)" (p. 95). And in his short appendix (the transcript of a television address in Fulda, Germany, in 1988), he states again, "if, after all that has occurred, there is still Jewish faith at all, it is, I am convinced, exclusively because of the fact that after the great catastrophe there arose a Jewish state" (p. 103).

In the Spring semester of 1992, a small group of scholars at Indiana University met with Professor Fackenheim to respond in a face-to-face conversation to the positions he adopts in this book. Present were Professors Michael Morgan, James Ackerman, Bernard Levinson, Alvin Rosenfeld, and Herbert Marks, all then of the faculty at Indiana University, and Professor Joseph Blenkinsopp of Notre Dame University. In the paragraphs that follow, I elaborate in somewhat greater detail the substance of the response I made to Professor Fackenheim at that time. I have retained the oral style of presentation, because my points have very much to do with the importance of personal witness as well as the limitations of any single perspective. As I apply these observations to Professor Fackenheim's work, I make the same point with respect to myself as well.

II

Professor Fackenheim begins his discussion with a wry reference to his *chutzpah*—he has indeed combined astonishing intellectual ambition and passionately personal testimony within the pages of a remarkably small book. I also begin with a quite sober recognition of my own *chutzpah* in entering the same conversation within the framework of a considerably smaller essay. In contemplating this response, I have become increasingly uncomfortable with the disparities between author and respondent. Professor Fackenheim speaks of Bultmann, Tillich, Barth, Bonhoeffer, and Buber as elder contemporaries. For me, they are figures in the history of ideas. More important, Professor Fackenheim lived through, suffered from, and had his entire life marked by the events of the Holocaust (which made him an emigrant to Canada) and the resurrection that is the state of Israel (which ultimately claimed him as an immigrant). In contrast, I grew up in the safe context of the midwestern and southern United States, in the sanctuaries of repose offered respectively by monastery and university. I perfectly exemplify those whom Fackenheim refers to somewhat scornfully as living "safe in seminaries" (p. 55).

Even more, perhaps, than others living in those sanctuaries, I was an observer—often a distracted and belated one—rather than a participant in history. In contrast, Professor Fackenheim is a personal witness to the events of the Holocaust that he terms a *novum*, an experience that has torn asunder any pretense that either history or thought can be regarded as seamless. Professor Fackenheim's passionate testimony and intellectual inquiry are located within a Judaism searching for a post-Holocaust identity that can be something more than purely secular survival, but must be at least secular survival. I am a Roman Catholic. My every conversation with Jews must be constrained by the acknowledgment of the role my tradition has played—and continues to play—in perpetuating antisemitic attitudes and actions that at least allowed the Holocaust to occur and may have been complicit in its occurrence.[2]

Recognizing the severe disproportion between author and reviewer at the level of personal experience and passionate witness, I want to begin by also acknowledging, at the level of personal experience and passionate witness, the truthfulness of Professor Fackenheim's book. If I add that I regard it as a subjective truthfulness, I mean no dishonor, for in personal experience and passionate testimony, subjective truthfulness is the highest truth. But because his book is not only passionate witness but also a serious intellectual inquiry concerning the reading of the Jewish Bible not only by Jews but also by Christians after the Holocaust, it is necessary also to respond to his invitation to intellectual engagement by others passionately concerned with that subject. I offer, then, a series of questions that occur to me as I read and reread his book, and, in imitation of Fackenheim's own simplicity and candor, state them as plainly as I can. My questions have less to do with this or that point of interpretation—there are many individual interpretive observations that any reader of the Bible can appreciate—than with some aspects of the project as a whole that genuinely puzzle me.

The first concept that gives me pause is that of the *novum* itself. In what sense can we, as *historians*, speak of the Holocaust in absolute, even eschatological terms? I perfectly understand how Fackenheim can testify passionately to the unprecedented character of the Holocaust—the way in which Jews were subjected to a process that destroyed their capacity to choose (p. 19), or the way in which birth as a Jew was defined as a crime in itself (p. 87). As historians, however, are we not obliged to ask whether in fact this monstrosity, this *mysterium tremendum* of evil, was unprecedented qualitatively, or only quantitatively, in that technology enabled murderous intent to be exercised with unparalleled ambition and efficiency? Fackenheim's own recollection of the people's 400 years of captivity under the Pharaohs, and the use of Jewish children's blood by a Pharaoh to heal his leprosy, suggest that other horrors in this people's history might have seemed to the victims, or even to the historical observer, qualitatively of the same order as the Holocaust. Josephus's descriptions of the terror and carnage at the fall of Jerusalem in the war against Rome cause the reader to blanche at the universal and indiscriminate nature of the slaughter. Similarly, the experience of those who put themselves and their children to death at Masada rather than face Roman rule was, in subjective terms, as total and final as the experience of those killed by Nazis in the camps. What is it, as historians, to declare that such precedents do not apply?

I ask the reader to bear with me here, for I know how sensitive a subject this is. I am well aware of the way in which many Jews today bristle at any attempt to relativize the Holocaust by means of comparison to other genocides, such as those of the Armenians, or Native Americans, or Cambodians, or those killed in the Soviet Gulag. They bristle because they suspect that the purpose of the exercise is to trivialize, then to normalize, and then finally, to deny the events of the Holocaust.[3] In the same way, they resent the astonishingly clumsy attempts to render the Holocaust "meaningful" by Christian theological cooptation.[4] I need to make clear that such trivialization is not my point. I am struggling, rather, with epistemology, and with the question of what kinds of claims can be made on the basis of what kinds of evidence. I want to suggest that there are different ways of knowing reality, and that each has its validity but also its limits, and that no one way of knowing has the privilege of dictating to other ways of knowing. Speaking as a participant, one can declare one's experience unique, and speak the truth. But speaking as a historian, one cannot declare one's own or anyone else's experience unique, for the rules of historiography do not allow that sort of declaration.

So I want to insist on the legitimacy of regarding the Holocaust as a *novum*, an unprecedented and unparalleled event, for those who experienced it and now testify to that experience with passionate intensity. But with another part of their minds, such witnesses need to be aware that other persons, without trying to minimize much less deny the truth of that testimony, may not be able to share that perception, simply because they have not shared in that event—and, for people of my generation and the ones following, could not have shared in that event in the same manner as those who testify to it as a *novum*. Indeed, to ask this and the following generations to act as though they had participated in the event, or bore personal responsibility for the event is to return, paradoxically, to the same sort of blood curse that Christians applied to Jews for centuries.

Here Professor Fackenheim the philosopher rather than the historian or witness may need to recognize the *aporia* between the truth of experience and the truths of history. It is an *aporia* similar to the one he cites from Lessing, between the "truths of reason," which can be absolute, and the "truths of history," which can never be more than relative and probable (p. 10). For Professor Fackenheim and other Jews of his generation, the drawing of a line in the sand to say, "this event is ultimate," is perfectly understandable. But the tides of time will surely wash past that line and erase it as surely as they have every other attempt to declare a *novum* within history that absolutely transcends history. The truth that subjective experience demands that we declare as absolute and final cannot be recognized as such by others who do not share the same experience. Even with different parts of our minds, if you allow the expression, each one of us is obliged to see the same thing quite differently: with that part of our mind that knows experientially (perhaps religiously), we declare the truth that this experience is ultimate; but with that part of our mind that functions analytically (perhaps as historians), we at the same time declare that this event is as other historical events, one among others.

A second question, or set of questions, occurs as I consider the connection between Fackenheim's *novum* and his proposed hermeneutics of Tanakh, or biblical interpretation. He derives from the historical *novum* a legitimation for encountering "the naked text" (see pp. 43, 57, 67, 74). From such reading, he hopes that both Jews and Christians will discover "a *novum* also in the self-understanding and the very being of the two remnants, the Jewish and the Christian" (p. 87). It is on this basis that he rejects, throughout the book, the "pious commentators" of the tradition (see pp. 30, 44), and seeks "a reading of the book as though it had never been read before" (pp. x–xi). His reading of the Tanakh is not really "naked," though, for it is a reading governed precisely by the twinned events of the Holocaust and the establishment of the State of Israel. Such a new experiential standpoint functions as his hermeneutical key, both for understanding texts and for the selection of certain texts as more pertinent or normative than others. The *novum* alone can justify making the Book of Esther the center of Fackenheim's post-Holocaust canon. And the reality of the state of Israel is the premise of his speaking of this new nation as "a new Mordecai for a new age in the history of Judaism, guarding the Jewish remnant" (p. 95). The same hermeneutical principle moves him to dismiss "sacral history" (*heilsgeschichte*), whether Jewish or Christian, in favor of "*geschichte* plain and simple, to which no higher—saving, divine—purpose is ascribed" (pp. 57–58).

Now in many ways, Fackenheim's return to the text resembles that traditionally taken by midrash, which always sought to bring a potentially shattering contemporary event under the umbrella of meaning provided by Torah. The closest analogies to Fackenheim's proposal, in fact, are found in the generative period of the first century of the common era, before the event of the Jewish war with Rome and the destruction of the Temple left the Pharisaic tradition to gain ascendency as the "normative" form of Judaism in the Rabbinic or Talmudic tradition. At least two Jewish groups in the first century, the sectarians at Qumran and the sectarians who gathered in the name of Jesus, followed just such interpretive procedures. Each group leaped over precedents and moved directly from an experience that they regarded as ultimate, back to the Tanakh read in the light of this central experience and conviction. In their respective sectarian hermeneutics, furthermore, certain texts were perceived as central to Torah that had never previously been considered so important. Even texts (like Isaiah) that had been central to all previous readers were read in an entirely new way because of the existential insight given by the shattering events they regarded as defining their present situation. They too were caught in cognitive dissonance between what the texts had always been thought to say and what their experience of reality had taught them. They too found it necessary to start their reading *ab novo*.

I take it as a historical lesson, however, that Jews outside their range of experience were not willing to acknowledge their *novum* as the necessary starting point for any authentic Jewish hermeneutics. No Jews except the sectarians at Qumran were willing to see the wilderness community and the Teacher of Righteousness as the key to all of Torah. No Jews except the followers of Jesus were willing to call a crucified Messiah the key to unlocking all of Scripture. In some ways, the Rabbinic revolution of the Mishnah, that centered life on the *halachic* reading of Torah, might be taken as an implicit rebuke of such claims of historical absolutizing.

What is truly novel in Fackenheim's proposal, then, is not the hermeneutical reflex, but the premises governing his return to the text "as though it had never been read before." The first-century Jews who practiced midrash to resolve the cognitive dissonance between their symbols and their experience were convinced that both their texts and their experiences came from God. The problem for their understanding was bringing them into some harmonious (if dialectical) relationship. They assumed that the Lord who created and sustained the world and had chosen this people for the Lord's own purposes had also revealed to this people the Torah. The life-giving authority of the text was not found in the accuracy of its depiction of history or in its legitimation of institutions, but in the Living God who continued to speak, even if obscurely, through each of its words. Fackenheim, in contrast, is able to assert neither of these convictions in a straightforward fashion. He does not consider the text to have a self-evident revelatory character based in divine authorship. He is not willing to consider the events either of the Holocaust or of the founding of Israel as falling under God's providential guidance of events. Even the possibility of a relationship with God is one that Fackenheim raises only cautiously and obliquely. The question inevitably arises, *why* turn to Tanakh at all? If neither the text nor the experience bears the mark of divinity, why should Jews make any attempt at a post-Holocaust reading of the Bible?

And if, as Fackenheim suggests, the Bible is now to be read not as the source of the *halakoth* by which the Jewish community is structured, still less as revelation of a *Heilsgeschichte*, but only as the record of a "*geschichte* pure and simple," does this not really amount to a *volksgeschichte* pure and simple? Does not Tanakh become nothing more than the source of the national myth of the nation of Israel? But if that is to be the status and function of the text, what possible interest should anybody outside the State of Israel have in the Tanakh? There seems to be an unbridgeable gap between the exclusive hermeneutical standpoint he will allow to Jews and his desire for a "fraternal reading" between Jews and Christians. Instead, the logic of his argument would seem to lead in the opposite direction from a shared reading of the text, and at most amount to an appeal to a mutual respect for interpretive starting points that have absolutely nothing in common except that they are absolutely different from each other. They can therefore no longer compete, but can they even converse? One might ask also whether Fackenheim's "naked text" (which, as we have seen, is not so naked) is not simply a reflex survival mechanism rather than a serious effort to engage what Torah has always meant to this people? Can it be a hermeneutics that nourishes the Jewish people in an identity more profound than that of simply being another nation among the nations?

It is in this respect that I find Professor Fackenheim's neglect and even dismissal of diaspora Judaism—both ancient and contemporary—to be strange. It is fair to say, I think, not only that many Christians have continued to think theologically in a seamless fashion despite the Holocaust, but that many religious Jews have continued to do so as well. The performance of midrash continues by many Jews who have not found the Holocaust, despite its profoundly evil character, to represent the fundamental rupture of all symbols or even the possibility of belief and trust in the Living God. Many of these Jews, though by no means all of them, practice their faith and their interpretation of Torah outside the State of Israel. They do not deny the Holocaust. Many of them are witnesses to its awful reality. They do not trivialize the Holocaust. But for them, the experience of the Holocaust does not have the same implications as it does for Fackenheim. There still exist communities of Jews for whom the observance of *mitzvoth* and the study of *halachic* midrash in continuity with the traditions of the elders still function to articulate faith and loyalty to the Living God of the people Israel. If this is the case, is their experience of classical, "diaspora" Judaism invalidated by the experience of the Holocaust? How seriously does Fackenheim intend his suggestion that Jewish belief in the Living God after the Holocaust is owed exclusively to the existence of the State of Israel (p. 103; see also p. 95)? It would seem that the more one insists on the *novum* of the Holocaust/State of Israel as the single legitimate hermeneutical fulcrum for reading the Jewish Bible in this generation, the more one risks dangerously narrowing the possibilities for Jewish existence in the future, and precipitously cutting off all the options for this future offered by the rich tradition of interpretation that preceded this novum. I suspect that Professor Fackenheim would not want to do this. His own practice of interpretation, in fact, demonstrates an intense willingness to continue engaging—albeit in a sharply dialectical fashion—all the voices preceding this generation within the tradition.

III

My final series of observations apply this same danger of narrow definition and closed possibilities to relations between Jews and Christians. I agree completely with Professor Fackenheim and other critics of supersessionist Christian theology—a group that includes Charlotte Klein, Rosemary Radford Ruether, Roy Eckardt, N. A. Beck, and Clark Williamson[5]—when they insist that definitions of Christianity that rely on a negative reading of Judaism (much less actual antisemitism) are theologically unacceptable. They are unacceptable not simply because they have done harm, but because they fall short of the truth of the Good News from God. I disagree with only some of these critics concerning the degree to which such anti-Jewish definitions are essential to Christian self-understanding and therefore critical to Christian theology. To illustrate my point autobiographically: I managed to grow up within the Roman Catholic tradition, attend minor and major seminary, and live as a Benedictine Monk for almost ten years, without once encountering the sort of crypto-Marcionite understanding of Paul and the Gospels that has so dominated some forms of Christian discourse. In fact, when I first encountered the term Atonement when studying theology, I had great difficulty connecting the various theories I was hearing about for the first time to any understanding of Christian existence that I had experienced in the previous twenty-five years. I don't deny that many Christians have been shaped theologically in the manner rightly despised by the authors I have mentioned. I only offer the observations that Christians have neither universally nor necessarily been so shaped.

Moreover, I reject the proposition that Christology is inherently antisemitic,[6] or that the writings of the New Testament lead inevitably to the Holocaust,[7] so that the only way Christianity can finally be purged of its antisemitism is by recasting the image of Jesus and abandoning its own canonical texts.[8] I emphatically agree, however, that European theology in particular has *used* Christology in the manner described, and has *read* the New Testament in ways that are functionally antisemitic. The fateful equation between Catholicism and Judaism within Reformation polemics ensured that mainstream Protestant theology, and the field of New Testament studies that fundamentally was shaped by Protestant theological premises, would consistently search for an "authentic" and "original" Christianity understood as distinct both from Judaism and from that Catholicism that was viewed as a recrudescence of Jewish and Pagan elements in the previously pure revelation of the Gospel.[9] So profoundly is New Testament scholarship over the past 200 years marked by this theological bias that the first thing required in reading much of the classical literature in this field is an ideological critique.

So I agree with Professor Fackenheim when he says that Christian theology cannot now proceed as though the Holocaust had not happened. But perhaps I mean something different even as I agree. I do not mean that Christian theology must completely reconstitute itself, using the Holocaust as a new starting point. For Christians, there can be no new starting point except that *novum* in their experience and conviction that is the resurrection of Jesus to share the life of God and become "life-giving Spirit' (I Corinthians 15:45) as the basis for a new humanity: 'If anyone is in Christ, there is a new creation" (II Corinthians 5:16). But I do mean that Christianity must take the Holocaust as God's judgment on Christians for what was wrong (conceptually) and evil (morally) in their theology, even from the start, and that no celebration of Christian identity can any longer proceed on the basis of an odious (and ignorant) contrast to Judaism.

This requires that Christians assess and critically engage those traditions of biblical scholarship that have helped form such privileging contrasts. Significant progress has been made, for example, in the study of Paul[10] and the Gospels.[11] Despite the many unfortunate aspects of historical Jesus research, one clear contribution made by what is sometimes called "the third quest" is the placement of Jesus squarely within the world of first-century Judaism.[12] Even more, Christians must also have the courage to critically engage the language and attitudes of the New Testament writings themselves that can perpetuate hostile perceptions and actions, both of Jews and of all those whom Christians regard as "other" and therefore as threatening.[13] Such an effort requires a combination of loyalty and moral courage. Loyalty, for these compositions remain powerfully transformative as witnesses to the truth of the good news that is in Jesus. But also moral courage, for that good news cannot take a form that denies the humanity or leads to the harm of people who do not—for God's own reasons—share in the experience of that good news. The easy temptation is to declare ourselves morally superior to the texts and eliminate all the passages that offend us. The difficult challenge is to humbly serve the integrity of God's Holy Word by finding within it the principles and images that enable a liberation from the language and attitudes that are morally incompatible with the Lord whom we confess.[14]

I also agree completely with Professor Fackenheim that the only way Jews and Christians can reach a more fraternal and less polemical reading of Torah is through coming to know each other better, not only as persons of good will, but also in terms of the basic commitments and presuppositions that we have as discrete reading communities.[15] But I wonder whether Fackenheim's hermeneutical proposals, if accepted by all Jews, might actually make this more difficult. I approach this point once more from personal experience. As a New Testament scholar, I have been extraordinarily fortunate to have learned Judaism mainly from Jews rather than through New Testament scholarship! My New Testament mentors had themselves learned from Jewish scholars. I was introduced to Talmudic studies at Indiana University in 1969 by Henry Fischel, who had earlier been the teacher of Wayne A. Meeks—Meeks had also studied with Erwin R. Goodenough. Fischel was a pioneer in bridging the worlds of Talmud and Hellenistic culture.[16] My paper for him on Merkabah Mysticism was a genuine initiation into a new world.[17] As a doctoral student in New Testament at Yale University, I studied Midrash—the *Aboth de Rabbi Nathan* and *Sifre on Deuteronomy*—with Judah Goldin.[18] Preparing for his rigorous seminars meant working side by side with such future scholars in Judaica as Rueven Kimmelman (who also shared in New Testament seminars together with Alan Segal), Bruce Zuckerman, and Alan Cooper. As a faculty member at Indiana University, I have had strong Jewish colleagues not only in Hebrew Bible (Bernard Levinson and Herbert Marks), but also in Mishnah (Howard Eilberg-Schwartz), Lurianic Mysticism (Lawrence Fine), and Kabbalah/Medieval Jewish Philosophy (Hava Tirosh-Rothschild). With such teachers and colleagues over a twenty-five year period, I have had intense conversations within an explicitly pluralistic and comparative context, and have learned a great deal about Judaism in all its stages and manifestations, ancient, medieval, and modern. The conversations have ranged widely and sometimes in spirited fashion across the biblical texts shared and disputed by the two traditions. I doubt that I have added much to my Jewish colleagues' understanding of the New Testament, but they have surely offered me a sense of Judaism that is rarely given to a New Testament scholar.

Here is the point of the personal recital. In this long conversation, never has the Holocaust/State of Israel been presented as a *novum* that demands the shedding of all the history of "pious commentary" in order to confront the naked text "as though it had never been read before." Only once in all these years, moreover, has it ever been presented to me by a Jewish colleague—not a student of Judaica so much as a student of Jewish Holocaust literature—that such should be the case. The novelty of the suggestion that nothing more could be discussed between Christians and Jews—nothing about God, nothing about tradition, nothing about the interpretation of the Bible—without a commitment to such a proposition seemed to me so out of line with all my years of studying with Jewish colleagues that I found it incomprehensible. My last question to Professor Fackenheim, therefore, is this: if he is correct about this *novum*, and all fraternal work on the Bible must take the Holocaust and the State of Israel as its nonnegotiable starting point, then what does that say about the authenticity or nonauthenticity of the conversations of which I have been a part for these many years? I would prefer that such judgments not be required, and that instead, every voice and every passionate testimony be allowed to speak within a continuous conversation into which all lovers of the Living God and all lovers of these texts find themselves irresistably drawn.

Professor Fackenheim's short book serves as an important reminder to all readers of the Bible, both Jewish and Christian, that each generation must stand responsible for the way it reads, that the experience of God (or the apparent absence of God) in each generation's experience necessarily must shape the context within which the Bible is read, that the pretense of a neutral, historical reading of the Bible that means the same to everyone is actually a way of avoiding the claims that these texts make on their readers, and that one's hermeneutical stance really matters. I am grateful to Professor Fackenheim for the forthrightness and clarity of his position, and to his implicit challenge to Christian readers to be equally clear in staking out their own way of reading the Bible passionately and "for the sake of their children."

No doubt Christian interpreters functioning as historians will continue, as will some of their Jewish counterparts, studying the Bible within the framework of the dominant historical–critical paradigm. There is no reason to scorn such efforts at historical contextualization and reconstruction, even though their usefulness for communities of faith is increasingly unclear.[19]

Christian scholars will also continue, together with their Jewish counterparts, to study the compositions of the Bible from the perspective of a variety of literary and social–scientific perspectives. Well and good, and with some gain to the imagination if not necessarily to the spirit. Fackenheim's real challenge to Christian readers, however, is to claim a hermeneutical place based on the experience of this generation for their tradition that he has staked for Jewish readers. If the Jewish Bible is not the Christian Bible—even though it contains many of the same writings—and if the standpoint of Christian readers is not to be that of post-Holocaust Israeli readers (for that would indeed be a form of alienation), then what is the distinctly Christian perspective that serves to address this generation and "save the children" of this generation?

Among the elements that I think must be included in an adequate response to that question are the affirmation of the *novum* that is the death and resurrection of Jesus as a *novum* that is as experientially real today as in the first century, and the conviction that for the life of the Christian community, the Jewish Bible *is* the "Old Testament," even though, as Origen has it, it is always new because of our way of reading it through the good news. Christians must also, in other words, be willing to let go of the false objectivity of history that it has too long used as a means of asserting its superiority to the Jewish mode of reading, and must be willing to embrace the passionately subjective standpoint of religious experience as defining the life of this community of faith. Christians must be willing, together with Jews, to acknowledge (and celebrate) the partial and particular perspective of its reading. Once having done that, however, further challenges remain, in the form of earlier and perhaps unfortunate decisions that now need reexamining.

I touch on only two interrelated issues. If Christians reading *as* Christians—that is, not as historians but as those marked by faith in the resurrection of Christ—must, to be theologically consistent, engage the "Hebrew Scriptures" as "Old (and always new) Testament," then the question of the place of the Septuagint (LXX) needs further theological discussion. The LXX *is* the Scripture of the New Testament and for much of the tradition of Christian interpretation, which shared the conviction of the Jews of the first century that the LXX was divinely inspired. What is the *theological* rationale for preferring the Hebrew text, when that is not the text taken up by the New Testament? Even stating the question points to the deeper theological problem hidden by the historical–critical approach. If we prefer the Hebrew text because we seek the original, human, meaning of the Bible, that is historically adequate, but not necessarily theologically pertinent. Does the quest for the historical meaning operate within the implicit denial of divine inspiration, the conviction that God truly seeks to speak through human words? Or do we choose the Hebrew because we think it was divinely inspired, whereas the LXX is a "mere translation" among other ancient versions? This gives rise to two further questions. If we think the Hebrew text inspired and therefore more truly "Scripture," why do we restrict our inquiry only to the historical dimensions of the text, and not to its prophetic dimensions? If we do not think it inspired, on what ground do we prefer it to the LXX, which the New Testament regarded as inspired? I am fully aware that this set of questions is faintly embarrassing to those who would prefer to deny or ignore the fact that Christianity does, in fact, have as distinctive and valid a hermeneutical starting point as that of Judaism, and needs to pay attention to that starting point if it is not, paradoxically, to veer either into the implicit supersessionism granted by "history" or the implicit alienation of taking the Jewish starting point as its own.

The final issue is the pertinence of the history of Christian interpretation of the Bible. It is another paradox that the "rupture" with tradition that Professor Fackenheim attributes to the Holocaust was, for Christians, self-inflicted by Christians through the hegemony of the historical–critical approach, whose premise was that the 1600 years of Christian interpretation preceding the Enlightenment contributes nothing to our understanding of the Bible.[20] In its claim to provide an objective, universal, noninterested, empirically verifiable reading of the Bible, the historical–critical paradigm can be seen as the perfect expression of the project of modernity. Professor Fackenheim's claim to an interested, partial, particular, and even local reading of the Jewish Bible reminds us that we have all, through the experiences of the past decades, been pulled out of the alienating comfort of modernity and must face the harsh but clarifying reality of diaspora. Willy-nilly, we are all postmodern, not as an intellectual fashion, but as a fact of existence. For Christians, this new situation enables a fresh appreciation of that history of interpretation of the Bible that was rejected by modernity. Postmodern Christians have, indeed, the most to learn from premodern Christians. We are at last free to engage Patristic and Medieval and Reformation interpreters, and learn what it meant for them to read the Bible as Scripture and as divinely inspired and as revealing one God. They might help us figure out what difference it makes to read the LXX rather than the Hebrew, or even to think in terms of figure rather than only in terms of fact. Our task is not to imitate them, for that would be another form of alienation from our own circumstances. Our task is not to go backward through false nostalgia, but to go forward enriched for having rejoined a conversation that is distinctively that of our own heritage.

NOTES

1. Emil Fackenheim, *The Jewish Bible after the Holocaust: A Re-reading* (Bloomington: Indiana University Press, 1990). Hereafter cited in text by page number.
2. For two recent Roman Catholic attempts to deal with this reality, see Garry Wills, *Papal Sin: Structures of Deceit* (New York: Doubleday, 2000), especially pages 11–70; and James Carroll, *Constantine's Sword: The Church and the Jews* (Boston: Houghton Mifflin, 2001).
3. See Deborah Lipstadt, *Denying the Holocaust: The Growing Assault on Truth and Memory* (New York: Penguin Books, 1994).
4. Fackenheim laments the foundation of a Carmelite monastery at Auschwitz (*Jewish Bible*, vii), and Carroll makes the erection of a cross at that site the key to his reading of Jewish–Christian relations in *The Sword of Constantine.*
5. See Charlotte Klein, *Anti-Judaism in Christian Theology* (Philadelphia: Fortress Press, 1975); Rosemary Radford Ruether *Faith and Fratricide: The Theological Roots of Anti-Semitism* (New York: Seabury Press, 1974); A. Roy Eckhardt, *Jews and Christians: The Contemporary Meeting* (Bloomington: Indiana University Press, 1986); N. A. Beck, *Mature Christianity in the 21st Century* (New York: Crossroad, 1994); Clark M. Williamson, *A Guest in the House of Israel: Post-Holocaust Church Theology* (Louisville: Westminster/John Knox Press, 1993).
6. Most famously stated by Ruether, *Faith and Fratricide*, 246–251.
7. See Eckhardt, *Jews and Christians*, 63.
8. See the strategies of Eckhardt, *Jews and Christians*, and Beck, *Mature Christianity.*
9. For an analysis of Protestant theological presuppositions governing "histories of Christianity," see, from quite different perspectives, J. Z. Smith, *Drudgery Divine: On the Comparison of Early Christianity and the Religions of Late Antiquity* (Chicago Studies in the History of Judaism; Chicago: University of Chicago Press, 1990), 1–35, 114–115, and L. T. Johnson, *Religious Experience in Earliest Christianity* (Minneapolis: Fortress Press, 1998), 1–37.
10. Credit here is deservedly given to the work of E. P. Sanders, *Paul and Palestinian Judaism: A Comparison of Patterns of Religion* (Philadelphia: Fortress Press, 1977), and K. Stendahl, *Paul among Jews and Gentiles* (Philadelphia: Fortress Press, 1976). Less visible though no less im-

portant is the contribution of Nils A. Dahl of Yale University, through his own teaching and through the publications of students like Terrance Callan.

11. Perhaps the simplest way to assess the tremendous progress in reading the Gospels within the framework of Judaism is to scan the volumes in the new Roman Catholic commentary series, *Sacra Pagina,* edited by Daniel J. Harrington: D. J. Harrington, *The Gospel of Matthew* (Collegeville: Liturgical Press, 1991), L. T. Johnson, *The Gospel of Luke* (1991), and F. J. Maloney, *The Gospel of John* (1998).
12. The point is made well by Charlotte Allen, *The Human Christ: The Search for the Historical Jesus* (New York: The Free Press, 1998), especially 285–328.
13. This is the aspect of the problem I have tried to address in my own work; see L. T. Johnson, "The New Testament's Anti-Jewish Slander and the Conventions of Ancient Rhetoric," *Journal of Biblical Literature* 108 (1989): 419–441; "Religious Rights and Christian Texts," in *Religious Human Rights in Global Perspective,* eds. J. Witte, Jr. and J. van der Vyver (The Hague: Martinus Nijhoff, 1996), 1:65–95; "Proselytism and Witness in Earliest Christianity: An Essay on Origins," in *Sharing the Book: Religious Perspectives on the Rights and Wrongs of Proselytism,* eds. J. Witte, Jr. and R. C. Martin (Maryknoll: Orbis Books, 1999), 145–157, 376–384.
14. For a serious engagement with this hermeneutical struggle with the language of the New Testament and the attitudes and actions of the Christian tradition, see Richard B. Hays, *The Moral Vision of the New Testament: A Contemporary Introduction to New Testament Ethics* (San Francisco: HarperSanFrancisco, 1996), 407–443.
15. A hopeful example is the recent volume of essays edited by Tikva Frymer-Kensky, David Novak, et al., *Christianity in Jewish Terms* (Bolder, CO: Westview Press, 2000).
16. See, e.g., Henry Fischel, *Rabbinic Literature and Greco-Roman Philosophy: A Study of Epicurea and Rhetorica in Early Midrashic Writings* (Leiden: E. J. Brill, 1973).
17. L. T. Johnson, "Gnosticism in the Rabbinic Tradition," *Resonance* 4 (1969): 5–17.
18. See Judah Goldin, *The Fathers according to Rabbi Nathan* (New Haven: Yale University Press, 1955); *The Song at the Sea: Being a Commentary on a Commentary in Two Parts* (New Haven: Yale University Press, 1971); *The Living Talmud: The Wisdom of the Fathers and Its Classical Commentaries* (Chicago: University of Chicago Press, 1957).
19. See Jon D. Levinson, *The Hebrew Bible, the Old Testament, and Historical Criticism* (Louisville: Westminster/John Knox Press, 1993).
20. A point wonderfully made by the standard history of New Testament scholarship by W. G. Kummel, *The New Testament: The History of the Investigation of its Problems,* trans. S. McL. Gilmour and H.C. Kee (Nashville: Abingdon Press, 1970), which devotes six pages (13–19) to the first 1600 years of Christian interpretation!

CHAPTER 17

The Killing Fields of Matthew's Gospel

GARY A. PHILLIPS

> No statement, theological or otherwise, should be made that would not be credible in the presence of the burning children.
>
> —Irving Greenberg

> The Holocaust-world touched none but the innocent. What is innocent if not birth? Who is innocent if not children?
>
> —Emil Fackenheim

Readers of the Bible find it an all-too-familiar and disturbing theme: the murder of innocent children. The violent plotline surfaces again and again in both Jewish narrative and Christian gospel: Pharaoh tosses newborn Jewish males into the Nile (Exodus 1:22); Herod slaughters all the Jewish children of Bethlehem and its neighborhood (Matthew 2:16); even God gets caught up in the action, slaughtering every Egyptian first-born human being and animal left unprotected by the blood sign (Exodus 11:12). And we are reminded of God's less than paternal dealings with other children: Job's ten children, Haman's ten sons, and those countless Canaanite children in the wrong place at the wrong time. Egyptian, Jewish, Persian, Canaanite innocents, all the objects of narrative violence.[1]

Readers get caught up in the narrative violence too. The Matthean story of Herod's slaughter of the innocents and the associated guilt for Jesus' death falling upon Jews and their children has established a powerful hold upon readers' imaginations for two millennia. The blood-libel narratively associated with the Jews, given theological legitimacy by no less than Augustine and Luther, reverberates across the twentieth century and shows every promise of continuing to foster vicious antisemitic attitudes and actions in the millennium to come. Practically everyone, I suspect, *knows* the Matthean identifications whether they have actually read the text or not, for these are more than narrative roles; they are mythic markers as indelible as tattooed concentration camp numbers. The Jews (i.e., the Scribes and Pharisees) are vilified as the killers of children and the Christ, the sons of those who murdered the prophets (23:31), "serpents, brood of vipers" (23:33), "hypocrites" (23:13, 23, 25, 27), the people from whom the promise of the future has been decisively withdrawn (23:37–38). The differences are absolute: the old and the new, Moses and Jesus, "us" and "them," those who are in and those out, the blessed and the cursed, the apocalyptically rewarded and punished. Matthew's narrative helps construct a "Judaism" and the "Jews" as a persistent historical and religious problem awaiting—and inviting—in the minds of some a final solution.[2] The biblical narrative is a mine field of antisemitic potential.[3] It is a figurative and literal killing field.

Some readers defuse the problems of violent gospel texts by appeal to history. Luke Timothy Johnson's oft-cited essay is a case in point.[4] Textual violence, he claims, reflects ancient polemical rhetorical practices: everyone spoke, and sometimes acted, violently against their opponents, Jew and Gentile alike. His is a rhetorical "everyone did it" explanation. Johnson calls for an "exercise of historical and literary imagination" to recenter the debate on "higher ground" where he can survey the situation.[5] He doesn't "worry about what to do with this language so much as about what the language was doing."[6] He ought to worry. By recasting the issue as a matter of rhetorical convention, Johnson diverts attention away from what readers actually do with these texts. He averts his eyes from the faces of the specific children who live out the Matthean narrative action. This self-described imaginative move is as ethically troubling as it is historically ineffective. In claiming the interpretive "high ground" he compartmentalizes the ancient meaning of the gospel narratives from the subsequent ways these texts get read and lived out. Furthermore, his conclusion that "grasping the conventional nature of the polemic can rob such language of its mythic force and thereby its capacity for mischief" woefully miscalculates the power of language, narrative, and myth, and the imaginative potential of texts to create worlds of meaning and mayhem notwithstanding what their original authorship might have intended them to mean. The cryptotheological effect of Johnson's own language is to sanitize the imaginative and material effects of the blood-libel in Matthew's gospel. To characterize these effects as "mischief" is simply offensive.

The National Rifle Association gun-lobby defense doesn't work either: "Gospel texts don't kill, readers do"—an interpretive distinction with hardly a difference to specific children, real or imagined. Such an argument presumes naively that texts and culture, imagination and imitation can be disentangled from one another. Evidence to the contrary is overwhelming. Experts who track youth violence have made a convincing case that the violence teenagers see, for example, on television and the movie screen is acted out in real life. What adults see and hear becomes reality too. One consequence of the 1991 Persian Gulf War with its video prosecution of the war has been an unsettling erasure of the line separating the imagined from the real, the visual from visceral reality, at a cost to live Iraqi men, women, and children.

There is no doubt that the Bible can be a text that cultivates the best in readers; but it is just as true that the Bible not only exposes the worst features of our humanity, it also amplifies and perpetuates them.[7] Biblical narratives have a robust cultural life of their own, independent of authors and original audiences. These narratives are generative of other narratives, of mythologies, and in important ways of forms of culture itself. In giving contour and texture to the way people live and die in the world, narratives are not only forms of cultural expression, they condition historical existence. Narratives are foundational to experience. In the words of Stephen Crites, "the formal quality of experience through time is inherently narrative."[8] This means that the *nature of the story* makes all the difference not only in the way we as readers live, but, to put it starkly, who gets to live and to die. What Johnson and others fail to appreciate is the autonomous and imaginative life of biblical texts and their readers and what little difference their explanatory distinctions make to real readers. Although the argument that antisemitic readers of Matthew are historically ill-informed about first-century polemical conventions may be true, it misses the pivotal historical and imaginative point altogether—what these texts do to the children.

For post-Holocaust readers of the Bible, to paraphrase Irving Greenberg, all commentary must meet a higher standard in order to be credible: the presence of the burning children. Historical and literary imagination is to be judged by the real innocents. Critics should ask: How does the Matthean story of the murder of the innocents and the defamation of Jewish children live on in contemporary culture shaping attitudes, imaginations, and actions? How does the text give warrant to the exclusion, even killing, of Jews and their children? These are hard questions that biblical scholars find difficult to address. For one thing modern biblical scholars do not routinely read the wealth of "cultural" texts that have for centuries complemented and glossed the written text. Written texts belong to the literary disciplines; visual and plastic renderings to the studio disciplines. Moreover, there are also deep-seated ideological and theological reasons for the downplaying of the visual media that trace their roots historically to the Reformation elevation of the written text over all else. Finally, critical responsibility and ethical responsibility remain largely disconnected domains. The ethics of criticism, to the extent it is reflected upon, is subordinated in key ways to methodological and theological principles. It is unclear how to conceive of ethics in other than traditional disciplinary terms. Notwithstanding the efforts of readers such as Johnson, different skills and sensibilities must be nurtured. What is clear is the reality of the dead children. Further, the imaginative staying power of these narratives is undeniable. And the link between the Matthean narrative and the Holocaust event is inescapable.

One place in which the narrative imagination comes to life is in visual culture. The nineteenth-century illustrator Gustavus Doré's stunning engravings of biblical stories that glossed the King James Bible have supplied readers with a lasting visual representation of these stories. More than that, these images are visual interpretations that lead readers back to the biblical narratives themselves, shaping the reading experience and the understanding of the text.[9] For anyone who has seen *The Ten Commandments*, in the mind's eye Charlton Heston *is* "Moses," just as Warner Sallman's portrait of Jesus *is* "Jesus." Cecil B. DeMille relied upon Doré's rendering of Moses with the Tablets of the Law to construct that visual scene, and its effects live on. What this points to is the inherent difficulty in distinguishing cleanly the read biblical text from its visual appropriation in culture, what we read from what we have already seen, and what we see from how we will read.

Whether in visual or written texts the pervasive and insidious triumphalism of Christian readers subordinates Jewish texts and Jewish experience. This apologetic stance effectively excuses or, worse, legitimates the violence in a text and the violence enacted with a text by a costly and careless downplaying of this as so much cultural "mischief." To his great credit John Dominic Crossan faces this issue squarely by chastising biblical scholars to do better in identifying the latent antisemitism in early Christian gospels. We must do a better job investigating the biblical narrative as a form of cultural expression past and present. Similarly, biblical critics must become better analysts and interpreters of their contemporary culture, attentive to the ways the biblical narrative is foundational to lived experience for better or worse. The Holocaust has given this critical task new urgency. Critical reading of the Bible must meet a higher standard to be credible today—namely the Jewish children of Terezin and all the children in all the other death camps.

Recentering the issue of gospel violence on historical terms as Johnson tries to do intensifies, rather than diminishes, the ethical pressure to meet this higher standard. The appeal to the truth of history and historical imagination that Johnson evokes already configures the facts, and in Matthew's case the "Jews," according to a cultural model of cognitive apprehension. Arguing against a kind of epistemological fundamentalism, Edith Wyschogrod shows that the historical imagination is already implicated in a "prediscursive ethics before it is a conveying of facts."[10] That being the case, the historian "assumes liability for the other, feels the pressure of an Ethics that is prior to historical judgment." Because historical reconstruction can replicate and reinforce cultural assumptions its first task is to recognize its moral responsibility to the dead whose story the historian attempts to bring to life.

The Matthean story of the murder of the innocents ripples through literature, theological and philosophical reflection, and the aesthetic and artistic imagination of the West. It leads readers right up to the gates of the Lager and into the crematoria. My claim is that the identification of Matthew 2 and 27 with the events that took place in Nazi Germany from 1933 to 1945 is not fanciful, but an unfortunate fact, a connection seared into cultural memory and imagination, which I believe is impossible to remove but indeed possible to forget. The critical issue is therefore twofold: first, to explore the cultural connections between biblical text and Lager, and what role Matthew's narrative plays explicitly in the effort to exterminate and erase from memory all of Rachel's children. The second task is moral: to face up to our responsibility before the children when reading and living out lethal texts. The critical task and the ethical task. The connection of Matthew's killing text with the Holocaust is as unavoidable as it is disturbing: unavoidable because it works as a pervasive intertext and gloss upon a mad moment in twentieth-century life; disturbing because of its formative role historically as a direct encouragement in the killing itself. Gospel fiction turned lethal, Crossan would say.[11] It is in making sense of the way we read the Matthean text and conversely the way the text reads us that our ethical responsibility to the children is to be measured.

Fraternal Reading/Unseamly Reading

Recently Emil Fackenheim has taken special note of the textual killing potential associated with the Biblical text. He reflects specifically upon the responsibility Christian readers have to Jewish texts and to Jewish and non-Jewish children. Dedicated "To the children—ours and all the others," *The Jewish Bible after the Holocaust* explores the possibility of a "fraternal reading of the Bible." Fackenheim writes: "Through the centuries Christians have imagined that Jews spend their days rejecting the Christ, or to put it into worse words, killing him all over again, as they are said to have done originally."[12] Who are the children of Rachel, of Haman? What does it mean to be a responsible reader of the Jewish Bible after Auschwitz? Commenting on Matthew 2:16–19 Fackenheim observes: "Without the New Testament passage, the children of Rachel, evidently, are Jews and they alone. With it . . . they are Christians and they alone, for in them Jeremiah's prophecy is 'fulfilled.' A fraternal Jewish–Christian reading of the Rachel-text, then, seems impossible both with Matthew and without it."[13] Fackenheim points to a double bind: after the Holocaust the Matthean text makes it impossible for Christians to read with Jews and impossible to live without them. Yet, in spite of Auschwitz and the murder of innocents there remains some slight hope of success. But that possibility demands an awareness of the period 1933–1945 and a rupture in what he calls "seamless" Christian reading.

"Seamless" reading is the sort that proceeds past the events of 1933–1945 without radical disruption. Seamless reading is what one hears in this assessment of the Matthean passion account: "the most effective theatre among the Synoptics, outclassed in that respect only by the Johannine masterpiece" and "a

Matthean composition on the basis of a popular tradition reflecting on the theme of Jesus' innocent blood and the responsibility it created."[14] "Capacity for mischief," Johnson's words, belong to the same genre. Whether theological, exegetical, or historical, seamless reading invites a complicity in the events that breathes life into the "naked text," as Fackenheim calls it. Seamless reading is one way Christian readers enable Matthew's text to murder the children again and again.

Instead, Fackenheim calls for an interruption or shock (*Erschuetterung*) in the Christian soul that is not mediated through theological categories but by the event of the Holocaust itself. This is comparable to what the Jewish philosopher and Talmudic reader Emmanuel Levinas calls a "shaken conscience" whereby consciousness is profoundly disturbed by conscience through the breaking through of the face of the other. The moment of ethical encounter is the coming face-to-face with the suffering children. For Levinas the face is the place where the infinite breaks through the finite, where the good in all of its height is encountered, where responsibility for the other is met. In a meditation on Amos 5:19 he says that "the death of the starving children thrusts us into the snake pit, into places that are no longer places, into places one cannot forget, but that do not succeed in placing themselves in memory, in organizing themselves in the form of memories. We have known such pits in this century."[15] To face up to the reality of the suffering innocents is to stand in that pit with them.

After the Holocaust the Bible itself has been ruptured and seamless critical scholarship discredited for good. Normative critical reading and normative ethics are ruptured. Nothing is the same again. There is a *novum* in history, encouraged by the Matthean text, namely the conjunction for the first time in history of *birth* and *crime*.[16] Readers of the Bible must read differently, deferentially, deliberately for the children, otherwise they contribute to the formation of a culture that makes the murder of the innocents natural and inevitable.

One step toward identifying the formative presence of this killing text and its intimate relation to the Holocaust is to read for the way the Matthean story and the Jewish Holocaust live on together, reinforcing each other, participating in the formation of mythic consciousness, particularly of national and cultural self-expressions, through contemporary literature and cinema, as well as other forms of modern culture. By noting examples of the way the biblical text glosses and underwrites literary and aesthetic expressions, biblical scholars may learn something about the capacity of texts to live on in complex ways. Conversely, reading the way Matthew's killing story glosses the Holocaust experience in Serbian, Russian, and American cultural texts might prompt a rereading of the biblical text and a more sober assessment of Matthew's neutralizing relationship to its Hebrew bible intertexts.

Matthew in Culture

It is winter 1999 in Kosovo and ethnic Albanian children are dying: Matthew's text and the Jewish Holocaust form a powerful accelerant to the suffering. The murder of the innocents narrative and the experience of the Nazi genocide directly inform Serbian national and ethnic identity. The 1389 Battle for Kosovo, dramatized poetically in *The Mountain Wreath*, serves as a mythologized historical event in Serbian self-understanding that directly shaped nineteenth-century Serbian Christological self-expression. "Christoslavism" is the argument that Slavs are by essence Christians and conversion to any other religion is a betrayal of race or people and massacre or sacred cleansing is one's religious duty.[17] In this legend Lazar is betrayed and subsequently put to death by turncoat Muslim Slavs. In this Slavic "passion play," Slav "christ-killers"—Muslim children, women, and men—are brutally slaughtered during advent season. Matthew 2 and 27 work in tandem as subtexts scripting Serbian mythic consciousness and justify subsequent cleansing actions.

Matthew's mythic power in feeding Serbian nationalism is public and real. Michael Sells reports that a 1989 production of *The Mountain Wreath* played to more than a million people in Kosovo.[18] With their memories painfully refreshed by their own World War II experience of Nazi genocide, the dramatized Matthean murder-of-the-innocents narrative helped inflame a new genocidal spirit directed now against the Serbs of Kosovo. Victims become victimizers; past and present converge; subtexts become pretexts; narrative events mythologize ethnic history. The outrage of German atrocities, mediated by the Matthean narrative, scripts a new wave of genocidal violence whose effects are being realized today in the murder of innocent ethnic Albanian children. Matthew's story of the killing of the children freely crosses cultural boundaries and historical periods. Not to be ignored is the direct impact of the same Matthean text upon the "narrative quality of experience" that shaped Croat attitudes toward and underwrote atrocities committed against their Bosnian Muslim neighbors only a few years ago in Bosnia-Herzegovina. The Matthean narrative is hard at work shaping Serbian mythic time as killing time.

The mutual shadowing of Matthean narrative and Holocaust camp is encountered in the Russian novel *Life and Fate*. The setting for Vasily Grossman's fiction is the horrendous battle for Stalingrad. An eyewitness to the Holocaust, Grossman was the first journalist to publish an account of a German death camp. Although his subsequent writings were suppressed by Soviet authorities for more than two decades, Grossman's manuscript was spirited out of Russia and published. Grossman wrestles with the question, was 350,000 souls lost in the Battle for Stalingrad in any sense a justifiable price to defeat evil? How does one justify the cost of innocent women and children in such a battle? Is there any reason to be confident that Western political and religious institutions provide the basis for knowing and doing the good? Grossman turns to the Matthean story and its Hebrew bible intertexts to gloss the character Mostovskoy's effort to provide an accounting:

> Many books have been written about the nature of good and evil and the struggle between them. There is a deep and undeniable sadness in all this: whenever we see the dawn of an eternal good that will never be overcome by evil . . . the blood of old people and children is always shed. Not only men, but even God himself is powerless to lessen this evil.
>
> 'In Rama was there a voice heard, lamentation, and weeping, and great mourning, Rachel weeping for her children, and would not be comforted, because they were not.'
>
> What does a woman who has lost her children care about a philosopher's definition of good and evil?[19]

Grossman laments the fact that "prophets, religious leaders, reformers, social and political leaders are impotent" in the face of evil, evil that lofty goals and texts ironically give stage to. In spite of Western political and religious institutions the words of Jeremiah 31:15 are fulfilled. Matthew 2 and 27 are fulfilled. The inevitability of human and divine complicity with Evil is affirmed. And inevitably the children bear the consequence when Good and Evil contest one another. As in Stalingrad so also in Bethlehem: innocent children die for the sake of some good theological or ideological cause. But Grossman finds this cost and its supporting logic unacceptable: "I do not believe in the good, I believe in kindness. . . . Not even Herod shed blood in the name of evil; he shed it for his version of the good. Herod's good."[20] The mythic battle does not justify the children's death.

At one point a German officer attempts to persuade Mostovskoy that Russians and Germans really have much in common, and that Russians have something to learn from German hatred of the Jews and, above all, their experience of liquidating them by the millions. Stalin's true genius, Liss suggests, is a definitional and associative one: he had "seen the hidden brotherhood between Fascism and the Pharisees." Liss says, "You and I both know that it's not on battlefields that the future is decided." Liss is right. The decisive battle is waged with those mythic narratives and logical arguments that link arms to justify the deaths of the innocents as an unfortunate but acceptable cost. The appropriate ethical response to such mayhem does not derive from a countermyth and counterrationality (for example, a better "historical" or "literary" argument) equally grounded in the same Western institutional culture, but from a goodness that Levinas says is "a goodness without witnesses, a little goodness without ideology. It could be called goodness without thought. The goodness of men outside the religious or social good . . . ."[21] The faceless and nameless peasant children of Siberia, the besieged children of Stalingrad, the future deaths of Russian children are already recorded before the fact in a Matthean narrative that has entered the Western mythic battle of Good against Evil. Their faces demand something better of us than an appeal to history or the Good.

Lest one think this an exclusively literary and European phenomenon, Matthew's narrative of the murder of the innocents and its tie to the Holocaust lives on richly in American pop culture. The third release in the highly successful *Planet of the Apes* film series reveals how natural it is to think Matthew's narrative in relation to the Final Solution and to sell it. *Escape from the Planet of the Apes*[22] plays upon a reversal of Matthew's murder-of-the-innocents plot: innocent chimpanzee adults and child, instead of human beings, are targeted for elimination. In this film biblical violence is shaded with humor and a thinly veiled political message. Needing to produce a winning script, one that would retain a predominately teenage following, and to capitalize on the growing youth culture opposition to the Vietnam War, the producers tap the all-too-familiar biblical plot. Entertainment, political opposition to the Vietnam War, biblical violence, and xenophobic mythology combine to produce "effective theatre" with a potent message.

The last-second switch of the speaking child Milo for a "dumb" chimpanzee child serves to disparage an unpopular American military that looks ever so much like the bumbling German captors of "Hogan's Heroes": the captives outsmart their captors at every turn. Most importantly, the turnabout ensures a potential plot for yet another sequel. Lost in the rush to celebrate the survival of the series and the intelligent chimpanzee is that "dumb" chimpanzee whose bullet-riddled body is unceremoniously dumped into the water in a manner that calls to mind Pharaoh's dispatch of male Hebrew children into the Nile. Like Matthew's Jesus, Milo lives for a future apocalyptic conflict, which becomes the theme of the final installment in the series; and like the dead children of Bethlehem, the death of this unnamed chimpanzee child is put to the service of the human-like child whose survival is ensured.

The allusions to the Jewish Holocaust are everywhere: the President's scientific adviser is a German Otto Hasslein, a scientist whose goal is to ensure racial and species dominance; a Commission that makes a "final" recommendation; an internment camp in which Mengele-type scientific experimentation (involuntary interrogation and abortion) takes place; and of course "transport cars" in the form of circus wagons used to move apes and other animals about. Himmler's lager, Herod's Bethlehem, and technoculture converge. The imaginative link is underscored in the following exchange in which the American President responds to Hasslein's proffered advice:

> Now what do you expect me . . . to do about it? Alter what you believe to be the course of the future by slaughtering two innocents, or rather three now that one of them is pregnant? Herod tried that and Christ survived.
>
> Mr. President, Herod lacked our facilities.

Narrative roles are reversed in several ways: chimpanzees for humans, chimpanzees for Jews, and Americans for Germans. Already identified with Nazis in the popular press after the Calley-led massacre at My Lai, American soldiers are portrayed as German killers of the innocent. From the point of view of anti-Vietnam war ideology operating at the surface of the film, Americans are cast in a negative moral light, but it relation to the "species" war that evokes deeper religious and technoscientific macronarratives and experiences, the moral status of the Americans' actions is more ambiguous, conflictual. Hasslein poses the question:

> How many futures are there? And which future has God, if there is a god, chosen for man's destiny. If I urge the destruction of these two apes am I defying God's will or obeying it? Am I his enemy or his instrument.
>
> An assassin would say the latter. Do you approve of assassination?
>
> Well, Mr. President, we condoned the attempted suicide of Hitler because he was evil.
>
> Yes, but would we have approved of killing him in babyhood when he was still innocent or killing his mother when he was still in her womb, or slaughtering his remote ancestors. We have no proof, Hasslein, that these apes are evil.
>
> Mr. President, the people must be told that the killers of today could become the mass murderers of tomorrow.

In Hasslein's struggle to discern the right moral action, the Matthean narrative script surfaces. The xenophobic response of killing the baby chimpanzee is given biblical legs on which to stand. With the human species and its destiny at stake, the murder of the innocents is rationalized in a way that the movie does not explicitly challenge. Grossman's worry is confirmed again: the killing of innocent children is legitimated when a basic cultural, theological, or philosophical principle needs defending.

Even if we grant that the film has purposefully conflated narrative elements in order to expose the ambiguity of moral action, other cultural texts have slipped in to reinforce a deadly message about the nonhumans. There is a more onerous twist in that the innocent chimpanzee becomes victimized twice. Not only does Matthew 2 forecast the present (1973 C.E.) death of the chimp, Matthew 27 anticipates a future (3955 C.E.) that has already happened, a future in which apes have committed atrocities against humans. While under interrogation Zera confesses to Hasslein that she has dissected human beings, a gruesome image championed in the original movie release. The identification of chimpanzee actions with Nazi practices turns victim into victimizer. Also evoked is the medieval charge that Jews ritually murdered and cannibalized Christian babies, which fueled pogroms since the Middle Ages, and the Christoserbian legitimation of the murder of ethnic Albanian children. The murder of innocent Milo is doubly legitimized as an efficient Herodian-like past action and a just response for a future atrocity that will already have been committed in the future. The past is the future, the future is the past. Killing them for the past, killing them for the future. Both victims and victimizers, the chimpanzees can't win for dying. The Matthean narrative with its Holocaust intertext crosses national, temporal, ethnic, and now species boundaries in order to neutralize the enemy.

Neutralizing the Hebrew Narrative

This brief look at the cinematic portrayal of the Matthean story/Holocaust connection brings us back to the point at which we began, namely the Matthean text. How does attention to the way the Matthean narrative visually scripts the elision of past and future, victim and victimizer in *Escape from the Planet of the Apes* offer a clue about the way Matthew uses story to neutralize the Jewish Exodus narrative as a Jewish foundation myth?

Matthew makes much of Hebrew scripture in the construction of the Jesus narrative. Traditional biblical scholarship resorts to explaining the intertextual[23] relationship of one text to another as a process of "influence": one text evokes another in the form of a direct citation or as an allusion. Matthean commentators have long centered on Matthew's "use" of the Old Testament in terms of the explicit citation of Hosea, Jeremiah, and Micah texts. Critics have also sought to pin-point the "allusions" in Matthew 2:13–23 to the beginning of Exodus (usually 4:19ff). Luz has noted the parallels between Matthew's text and a second story, namely the rescue of the Moses child and the murder of Israelite boys by Pharaoh in Exodus 1 and 2.[24] The parallels between Moses and Jesus are thick and conflictual, and they are routinely accounted for in terms of the "influence" of the Old Testament text upon Matthew.

But what about a reverse "influence"? In terms of the lived nature of this intertextual relationship, as Fackenheim shows, Matthew's text is the one with far greater "influence." Reading the texts unidirectionally and piecemeal obscures the narrative and mythic conflict at work in the heart of the Matthean foundation story, a conflict that is constantly repeated. Matthew and Exodus follow a common narrative course, one that extends beyond the boundaries of the killing stories themselves where critics traditionally draw the citational limits when charting Matthew's relationship to his Hebrew intertexts. Against Brown and others who suggest that Matthew's text repeats or augments that structure by "inserting" into it prophetic citations, I suggest a more basic deformation of narrative structure and meaning is underway, one that has profound effects on the way Matthew's readers henceforth will understand the foundation story that shapes Jewish life and faith. The Matthean narrative takes the Mosaic infancy and adult death stories, which form *in nuncio* the body of the Jews' Exodus and Conquest foundation myths, and interpretively trumps them with the Jews' very own prophetic texts. Matthew "kills" the Jews' foundation narrative with the aid of prophetic discursive material.[25]

Matthew 2:15 // Exodus 4:22 (calls son out of Egypt)
    Hosea 11:1 citation
Matthew 2:16 // Exodus 4:23 (killing of male children)
Matthew 2:18 // Exodus 4:23/24 (allusion to Rachel's death); Genesis 35:16–20, Genesis 32 (Jacob's struggle with the "Angel of God")
    Jeremiah 31.15 citation
Matthew 2:20 // Exodus 4:19 (mother and child to safety)
Matthew 2:23 // Exodus 4:13–15 (naming Jesus/God) (naming Jacob, Genesis 32:28)
    Isaiah 11:1 citation(?)
Matthew 3:1 // Exodus 4:27 (exit to wilderness, *erēmō*)
Matthew 3:6 // Exodus 4:31 [people (*laos*) repent/believe]
Matthew 3:7 // Exodus 5:1 (*Pharisaiōn, Pharaō*)

When presented this ways as an intersection of stories, the neutralizing effect is severe. Matthew's text employs Hebrew texts to subvert the original Mosaic mythic story and to kill it off by radically distorting its characters and action just as the Serbian myth of Lazar recasts Kosovo Muslims as the enemy and Hassleim makes chimpanzees the victimizers. The intertextual effect of recalling the Exodus stories and then prophetically attacking them, by trumping Moses with Jesus (especially in Chapters 5–7), is painful enough. But Matthew's text does even greater damage to the Jews. This, I suggest, is where the Matthean narrative draws its turbo power and potential for imaginative and lived damage. In the process of beginning afresh with the wilderness narrative (Matthew 3:1 ff.) in which Jesus and John the Baptist now displace Moses and Aaron in their lead roles, Matthew fashions one more deadly narrative insult that turns the text figuratively and literally against the Jews. The larger matrix distortion invites readers to identify the Pharisees and Scribes as the opponents of Jesus who first make their appearance on the Gospel scene in 3:7 as structurally and homophonically identified with Pharaoh's appearance in Exodus 5:1. With the identification of

Pharisees and Pharaoh (*Pharisaion // Pharao*) the meaning of the narrative of the killing of the Jewish innocent is now shockingly turned on its head: Egyptian political and religious leaders are identified narratively within the matrix of texts with Jewish political and religious leaders. The *Jews* under Herod's leadership become responsible for the death of their own children just as the narrator will later identify the Pharisees as responsible for the killing of their own prophets (23:37). This is the reversal pattern found in *Escape from the Planet of the Apes.* Future "nonhumans" are ultimately responsible for their own past innocent's death.

In the Jewish associative identification with Pharaoh a vile portrait of a people wicked enough to kill their own children emerges, ironically and pitifully reinforced and condemned by their own narratives and foundation stories. An old foundational narrative in which Jewish children are murdered by Egyptians now becomes a new foundation story for Christians in which the Jews are murderers and are to be murdered. It is the acceptance of responsibility for infanticide associated with Jews that is reiterated in that most horrific of statements in Matthew 27:25: "And all the people answered, 'His blood be on us and on our children.'"[26] Out of their own mouths and narratives the Jews condemn themselves and their children. We do not have far to go to arrive at the killing of Jews as legitimated by their very own "rewritten" Scriptures. We are at the gates of Kosovo and Auschwitz.

By identifying the Jews with Pharaoh, with their own bondage and their own complicity in the death of their children, Matthew invites—no trains—the reader to share this reading of their texts and his own anti-Jewish violence. Through the juxtaposition not just of individual texts but a matrix of textual and narrative roles and actions, the Matthean text encourages the reader to join in constructing "the Jews" as vile perpetrators of one of the most horrendous crime imaginable—killing the infants—a charge that Christians have kept alive for centuries. Matthew encourages a narrative and theological triumphalism by shaping the reader to be a "scribe fit for the Kingdom" and to pull from the treasure room what is new and old (13:52). In other words, readers are to appropriate for their own purposes those living texts and narratives and turn them back in an aggressive, murderous way against their very authors. It is precisely what *Escape from the Planet of the Apes* does. It is a double homicide: of infants and of foundation stories.

A Respite from the Killing

Matthew's intertextual reading of Exodus and the gospel's close association with the Holocaust event challenge us as critical, post-Holocaust readers to speak out against a reading of Jewish narratives that is exclusionary and murderous. We come face-to-face with the ethical challenge and responsibility as Grossman says, to say "No" to Matthew's use of Hebrew scripture, "No" to the commentary tradition that averts the eyes or relativizes the problem, "No" to a critical interpretive practice that resists recognizing its own cultural implicature in readings that kill. In addition to reading biblical texts and narrative matrices differently, we must learn to read a range of cultural texts for the elision, conflicts, and displacements that these texts generate. Only then will we take the full measure of the place of the Bible in culture. Only in this way can we begin to take responsibility as critical readers of the Bible for the place this text occupies in our world. By reading for the social and cultural formations that inform Matthew's narrative distortions in a post-Holocaust context we resist becoming the reader Matthew's script invites.

How and why the Matthean narrative survives literarily and aesthetically as a textual killing field at the same time as the children it speaks of are silenced is a deeply disturbing irony. It opens the door to fundamental textual, interpretive, and ethical questions about the subtle and not-so-subtle role of the Bible in culture in perpetuating violence, and about critical reading originating first and foremost as a moral activity that sets out quite deliberately to defeat such violence. Levinas reminds us again that the death of the innocents "thrusts us into the snake pit, into places that are no longer places, into places one cannot forget, but that do not succeed in placing themselves in memory, in organizing themselves in the form of memories. We have known such pits in this century."[27] Pits are being dug today as you read this.

Becoming better, more critically imaginative readers of contemporary culture is in part what is required. The credibility of biblical scholarship is at stake. With some notable exceptions, the field has not adequately come to terms with the event of the Holocaust, much less the broader phenomenon of genocide, and the subtle ways the biblical text, especially the Matthean narrative, makes the worst possible.

Simply being better is, however, the most important thing. We can do a better job of acknowledging directly the innocents and the power biblical texts have over us in shaping our perceptions and informing our world. By attending to the reality of these children whose deaths rupture our memory, we open ourselves to the possibility of saying "No" to all texts, biblical or otherwise, that kill children, biblical or otherwise. Short of a shaken conscience nothing is credible.

NOTES

1. On the issue of the ethics of reading and children see Danna Nolan Fewell's *The Children of Israel: Reading the Bible for the Sake of Our Children* (Nashville: Abingdon Press, forthcoming).
2. It is a toss-up which gospel narrative is finally the most anti-Jewish and gets used for antisemitic purposes. See J. T. Sanders, "The Salvation of the Jews in Luke-Acts," in *Luke-Acts: New*

Perspectives from the Society of Biblical Literature Seminar, ed. C. H. Talbert (New York: Crossroad Press, 1984), 115.

3. Note Fred Burnett, "Exposing the Anti-Jewish Ideology of Matthew's Implied Author: The Characterization of God as Father," *Semeia* 59 (1992): 155–191.
4. Luke Timothy Johnson, "The New Testament's Anti-Jewish Slander and the Conventions of Ancient Polemic." *Journal of Biblical Literature* 108 (1989): 419–441.
5. Ibid., 421.
6. Ibid., 419.
7. Gary A. Phillips and Danna Nolan Fewell, "Ethics, Bible, Reading *As If*," *Semeia* 77 (1997): 1–21.
8. Stephen Crites, "The Narrative Quality of Existence," *Journal of the American Academy of Religion* 39 (1977): 291–311.
9. For a reading of Doré's biblical engraving see Danna Nolan Fewell and Gary Phillips "Drawn to Excess, or Reading Beyond Betrothal," *Semeia* 77 (1997): 22–47.
10. Edith Wyschogrod, *An Ethics of Remembering: Histroy, Heterology, and the Nameless Others* (Chicago: University of Chicago Press, 1998), 3.
11. John Dominic Crossan, *Who Killed Jesus? Exposing the Roots of Anti-Semitism in the Gospel Story of the Death of Jesus* (San Francisco: HarperSanFrancisco, 1991), xi.
12. Emil Fackenheim, *The Jewish Bible after the Holocaust: A Rereading* (Bloomington: Indiana University Press), 102.
13. Ibid., 81.
14. Crossan, *Who Killed Jesus?*, xi (quoting Raymond Brown).
15. Emmanuel Levinas, "Beyond Memory: From the tractate *Berakhot, 12b-13*," in *In the Time of the Nations* (Bloomington: Indiana University Press, 1994), 85.
16. Fackenheim, *The Jewish Bible after the Holocaust*, 87.
17. Michael Sells, *The Bridge Betrayed: Religion and Genocide in Bosnia* (Berkeley, CA: University of California Press, 1996), 51.
18. Michael Sells, "'Christ Killer' Mythology and the Tragedy in the Balkans," *Explorations* 11 (1997): 5.
19. Vasily Grossman, *Life and Fate* (London: The Harvill Press, 1985), 406.
20. Ibid., 405.
21. Levinas, *In the Time of the Nations*, 91.
22. *Escape From the Planet of the Apes*, Twentieth Century Fox Home Entertainment (Beverly Hills, CA, 1977).
23. Julia Kristiva, regarded as the author of the phrase, defines intertextuality as a "permutation of texts . . . in the space of a text several utterances drawn from *other texts intersect and neutralize one another*" [*Semeiotiké: Recherches pour une sémanalyse* (Paris: le Seuil, 1969), 113; translation and emphasis mine].
24. Ulrich Luz, *Matthew 1–7: A Commentary*, trans Wilhelm Linss (Minneapolis: Augsburg Fortress, 1985). Luz (144) has compared and contrasted stories of persecution and preservation of other royal children. He charts more than 25 different traditions including Moses, Abraham, Cypselus, Mithridates, Romulus and Remus, Augustus, Nero, Gilgamesh, Sargon I, Cyrus, Zoroaster legend, Fredun, Krishna, Perseus, Heracles, as well as substantial first-century midrashim on the infancy of Moses.
25. The aspect of *neutralization* is pivotal for Kristeva because it underscores intertextuality's ideological and cultural-critical edge. Intertextuality is an act of cultural production and reproduction (a "signifying practice" following Barthes, a "writing" following Derrida) in which the text (be it linguistic, somatic, visual, etc.) is a field traversed by lines of force in which various signifying systems undergo transposition of varying sorts and in varying degrees of magnitude.

26. Johnson concludes his essay by saying that knowing the polemical patterns of antiquity enables us to "relativize our party's version. To take only the most hurtful example, we cannot view with the same seriousness the 'curse' laid on Jews by Matthew's Gospel when we recognize that curses were common coinage in those fights, and there were not many Jews or Gentiles who did not have at least one curse to deal with" (441). I suggest Johnson "relativizes" not only the reality of the Matthean text's power but the ethical responsibility of the historian to take that deadly power and its victims seriously.
27. Levinas, *In the Time of the Nations*, 85.

Contributors

Timothy K. Beal is the Florence Harkness Professor of Biblical Studies at Case Western Reserve University.

Walter Brueggemann is the William Marcellus McPheeters Professor of Old Testament at Columbia Theological Seminary.

John Dominic Crossan is professor emeritus of biblical studies at DePaul University in Chicago and co-director of the Jesus Seminar.

James D. G. Dunn is professor of New Testament at the University of Durham.

Pamela Eisenbaum is associate professor of Biblical Studies and Christian Origins at the Iliff School of Theology.

Lloyd Gaston is professor emeritus of New Testament at Vancouver School of Theology.

Mark K. George is assistant professor of Hebrew Bible at the Iliff School of Theology.

Susannah Heschel is the Eli Black Professor of Jewish Studies at Dartmouth College.

Craig C. Hill is professor of New Testament at Wesley Theological Seminary.

Steven L. Jacobs holds the Aaron Aronov Chair of Judaic Studies at the University of Alabama.

Luke Timothy Johnson is Robert Woodruff Professor of New Testament and Christian Origins at Emory University's Candler School of Theology.

Jennifer L. Koosed is assistant professor of biblical studies at Albright College.

Deborah Krause is associate professor of New Testament at Eden Theological Seminary.

Tania Oldenhage is assistant professor of religion at Mount Union College.

Gary A. Phillips is professor of New Testament and Chair of the Religion Department at Sewanee, The University of the South.

Rolf Rendtorff is professor emeritus at the University of Heidelberg.

Richard L. Rubenstein is President Emeritus of the University of Bridgeport, where he is currently Distinguished Professor of Religion and director of the Center for the Study of Ethics, Religion, and International Affairs.

Margie Tolstoy lectures and supervises in the Divinity Faculty at the University of Cambridge, where she also teaches in the Centre for Jewish and Christian Relations.

Index

ANCIENT SOURCES

a. Biblical

b. Apocryphal and Extrabiblical